Creativity and Public Policy
Generating Super-Optimum Solutions

STUART S. NAGEL
University of Illinois

Ashgate

Aldershot • Burlington USA • Singapore • Sydney

Published by
Ashgate Publishing Limited
Gower House
Croft Road
Aldershot
Hants GU11 3HR
England

Ashgate Publishing Company
131 Main Street
Burlington
Vermont 05401
USA

Ashgate website: http://www.ashgate.com

British Library Cataloguing in Publication Data
Nagel, Stuart S., 1934–
  Creativity and public policy : generating super-optimum
  solutions. – (Policy studies organization)
  1. Public policy
  I. Title
  320.6

Library of Congress Cataloging-in-Publication Data
Nagel, Stuart S., 1934–
    Creativity and public policy : generating super-optimum solutions
  /Stuart S. Nagel.
      p. cm.
    ISBN 1–84014–018–6 (hb)
    1. Policy sciences–Decision making.   2. Creative ability.
  I. Title.
  H96. N54   1998
  320'.6—dc21   98–35235
                                                                   CIP

ISBN 1 84014 018 6

Typeset by Manton Typesetters, Louth, Lincolnshire, UK.
Printed in Great Britain by MPG Books Ltd, Bodmin, Cornwall

Summary Table of Contents

PART IV   INTEGRATION

Contents

List of Tables

List of Figures

Introduction

Creativity and Super-optimum Solutions

Creativity

Creativity in general can be defined as an ability or an occurrence. Either way, it refers to developing an alternative way of (1) explaining gravity, (2) writing a symphony, (3) lessening the problem of poverty or (4) dealing with some other subject. The distinctive aspect of a creative alternative is that it is better on whatever criteria are considered relevant than the alternatives that were previously being considered.

Super-optimum Solutions

A special kind of creativity involves not merely finding a better way of doing things, but finding a way that exceeds the best initial expectations of whatever sides or viewpoints may have been in contention over how to deal with the problem. That kind of creativity can be referred to as 'super-optimizing creativity'. It does more than just find a new better or best alternative: it finds an alternative that is better than what the previous perspectives had as their best expectations, simultaneously across all those previous perspectives. Super-optimizing creativity is closely related to super-optimizing analysis, which refers to methods that are useful in finding alternatives that are capable of exceeding the best expectation of all sides and viewpoints to disputes or dilemmas.

Creativity in the context of public policy evaluation tends to refer to finding alternative ways of dealing with public policy that are better than those which have previously been proposed. The relevant criteria may include effectiveness, efficiency, equity, public participation, predictability, procedural due process or other more specific criteria. Super-optimizing creativity refers to finding alternative ways of dealing with public policy problems that exceed the best expectations simultaneously of conservatives, liberals and other major viewpoints on whatever the policy problem is, using their own criteria and relative weights for those criteria.

Overview of the Book

This book contains a variety of experiences of the author around the world, including Africa (Ghana, Kenya, Malawi, Morocco, South Africa, Togo and Zambia), Asia (China, Hong Kong, India, Israel, Japan, Palestine, the Philippines, Qatar, Sri Lanka, Taiwan, Thailand and the United Arab Emirates), Latin America (Argentina, Brazil, Mexico and Panama) and Europe (Croatia, England, France, Germany, Italy, the Netherlands, Switzerland and Russia). Those experiences also include conducting workshops with numerous US government agencies, such as the Air Force, Central Intelligence Agency, Congressional Budget Office, Defense Department, Justice Department and Veterans Administration. Other sources of ideas for generating case studies of super-optimum solutions include the conducting of workshops for adult education programmes, students at the University of Illinois and conventions of such associations as the American Political Science Association (APSA), Association for Public Policy Analysis and Management (APPAM), American Bar Association (ABA), International Political Science Association (IPSA), Midwest Political Science Association (MWPSA), American Society for Public Administration (ASPA) and International Association for Schools and Institutes of Administration (IASIA). These sources deserve credit for having stimulated the ideas and examples presented in this book.

Super-optimum solutions (SOS) in public controversies involve solutions that exceed the best expectations of liberals and conservatives simultaneously, within public or government controversies. An optimum solution is one that is best on a list of alternatives in achieving a set of goals. A super-optimum solution is one that is simultaneously best on two separate sets of goals. One set is a liberal set and the second set is a conservative set. They may share many or all of the goals, but they are likely to differ in terms of the relative weights they give to the same goals.

In general terms, a super-optimum solution is a solution to a decision-making problem where the solution is considered to be objectively better than what has traditionally been considered to be the best possible solution to that type of problem. In recent times, there has been a growing literature advocating dispute resolution in which all sides come out ahead. Such solutions are associated with the concept of settlement through mediation or through win–win negotiation, as contrasted to the adversarial determination of who is right and who is wrong. Win–win negotiations, however, may merely involve each side coming out ahead of their worst expectations.

The concept of super-optimum solutions goes beyond settlement mediation and win–win negotiation by emphasizing the possibility and desirability of each side in a dispute coming out ahead of their best expectations. That kind of dispute resolution partly stems from new philosophies that relate to supply-side economics, industrial policy and other forms of expansionist thinking, rather than zero-sum or fixed pie thinking, which assumes that the total resources are constant.

There are at least seven different ways of arriving at super-optimum solutions. The first way is by *expanding the resources available*. An example might include well-placed subsidies and tax breaks that would increase national productivity and thus increase the gross national product and income. Doing this would enable the tax revenue to the government to increase even if the tax rate decreases. That would provide for a lowering of taxes, instead of trying to choose between the liberal and conservative ways of raising them. It would also provide for increasing both domestic and defense expenditures, instead of having to choose between the two.

The second way is by *setting higher goals* than those previously considered the best, while still preserving realism. An example might include the Hong Kong labor shortage, with unemployment at only 1 per cent. Hong Kong is faced with the seeming dilemma of having to choose between forgoing profits (by not being able to fill orders because of lack of labor) and opening the floodgates to mainland Chinese and Vietnamese (in order to obtain more labor). A super-optimum solution might involve adding to the labor force by way of the elderly, the disabled and mothers of pre-school children. It also would provide more and better jobs for those who are seasonally employed, part-time employed, full-time employed but looking for a second job, and full-time employed but not working up to their productive capacity.

Situations where *one side can receive big benefits but the other side incurs only small costs* provide a third way. An example is in litigation where the defendant gives products that it makes, in lieu of cash. The products may have high market value to the plaintiff, but low variable or incremental cost to the defendant, since the defendant has already manufactured the products or can quickly do so.

Fourth, there are situations involving a *third-party benefactor*, which is usually a government agency. An example is provided by government food stamps which allow the poor to obtain food at low prices, while farmers receive high prices when they submit the food stamps they have for reimbursement. Another example is rent supplements which allow the poor to pay low rents, but with landlords receiving even higher rents than they would otherwise expect.

A fifth way is *combining alternatives* that are not mutually exclusive. An example is combining government-salaried legal aid attorneys with volunteer attorneys. Doing so could give the best of both the public sector and private sector approaches to legal services for the poor. Another example is combining (1) tax-supported higher education plus democratic admission standards with (2) contributions from alumni, tuition and merit standards. Doing this results in universities that are better than under pure government ownership or pure private enterprise.

A sixth way lies in *removing or decreasing the source of the conflict* between liberals and conservatives, rather than trying to synthesize their separate proposals. An example would be concentrating on having a highly effective and acceptable birth control program to satisfy both the proponents and opponents of abortion, since abortions would then seldom be needed. Another example would be concentrating on a highly effective murder-reduction program to satisfy both the proponents and opponents of capital punishment. Such a murder-reduction program might emphasize gun control, drug medicalization (treating addicts as people who are sick) and reduction of violence socialization by fostering peaceful resolution of disputes during childhood.

Developing a *package of alternatives* that would satisfy both liberal and conservative goals provides a final way. An example is pre-trial release where liberals want more arrested defendants released prior to trial, and conservatives want (a) a higher rate of appearances in court and (b) fewer crimes committed while prisoners are out on release. The package that increases the achievement of both liberal and conservative goals includes better screening, reporting in, notification and prosecution of those scheduled to appear in court who do not show up, as well as reduction of delay between arrest and trial.

This book will provide case examples from the public sector examining different ways to achieve super-optimum solutions. The theoretical aspects and principles will be consolidated and discussed in the following section, where the significance of SOS for various public administration concerns is demonstrated. Decision makers striving to make more informed and more responsive choices may well find the techniques described conducive to greater organizational creativity.

Basic Principles of Super-optimizing

One of the most exciting waves of the future in human interaction will be the movement that relates to alternative dispute resolution. That movement began with the rather mundane purpose of decreasing delay in resolving disputes. It has now shifted toward the more important purpose of resolving disputes in mutually beneficial ways, or even in ways in which all sides come out ahead of their best expectations.

To put the subject into a broader historical context, one might note that human beings have been having and resolving disputes since prehistoric times. The traditional method of resolving disputes (as with other primates and mammals) is for one side to dominate the other either by brute force or by verbal argument. A higher form of dispute resolution is to arrive at a compromise whereby there is a splitting of the difference between the two sides, either with or without the aid of a neutral third party. Compromising is considered to be a more civilized form of human interaction, at least where it does not involve retreating from fundamental principles.

The purpose of this introduction is to discuss the new, almost futuristic concept of achieving super-optimum solutions in public controversies. The discussion covers the essence of super-optimum solutions, examples from dispute resolution and from policy making, contrasts with other types of solution, procedures for arriving at super-optimum solutions, the helpfulness of decision-aiding software, the generic super-optimum solution from a spreadsheet perspective, classifying super-optimum solutions and streams of relevant ideas and literature. It also helps add to the bridge-building between futures research and policy studies. Futures research tends to emphasize describing what the future is likely to be. Policy studies emphasize the development of public policies for achieving a desired future. Both futures research and policy studies are currently undergoing change in the direction of becoming more global, more long-term and more interdisciplinary or cross-cutting as regards traditional fields of knowledge.

The Essence of Super-optimum Solutions

One type of super-optimum solution is a solution that achieves a super-optimum goal. A super-optimum goal is one that is far higher than is traditionally considered to be the best attainable. An example would be improving on 0 per cent unemployment by simultaneously eliminating or reducing traditional unemployment and greatly increasing job opportunities for those who are willing and able to work more, but who were formerly considered outside the labor force or formerly considered fully employed.

A second type of super-optimum solution occurs in resolving public policy disputes. It is a solution that provides a way of satisfying liberals and conservatives in a policy dispute so that both the liberal and the conservatives consider the solution to be better than their original best expectations by their own respective goals and priorities. The minimum wage policy dispute discussed below is an example.

A third type occurs in resolving adjudicative or rule-applying controversies, rather than policy-making disputes. It is a solution that provides a way of satisfying the disputants that is better than their respective best expectations. An example is where a plaintiff demands $900 000, the defendant refuses to pay more than $300 000 and they agree that the defendant will turn over merchandise which the defendant manufactures that is worth more than $1 000 000 to the plaintiff, but whose variable cost is worth less than $200 000 to the defendant.

A fourth type enables all sides in a dispute to add substantially to their original net worth. An example would be in the same litigation dispute where the defendant agrees to give the plaintiff a franchise for selling the defendant's products and the franchise brings in a net $1 000 000 a year, with $500 000 a year for the plaintiff and $500 000 a year for the defendant. This type of expanded-sum solution would still be met if the total net worth of all participants increased substantially, even if the net worth of some of the participants decreased slightly, provided that the decrease did not cause those participants to go below a minimum level of satisfaction.

Whatever solution is reached, it should not only be optimum in one or more of the above four ways, but should also enable affected outsiders who are not parties to the dispute or the negotiations to come out ahead. That excludes an agreement which greatly benefits the immediate parties, but at the substantial expense of others.

An Example from Dispute Resolution

The situation   A good example from the field of resolving litigation disputes is where the plaintiff (or one side) demands $800 as a minimum to avoid going to trial or resorting to other non-settlement action. The defendant (or the other side) insists that it will not part with more than $200. So long as the dispute remains on that single dimension, there is no way that both sides can come out truly ahead. Whatever the plaintiff gains, the defendant loses, and vice versa. A traditional compromise would involve splitting the difference to settle for $500, or else going to trial. The plaintiff might console himself by saying that it could have been worse if liability were rejected at trial, since the plaintiff would then get nothing. The defendant might console himself by saying that it could have been worse if liability were established at trial, since the defendant might then wind up paying $800 or more. In reality, the plaintiff has lost $300 if he really thought that $800 is what he deserved to get, and the defendant also lost $300 if he really thought that $200 is what he deserved to pay.

The solution of small costs and big benefits   The same problem might be approached from a multi-criteria perspective by adding one or more additional criteria to the plaintiff's goal of maximizing dollars paid. The additional criteria could include products of the defendant. Those products might include insurance annuities, manufactured goods or free transport. These criteria have in common that they cost relatively little per incremental unit for the defendant to produce if he is already in the business of producing them. However, they may have considerable value to the plaintiff in view of their market price, even with liberal discounts.

For example, in the case just mentioned, suppose the defendant manufactures electronic equipment, including television sets or other electronic equipment worth over $800 to the plaintiff. The same equipment might be worth less than $200 to the defendant, since the equipment has already been manufactured by the defendant. An exchange of a product like that is possible, maybe along with some cash to pay the plaintiff's attorney. It could result in the plaintiff gaining more than $800 in terms of the plaintiff's values and the defendant losing less than $200 in terms of the defendant's values. That is a multi-criteria dispute resolution in a litigation or rule-applying situation with mutually beneficial results. The best expectation of the plaintiff in the litigation example was probably to collect $800, since the plaintiff's initial demand tends to reflect an exaggerated high starting point. Likewise, the best expectation of the defendant was probably to have to pay only $200, since the defendant's initial offer also tends to reflect an exaggerated low starting point. Solutions like these can be referred to as super-optimum solutions because they are above the optimum or best that each side was initially expecting to achieve.

Examples from Policy Making

The outside offer   The minimum wage dispute could be used as an example of a potential super-optimum solution. The liberals in Congress are arguing for a minimum wage of approximately $4.50 an hour. The conservatives are arguing for approximately $4.00 an hour. A traditional compromise would be $4.25 an hour. That might be greeted as a victory by liberals since it is $0.90 more than the current $3.35. It might be greeted as a victory by conservatives since it is $0.25 less than what the liberals are seeking.

A wage of $4.25 an hour, though, could be considered a loss for both sides. It is a loss to liberals if $4.50 an hour is necessary for minimum food, shelter, clothing and other necessities for an average family of four. The $4.25 is a loss to conservatives if $4.00 an hour is the maximum that business firms can afford to pay to minimum-wage employees and thus anything higher than $4.00 an hour will mean laying off workers who will thereby suffer a lack of minimum food, shelter, clothing and other necessities.

A super-optimum solution might involve the minimum wage being raised to $4.75 an hour in terms of what each worker would receive, but simultaneously requiring each employer to pay only $3.75 an hour. The $1.00 difference would be paid by the government for every minimum-wage worker who would otherwise be unemployed either because the firm could not afford to hire the worker or because the worker would not be sufficiently inspired to take the job at less than the increased minimum wage.

Under such an arrangement the liberals come out ahead of their initial bargaining position of $4.50 and probably ahead of their best expectations. Likewise, the conservatives come out ahead of their initial bargaining position of $4.00 and probably ahead of their best expectations. The government and the taxpayers might especially come out ahead by virtue of (1) the money saved in terms of public aid, public housing, Medicaid and unemployment compensation, (2) the decreased cost of anti-social behavior associated with people who are embittered by unemployment or who resort to criminal sources of income, (3) the increase in the gross national product (GNP) as a result of the product these people produce and the accompanying increase in the taxes they pay, and (4) the better role models they now provide for their children and grandchildren who might otherwise be caught in a cycle of unemployment, public aid, criminal activity and lack of productivity.

As an additional requirement for a business firm to be eligible to pay only $3.75 an hour, the firm would be expected to provide on-the-job training so the workers would become even more productive to the firm, the economy and themselves. One thing in particular to point out regarding this example is that, by getting off the single track of the exchange of dollars between an employer and an employee, one can arrive not only at mutually beneficial solutions, but also at solutions that exceed the initial best expectations of both sides.

This example is summarized in Table 1. Table 1(A) shows the liberal, neutral and conservative alternatives, as well as the super-optimum solution. Table 1(B) shows six criteria for judging among the alternatives, although the emphasis in the subsequent analysis for the sake of simplicity is just on the first two criteria. Table 1(B) also shows that liberals place a relatively high weight on paying a decent wage compared to conservatives. On the other hand, conservatives place a relatively high weight on avoiding overpayment compared to liberals. The other criteria are given middling weights on a 1–3 weighting scale for the criteria, where a 3 means relatively high importance, 2 means middling importance and 1 means relatively low importance.

Table 1(C) shows how each alternative is scored on each criterion using a 1–5 scoring scale for the relations. A 5 means the alternative is highly conducive to the goal relatively speaking, a 4 means mildly conducive, a 3 means neither conducive nor adverse, a 2 means mildly adverse and a 1 means highly adverse. Thus the liberal solution has at least a mildly conducive effect on paying a decent wage, but a rather neutral effect on avoiding overpayment. The conservative solution is rather neutral on paying a decent wage, but mildly conducive on avoiding overpayment.

Table 1(D) shows the total scores for the liberal, neutral and conservative alternatives. The first total column involves the liberal weights or multipliers of a 3 for paying a decent wage and a 1 for avoiding overpayment. With those weights the liberal alternative gets a total score of 15, which is 3 × 4 plus 1 × 3. The conservative alternative gets a total score of 13, which is 3 × 3 plus 1 × 4. The second total column involves the neutral weights of a middling 2 for each goal. With those weights, the liberal alternative gets a total score of 14, which is 2 × 4 plus 2 × 3. The third total column involves the conservative weights of a 1 for paying a decent wage and a 3 for avoiding overpayment. With those weights, the liberal alternative gets a relatively low score of 13, which is 1 × 4 plus 3 × 3.

Combining alternatives into a creative synthesis   The kind of dispute resolution with which we are especially concerned is that of disputes over public policies for dealing with various social problems. For example, in the controversy over how to provide legal services for the poor, liberals and Congress advocate salaried government lawyers by way of the Legal Services Corporation. Conservatives and the Reagan White House advocate a program of volunteer lawyers serving the poor. Both sides agree that the key criteria for deciding among the alternative delivery systems are (1) inexpensiveness, (2) accessibility, (3) political feasibility, and (4) competence. There is also rough agreement that volunteers are better on inexpensiveness and political feasibility, whereas salaried government lawyers are better on accessibility and competence. The big dispute as to the inputs for arriving at a conclusion is over the relative weights of the goals. The liberals place a higher weight on accessibility and competence, whereas the conservatives place a higher weight on inexpensiveness and political feasibility.

Perhaps the best way to resolve disputes over the relative weights of the goals (or for that matter over any disputed policy problem) is to try to find a new alternative that will please both sides in light of their differing weights, goals, perceptions, constraints or other inputs. An example is working with the existing Legal Services Corporation, but requiring all Legal Services Agencies to use 10 per cent of their budgets to improve the accessibility and competence of volunteer lawyers. Accessibility can be improved by bringing the volunteer lawyers to the agency offices to meet relevant clients. Competence can be improved through training manuals, training workshops

Table 1   Minimum wages as an SOS policy example involving a third-party offer

A   The Alternatives

1	SOS wage supp.	($4.75) (to workers)
2	Substantial increase	($4.50) (liberal)
3	Compromise	($4.25) (neutral)
4	Slight increase	($4.00) (conservative)
5	SOS wage supp.	($3.75) (from employers)

B   The Criteria

		Liberal weights	Neutral weights	Conserv. weights
1	Pay decent wage	3.00	2.00	1.00
2	Avoid overpayment	1.00	2.00	3.00
3	Save taxes	2.00	2.00	2.00
4	Employ unemployed	2.00	2.00	2.00
5	On-job training	2.00	2.00	2.00
6	Better role models	2.00	2.00	2.00

C   Scores of Alternatives on Criteria

	Pay decent wage	Avoid over- payment	Save taxes	Employ un- employed	On-job training	Better role models
Substantial increase	4.00	3.00	3.00	2.00	2.00	2.00
Compromise	3.50	3.50	3.00	2.50	2.50	2.50
Slight increase	3.00	4.00	3.00	3.00	3.00	3.00
SOS wage supp.	5.00	5.00	4.00	4.00	4.00	4.00

D   Initial Analyses

		Liberal combined raw scores	Neutral combined raw scores	Conserv. combined raw scores
1	Substantial increase	15.00	14.00	13.00
2	Compromise	14.00	14.00	14.00
3	Slight increase	13.00	14.00	15.00
4	SOS wage supp.	20.00	20.00	20.00

Notes on how the wage supplement operates:
1. The minimum wage is raised to $4.75 per hour.
2. Employers need pay only $3.75 per hour for workers who were otherwise unemployed and who are provided with on-the-job training.
3. Those workers receive a wage supplement of $1 per hour from the government, bringing their total wage up to the $4.75 per hour new minimum wage.
4. The government gives the $1 per hour supplement to the employer to cover the minimum wage as an incentive to get the employer to hire an unemployed worker and to provide on-the-job training.
5. The government gives the $1 per hour supplement to the worker to cover the minimum wage as an incentive to get the worker to accept the job and to provide the worker with a decent wage to cover necessities.
6. The government provides the $1 per hour supplement which helps both the employer and the worker partly because: (a) it relieves the taxpayer from various welfare burdens such as Medicaid, Medicare, food stamps, unemployment compensation, public housing, aid to dependent children, social security, disability aid and so on; (b) it facilitates better role models, thereby relieving the taxpayer of the welfare burdens of future generations; (c) the new employment reduces costly anti-social behavior and attitudes such as crime, drug-taking, vice, bitterness and depression; (d) the employment adds to the gross national product, helps create jobs for others and adds to the tax base.

Notes on the general analysis:
1. The alternatives can be generalized into the four basic alternatives of liberal, neutral, conservative and super-optimum alternatives. (Table 1(A))
2. The dollar amounts of $4.75, $4.50, $4.25, $4.00 and $3.75 are approximations, partly for easy arithmetic. They do, however, approximate the actual minimum wage amount over which liberals and conservatives were arguing in Congress in 1989. (Table 1(A))
3. Liberals and conservatives both place a positive weight on paying a decent wage and avoiding overpayment. They differ, however, in the relative weights which they are likely to assign to those two key criteria. (Table 1(B))
4. The alternatives are scored on the criteria using a 1–5 scale where 5 means highly conducive to the goal, 4 means mildly conducive, 3 means neither conducive nor adverse, 2 means mildly adverse and 1 means highly adverse to the goal. (Table 1(C))
5. Liberals and conservatives tend to be roughly in agreement on the scores relating to the alternatives to the criteria, even though they disagree on the relative importance of the key criteria. (Table 1(C))
6. The combined raw scores are determined by adding the weighted relation scores together. For example, a substantial increase receives 15 points in the liberal total by adding 3×4 to 1×3. For the sake of simplicity in this introductory analysis, only the two key criteria of paying a decent wage and avoiding overpayment are used. (Table 1 (D))
7. The wage supplement comes out so far ahead of the second-place alternative on each of the three totals that the only way the second-place alternative could be a winner is (a) if one or more of the goals were to be given a negative weight, or (b) if one or more of the relation scores were to go above 5, below 1 or otherwise be unreasonable. (Table 1(D))

and matching specialist lawyers with clients who relate to their specialties. Such a 10 per cent system may be better than a pure Legal Services Corporation even for those with liberal weights, because it provides a better benefit/cost ratio and greater political feasibility without decreasing accessibility or competence. Such a system is also better than the existing Legal Services Corporation from a perspective with conservative weights because it represents an improvement on all four goals over the existing system. Also, if volunteering becomes mandatory for license renewal, the volunteers are likely to dominate the system.

Computer output for the legal service example is given in Table 2. The first part of the Table shows how the two original alternatives and the new alternative score on the four criteria on a scale of 1–2, corresponding to 'relatively no' and 'relatively yes'. The second part of the Table shows the same data, but with the scores on inexpensiveness and political feasibility doubled to reflect conservative values. The third part shows the same data as the first part, but with the scores doubled on accessibility and competence to reflect the liberal emphasis. The key feature to note is that the optimizing compromise scores better than the favored alternative of either side using each side's own value system. Finding such optimizing compromises is facilitated by this kind of analysis.

Contrasted with Other Types of Solutions

Disputes in adjudication or policy making can take various forms. Perhaps the most basic form relates to the winning and losing dimension. In that regard, the solutions to disputes can be classified as follows:

1   Super-optimum solutions in which all sides come out ahead of their initial best expectations, as described above. At the opposite extreme is a super-malimum solution in which all sides come out worse than their initial worst expectations. That can be the case in a mutually destructive war, labor strike or highly expensive litigation.
2   Pareto optimum solutions in which nobody comes out worse off and at least one side comes out better off. This is not a very favorable solution compared to a super-optimum solution. A Pareto malimum solution would be one in which nobody is better off and at least one side is worse off.
3   A win–lose solution, where what one side wins the other side loses. The net effect is zero when the losses are subtracted from the gains. This is the typical litigation dispute when one ignores the litigation costs.
4   A lose–lose solution, where both sides are worse off than they were before the dispute began. This may often be the typical litigation dis-

Table 2   An example of computer-aided mediation

	Inexpensiveness	Accessibility	Political feasibility	Competence
A With Unweighted Criteria				
Volunteer	2.00	1.00	2.00	1.00
Salaried	1.00	2.00	1.00	2.00
SOS	1.50	2.00	2.00	2.00
B With Conservative Values				
Volunteer	4.00	1.00	4.00	1.00
Salaried	2.00	2.00	2.00	2.00
SOS	3.00	2.00	4.00	2.00
C With Liberal Values				
Volunteer	2.00	2.00	2.00	2.00
Salaried	1.00	4.00	1.00	4.00
SOS	1.50	4.00	2.00	4.00

Notes:
1. The alternative ways of providing legal counsel to the poor include: (a) volunteer attorneys, favored by the White House; (b) salaried government attorneys, favored by Congress; (c) a compromise that involves continuing the salaried system, but requiring that 10 per cent of its funding go to making volunteers more accessible and competent. (Table rows)
2. The criteria are inexpensiveness, accessibility, political feasibility and competence. Each alternative is scored on each criterion on a scale from 1.00 to 2.00 (Table columns and cells)
3. Conservative values involve giving a weight of 2 to inexpensiveness and political feasibility when the other criteria receive a weight of 1. (Table 2(B)) Liberal values involve giving a weight of 2 to accessibility and competence when the other criteria receive a weight of 1. (Table 2(C))
4. With conservative values, the volunteer system wins over the salaried system by 10 points to 8. The compromise is an overall winner with 11.5 points. (Table 2(B))
5. With liberal values, the salaried system wins over the volunteer system by 10 points to 8. The compromise is an overall winner with 11.5 points. (Table 2(C))
6. The '10 per cent compromise' is thus a super winner in being better than the original best solution of both the conservatives and the liberals. (The third row in tables 2(A), 2(B) and 2(C))

pute, or close to it when one includes litigation costs. These costs are often so high that the so-called winner is also a loser. This is also often the case in labor–management disputes that result in a strike, and even more so in international disputes that result in going to war.

5   The so-called win–win solution. At first glance this looks like a solution where everybody comes out ahead. What it typically refers to, though, is an illusion, since the parties are only coming out ahead relative to their worst expectations. In this sense, the plaintiff is a winner no matter what the settlement is because the plaintiff could have won nothing if liability had been rejected at trial. Likewise, the defendant is a winner no matter what the settlement is because the defendant could have lost everything the plaintiff was asking for if liability had been established at trial. The parties are only fooling themselves in the same sense that someone who is obviously a loser tells himself he won because he could have done worse.

Another common way of classifying dispute resolutions is in terms of whether there is a third party present. In that sense, adjudication, arbitration and mediation are frequently referred to as forms of three-party dispute resolution, and negotiation refers to two-party dispute resolution. Adjudication tends to mean a court or administrative agency that resolves disputes, usually in a win–lose way. Arbitration tends to involve an ad hoc third party who is hired or obtained just for the immediate dispute, but who also tends to operate from a win–lose perspective. A mediator, like an arbitrator, tends to be ad hoc but seeks to have both sides arrive at mutually beneficial settlements which could be win–win, Pareto optimum, or even super-optimum, but not win–lose or lose–lose. This distinction between three-party and two-party dispute resolution may be undesirable because it encourages two-party negotiation to go for a win–lose solution. It is possible, when two negotiators are present, for one or both of them to have a mediation perspective in the sense of seeking truly to bring about a super-optimum or Pareto optimum solution.

Another way of classifying dispute resolutions or policy solutions is in terms of the substance or subject matter. This can include such categories as disputes involving family members, neighbors, merchant–consumer situations, management–labor situations, litigation or rule-applying, legislation or rule-making, and international disputes. Those categories are meaningful in the sense that it is possible to tell a family dispute from an international dispute. Emphasizing those distinctions, however, may be undesirable because the same underlying principles may apply regardless of the subject matter. These principles include (1) the desirability of getting off a single dimension into multiple criteria, (2) the desirability of generally seeking super-optimum solutions where all sides, including society, come out ahead of their best expectations, and (3) the usefulness of decision-aiding software for dealing with multi-criteria dispute resolution toward achieving super-optimum solutions.

Still another way of classifying solutions to policy controversies is in terms of the directions in which benefits and costs move. In a super-optimum solution, the benefits go up, and the costs go down. In a traditional solution, the benefits may go up, but at the expense of increased costs; or the costs may go down, but at the expense of decreased benefits. In a super-malimum solution, the benefits go down and the costs go up, which is the opposite of a super-optimum solution. Drug crackdowns can have that effect by being highly expensive and yet encouraging more suppliers to enter the market by raising the sale price of drugs.

Procedures for Arriving at Super-optimum Solutions

New alternatives   One procedure for arriving at super-optimum solutions is to think in terms of what is in the conservative alternative that liberals might like and, likewise, what is in the liberal alternative that conservatives might like; then to think whether it is possible to make a new alternative that will emphasize those two aspects. Another technique is to emphasize the opposite: it involves saying what is in a conservative alternative that liberals especially dislike and what is in the liberal alternative that conservatives especially dislike; then to think about making a new alternative that eliminates those two aspects.

In arriving at super-optimum solutions in litigation settlements, one should especially try to find something that the defendant can give to the plaintiff that is not worth so much to the defendant but is worth a lot to the plaintiff. This may relate to a product that the defendant manufactures or sells which has a low variable cost to the defendant but a high market value to the plaintiff. An example is the defendant insurance company giving a valuable annuity to the plaintiff. Another example is the defendant manufacturer giving manufactured products to the plaintiff which the plaintiff can use. This kind of trade can be generalized to policy-making situations as well as litigation situations.

New goals   Another technique is not to concentrate on the alternatives as the above procedures do, but instead to concentrate on the goals. One way of doing this is to ask what goals are especially important to liberals, and what goals are especially important to conservatives, then to try to find alternatives that can simultaneously satisfy both of those goals. This technique could be illustrated by the minimum wage example, where the goals do not change at all. Conservatives endorse the goal of low wages and liberals endorse the goal of high wages; or, to put it differently, conservatives endorse the goal of providing a stimulating environment for business, whereas liberals endorse the goal of preventing the abuse of workers. The minimum wage supplement allows business to pay as low as $1.00 per hour while the worker receives $5.00 per hour as a result of the voucher supplement.

A variation on this is to add new goals. The usual procedure starts with the conservative goals as givens in light of how they justify their current best alternative, and it starts with the liberal goals as givens in light of how they justify their current best alternative. This technique calls for thinking about the goals conservatives tend to endorse that are not currently involved in the controversy, but that could be brought in to justify a new alternative, and, likewise, what goals liberals tend to endorse that are not currently involved in the controversy, but that could also be brought in. For this technique, a good example is the free speech controversy, where liberals want virtually unrestricted free speech, in order to stimulate creativity, and conservatives want restrictions on free speech in order to have more order in the legal system. However, liberals also like due process, equal protection and right to privacy. This raises questions as to whether it might be permissible to restrict free speech in order to satisfy those constitutional rights, where the restrictions are not so great, but the jeopardy of those other rights might be great. Likewise, conservatives like policies that are good for business. They might therefore readily endorse permissive free speech that relates to advertising, to trying to convince workers that they should not join unions, or that relates to lobbying.

Combining alternatives   An important technique is to find a policy that in effect combines two policies into one. On the first policy, liberals receive a lot, but conservatives give up relatively little; on the second policy, conservatives receive a lot but liberals give up relatively little.

Bringing in a third party   In the minimum wage example, conservatives get more than what they want, and liberals also get more than what they want. The important thing is that conservatives do not get it by taking it from liberals, and liberals do not get it by taking from conservatives. Instead, at least on the surface, they are both taking from a third party. In this context the third party in the short run is the federal government and the American taxpayer. In the long run, though, the taxpayer benefits if subsidizing the minimum wage results in putting to work people who otherwise would be receiving public aid or would be engaging in anti-social or possibly criminal behavior. The taxpayer especially benefits if, combined with that minimum wage, is an on-the-job training requirement that upgrades the skills of the workers so that they substantially add to national productivity.

Getting the solution adopted One problem with super-optimum solutions is that they look so good that they may cause some people to think they might be some kind of trap. An example is the Camp David Accords. That example is a classic super-optimum solution where Israel, Egypt, the United States and everybody involved came out ahead of their original best expectations. According to the *New York Times* for 26 March 1989, however, Israeli intelligence at least initially opposed Anwar Sadat's visit to Israel and the Camp David Accords until close to the signing on the grounds that it all sounded so good that it must be a trap. Israeli intelligence felt that Israel was being set up for a variation on the Yom Kippur war, whereby Israel got into big trouble by relaxing its guard because of the holidays. They viewed this as an attempt to get them to relax their guard again, and believed that any minute the attack would begin. They were on a more intense alert at the time of the Camp David negotiations than they were at any other time during Israel's history. This nicely illustrates how super-optimum solutions can easily be viewed by people as a trap because they look so good that they are unbelievable. Traditional solutions are not so likely to be viewed as traps, and they are taken more at their face value, which is generally not much.

The Helpfulness of Decision-aiding Software

Super-optimum solutions are facilitated, not only by multi-criteria thinking, but also by decision-aiding software that is based on multi-criteria spreadsheets. A spreadsheet is nothing more than a table, matrix or chart that has rows, columns and cells which can be subject to manipulation in various ways.

In that context, the goals of each side are put in the columns. The alternatives available to them are put in the rows. The cells shows how each alternative scores on each goal. A column at the far right shows the total scores for each alternative when adding across to take into consideration that the goals may be measured in different ways. The whole system is subject to 'what if?' analysis, which can be especially useful for dealing with missing information.

Each side has its own spreadsheet perspective on the dispute that needs to be resolved. A super-optimum solution has been achieved if settling becomes the most desired alternative on each of those spreadsheets, and if such settling results in more net benefit to each side than its original favored alternative.

From the examples that have thus far been given (especially Tables 1 and 2) one can talk about the generic super-optimum solution from a spreadsheet perspective. Table 3 is designed to achieve that purpose. It shows the alter-

Table 3   The generic SOS solution from a spreadsheet perspective

A   The Alternatives
1   Conservative
2   Compromise
3   Liberal
4   SOS1 (dominating SOS)
5   SOS2 (non-dominating SOS)
6   SOS3 (new-goal SOS)

B   The Criteria

		Conserv. weights	Liberal weights
1	Conservative goal	3.00	1.00
2	Liberal goal	1.00	3.00
3	Neutral goal	2.00	2.00

C   Scores of Alternatives
     on Criteria

	Cons. goal	Lib. goal	Neut. goal
Conservative	5.00	1.00	3.00
Compromise	3.10	3.10	3.00
Liberal	1.00	5.00	3.00
SOS1	5.10	5.10	3.10
SOS2	4.50	4.50	2.90
SOS3	4.00	4.00	4.00

D   Initial Analyses

		Conservative combined raw scores	Liberal combined raw scores
1	Conservative alt.	16.00	8.00
2	Compromise	12.40	12.40
3	Liberal alt.	8.00	16.00
4	SOS1	20.40	20.40
5	SOS2	18.00	18.00
6	SOS3	16.00	16.00

Notes on the alternatives:
1. The conservative alternative is shown first because it tends to be the current alternative on which we would like to improve. The conservative alternative or set of alternatives in a policy problem tends to differ from the liberal alternatives in the relative extent to which it favors those who are relatively well off in a society, whereas the liberal alternative tends to favor those who are relatively not so well off.
2. The first super-optimum solution (and the most difficult to achieve) is to find an

alternative that is better than the conservative, liberal and compromise alternatives on all the goals. The second super-optimum solution is an alternative that is not better on all the goals than the other alternatives, but is better on the overall or combined score adding across the goals. The third super-optimum solution is not better on all the goals and is not better on the overall score with the initial goals, but is better on the overall score than the non-SOS alternatives when another goal is added.

Notes on the criteria:
1. The conservative goal or goals in this context are by definition goals that conservatives disproportionately favor, as indicated by the fact that those goals are given relatively high weight by conservatives. The liberal goals are likewise given relatively high weight by liberals. Note, however, that, in a typical policy problem, conservatives tend to give positive weight to liberal goals (although relatively less weight than to conservative goals) and vice versa with liberals.
2. The scores of the alternatives on the criteria are based on a 1–5 scale for the sake of simplicity, although that does not have to be. On a 1–5 scale, 5 means highly conducive to the goal, 4 means mildly conducive, 3 means neither conducive nor adverse, 2 means mildly adverse and 1 means the alternative is highly adverse to the goal.

Notes on the relation scores:
1. The conservative alternatives logically score high on the conservative goals and low on the liberal goals, and vice versa for the liberal alternatives. The compromise alternative scores slightly above the middle on each goal. That avoids ties in this analysis, and that is the general nature of compromises.
2. The scores of the super-optimum solutions on the conservative, liberal and neutral goals are consistent with their definitions. Likewise, the scores of the alternatives on the neutral goal are consistent with the definition of the neutral goal as being between the conservative goal and the liberal goal in its normative direction.

Notes on the initial analyses:
1. The combined raw scores are determined by adding the weighted relation scores together. For example, the conservative alternative receives 16 points using the conservative weights by adding 3×5 to 1×1. Using the liberal weights, the conservative alternative receives only 8 points by adding 1×5 to 3×1. For the sake of simplicity in this generic analysis, only the conservative goal and the liberal goal are used. The neutral goal has to be activated to enable the 'new-goal SOS' to be a super-optimum solution.
2. Using the conservative weights, the conservative alternative logically comes out ahead of the liberal alternative, and vice versa using the liberal weights. The compromise alternative is the winner among those three alternatives with an aggregate score of 24.80 versus 24.00 for either the conservative or the liberal alternative, but the compromise alternative is only the second choice of both groups.
3. The three super-optimum alternatives all do better than the traditional compromise. What is more important, the three super-optimum alternatives all simultaneously do better than the conservative alternative using the conservative weights and they do better than the liberal alternative using the liberal weights. That is the essential characteristic of a super-optimum alternative. It is the new first choice of both groups.
4. Even the worst of all three super-optimum solutions comes out so far ahead of the traditional compromise that the only way the traditional compromise could be a winner is (a) if one or more of the goals were to be given a negative weight, or (b) if one or more of the relation scores were to go above 5, below 1 or otherwise be unreasonable.

natives, criteria, scores of the alternatives on the criteria and the initial analyses using general language. The alternatives are referred to as the conservative, compromise, liberal or super-optimum alternatives. The criteria are referred to as the conservative, liberal or neutral goals.

Each goal has a conservative weight and a liberal weight, since the conservatives and liberals especially differ in terms of the relative weights they assign to goals. The scores are expressed on a 1–5 scale to bring out the relations more clearly. The initial analyses show how well each alternative scores overall in terms of the conservative weights and then in terms of the liberal weights.

Among the three basic alternatives, the conservative alternative is the winner using the conservative weights, as expected. The liberal alternative is then the loser, with the compromise in between. The opposite is true using the liberal weights. The super-optimum solution does better than any of the three basic alternatives using the conservative weights. It also does better than any of the three alternatives using the liberal weights. That is the essence of a super-optimum solution.

Three different types of super-optimum solution are presented, but they all have that essential characteristic of being simultaneously better than the conservative first choice in light of the conservative goals and better than the liberal first choice in light of the liberal goals. Further details are given in the notes to the table corresponding to the sections of the table dealing with the alternatives, the criteria, the relation scores and the initial analyses.

Classifying Super-optimum Solutions

Dimensions for classifying super-optimum solutions are as follows.

1   Whether or not super-optimum goals are involved.
2   Whether we are talking about dispute resolution or policy making.
3   Whether we are talking about all sides coming out ahead of their best expectations, or coming out ahead in a more absolute sense.
4   A typology that emphasizes the ways of arriving at super-optimum solutions, including
    (a)   an alternative that involves small costs to one side and big benefits to the other;
    (b)   the outside offer;
    (c)   the combination alternative that does well on everybody's goals;
    (d)   a package of items that does not simply involve combining the liberal and conservative alternatives into a new synthesis. An example would be the Vera system for dealing with pre-trial release so as to increase simultaneously the probability of re-

leased defendants showing up without committing crimes (in order to please conservatives) and the percentage of defendants who are released prior to trial (in order to please liberals). The Vera package of items includes screening for good risks, having released defendants report to the courthouse periodically prior to trial, notification immediately prior to trial, prosecution of those who fail to appear in court, and reduction of delay between arrest and trial;

(e) a super-optimum solution which involves removing the problem rather than trying to synthesize the liberal and conservative solutions. An example would be better birth control to deal with the abortion problem.

5   Whether or not a third party is present as a mediator, arbitrator or adjudicator.

6   The situation can be classified by the substance or subject matter.

7   Whether or not decision-aiding software is present.

8   Ways of arriving at super-optimum solutions in terms of concentrating on the alternatives, the goals or a better sub-classification might be

(a) developing a new alternative that is not a combination of the old alternatives;

(b) developing a new alternative that is a combination of the old alternatives;

(c) bringing in a new goal which enables an old or new alternative to become super-optimum, which it would not be without the new goal.

9   Classifying the super-optimum solutions in terms of

(a) whether the solution is better or at least as good on all goals as the original alternatives. This is a solution that is dominating.

(b) whether the solution is better than all the original alternatives on the summation score but not necessarily on every criterion. This is the non-dominating super-optimum solution.

(c) the non-dominating super-optimum solution that requires an additional goal to receive the highest summation score.

10 A distinction can also be made between prescriptive and predictive SOS analysis. Prescriptive is concerned with determining the policy that should be adopted in order to enable conservatives, liberals and other major viewpoints all to come out ahead of their best initial expectations simultaneously. Predictive analysis is concerned with determining the policy that will be adopted and why, or why a previous policy was adopted. The prescriptive–predictive categories roughly correspond to evaluative and explanatory or to normative and causal.

Table 4 Some trends in specific policy fields

Policy fields	Benefits for the have-nots	Benefits for the haves or all
Economic policy		
Labor	Better wages, hours, working conditions No child labor. Less discrimination	Stimulus to labor-saving technology. Happier and more productive workers
Consumer	More rights concerning product liability	Stimulus to prove better products & greater sales
Political–Legal Policy		
Free speech	More rights in politics, art and commerce	Stimulus to creativity
Due process & criminal justice	More rights to counsel, notice, hearings	More respect for the law
Equal treatment	More rights for blacks, women & the poor on voting, criminal justice, schools, employment, housing & consumer protection rights	More equality of opportunity and allocation on the basis of merit
Government reform	Less corruption, intimidation & incompetence	More effectiveness & efficiency
World peace & trade	Increased standards of living for developing countries	Uplifted countries become good trading partners
Social Policy		
Poverty	More rights as employees, consumers, tenants, welfare recipients & family members	The same rights apply to middle-class employees, consumers, tenants & family members
Education	More access to more education	More efficient economy from better training Less welfare
Science Policy		
Environment	More rights regarding cleaner air, water, solid waste, noise, radiation and conservation	The same rights are important to all people
Health	More access to medical help	This includes help with devastating diseases that even the rich cannot deal with

Mutually Beneficial Trends

Table 4 summarizes some of the trends in specific policy fields. The overall idea is that there have been increased benefits for people who had few rights as of the base years of 1910, 1930 or 1950. These people have been the immediate beneficiaries of the policy changes. It is, however, unduly narrow to limit the analysis to these immediate effects. The longer-term and broader effects have also been to benefit the dominant groups and the whole of society.

This is shown, for example, in the top row. Labor has benefited from better wages, shorter hours, better working conditions, the ending of child labor and the lessening of race and sex discrimination. Also highly important is the stimulus those labor policies have had in encouraging the development and adoption of labor-saving technology. The United States of 1980 might still be using slave labor or cheap immigrant labor and be a backward low-technology country if it had not been for the successful efforts of labor unions and working-class people to increase the cost of their labor. A third-level result is that the labor-saving technology has made labor more productive and more skilled. This has the effect of increasing wages still further, thereby stimulating greater consumption and the creation of new jobs, especially in service fields.

Likewise, one can go through each of the 11 policy fields and see that the initial policy changes have tended in a direction of increasing the rights of the have-nots. Those increases have in turn stimulated benefits for the whole society, regardless of whether one is talking about consumer rights, free speech, criminal justice, equal treatment, government reform, world peace and trade, poverty, education, environment or health.

Notes

For further details on the general nature of and need for super-optimum solutions, see Susskind and Cruikshank (1987), Nagel (1991), Sawhill (1988) and Nagel (1989).

On expanding the total resources, especially the gross national product, see Magaziner and Reich (1982), Etzioni (1983), Alperovitz and Faux (1984), Dermer (1986) and Lindsey (1990). On increasing productivity in the public and private sectors, see Holzer and Nagel (1984), Kelly (1988), Holzer and Halachmi (1988), LeBoeuf (1982) and Sato and Suzawa (1983). On increasing relevant innovation and creativity, see Kash (1989), Palda (1984), Mole and Elliott (1987), Agnew (1980) and Osborn (1963).

PART I
MORE RESOURCES TO
SATISFY ALL SIDES

1 Expanding the Resources

Dealing with the Deficit

The Alternatives

A basic illustrative problem is how to deal with deficits. One effective approach is to expand the total resources. If one examines the positions of the respective sides, one sees that approach taken.

The *liberals* want to increase taxes on the rich, hold constant taxes on the poor, decrease military spending and hold constant domestic spending. One might say they want to decrease taxes on the poor, but the poor pay very few taxes right now and there is not much potential for a decrease. One might say they want to increase domestic spending. That might be unrealistic if we are talking about traditional ways of dealing with the deficit. One does not increase spending or decrease taxes.

The *conservatives* want to hold constant taxes on the rich and increase taxes on the poor by way of sales taxes and other regressive taxes, or a value added tax. They want to hold constant military spending and decrease domestic spending.

The *compromise position* wants to do a little bit of everything. It would have a medium increase of taxes on the rich and on the poor, and a medium cutting of military spending and domestic spending.

SOS wants to decrease taxes on both the rich and the poor, especially by way of tax breaks that will stimulate increased productivity. However, the main way in which the tax decrease occurs is by way of decreasing the tax rate, not the quantity of tax dollars. The rate goes down and the quantity of dollars taken in goes up if the GNP goes up by way of well-placed tax breaks and subsidies. The SOS wants to increase spending in the form of productivity-encouraging subsidies. The increased spending can come from the increased GNP. The increased GNP can be a result of the well-placed subsidies.

The SOS Table

Tables 1.1 and Table 1.2 show these alternatives in the context of an SOS table. The first goal listed is to increase the gross national product. That means the same thing as increasing gross national income and gross national consumption or spending. This is an effective measure. The second goal is to decrease taxes or the amount or percentage of the GNP that people spend on government activities. That is an efficiency measure.

The conservative alternative constitutes at least a mild reduction in goal achievement on both increased national spending and decreased taxes since the conservative alternative decreases domestic spending and increases taxes at least on the poor. The liberal alternative also constitutes a mild reduction on both goals since the liberal alternative decreases defense spending and increases taxes at least on the rich. The compromise alternative decreases both kinds of spending and increases both kinds of taxes, although not as

Table 1.1   Dealing with the deficit (initial perspective)

Alternatives \ Criteria	L Goal Increase GNP	C Goal Reduce taxes	N Total (neutral weights)	L Total (liberal weights)	C Total (conservative weights)
C Alternative Reduce domestic spending, increase taxes on poor	2	2	8	8	8
L Alternative Reduce defense spending, increase taxes on rich	2	2	8	8	8
N Alternative Reduce both types of spending, increase taxes on both	2	2	8	8	8
SOS Alternative Increase spending, reduce taxes	4	4	16	16**	16**

Notes:
1. The double asterisk (here and throughout the volume) indicates an alternative that is capable of winning on both the liberal and the conservative totals.
2. The increased spending under the SOS alternative is for productivity-encouraging subsidies.
3. The decrease in taxes is for productivity-encouraging tax benefits.

much as the conservatives or liberals would do. The SOS alternative has at least a mildly positive effect on increasing the gross national product and decreasing taxes.

The neutral totals are calculated by summing the raw scores after doubling each one. This reflects the idea that a neutral weight is a 2 on a 1–3 scale where 1 is relatively low importance, 2 is middling and 3 is high importance. The liberal totals reflect a relatively low weight for the goal of decreasing taxes. The conservative totals reflect a relatively low weight for the goal of decreasing taxes. The conservative totals reflect a relatively low weight for increasing national spending, and a relatively high weight for decreasing taxes. Both liberals and conservatives, however, give positive weight to increased GNP and decreased taxes. The bottom row of Table 1.1 shows the SOS alternative as a clear winner on both the liberal totals and the conservative totals, as well as the neutral totals. A key question is how is that possible?

The Causal Arrow Diagram

This is better shown with a system of arrows plus Table 1.1 instead of verbally. Figure 1.1. shows what the arrows would look like.

As is shown, the increased GNP results in increased tax revenue even if the tax rate remains constant at approximately 20 per cent. However, we are talking about a decreased tax rate. If, for example, the GNP is $4 trillion in the before period and is $8 trillion in the after period, then, with a constant 25 per cent tax rate, the tax intake will double. Even if the tax rate drops below 25 per cent, the tax intake will still increase so long as it does not drop below 12.5 per cent. At a 25 per cent tax rate with $4 trillion, the income to the government is $1 trillion. At a 25 per cent tax rate with $8 trillion, the income is $2 trillion. Thus, so long as the tax rate falls to anything above 12.5 per cent, the tax intake will still increase.

We could add a circle, although maybe just verbally, without it being in the diagram, to say that, in order to have the right kind of subsidies and tax breaks, systematic public policy analysis is necessary. Without such analysis, subsidies could wind up supporting inefficient, unproductive activities in a kind of bail-out dole system rather than a system designed to provide incentives.

The increased government spending and tax reduction relate to production-encouraging subsidies and tax breaks. Well-placed subsidies increase productivity, GNP, tax revenue and money available for well-placed subsidies. It becomes the opposite of a vicious circle – a virtuous circle. It could be called an SOS circle, although that has a specialized meaning of being better than the best expectations of both sides to a dispute, or all sides to a dispute.

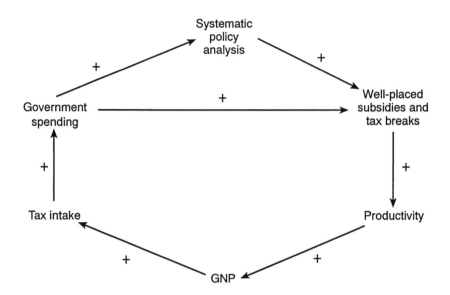

Figure 1.1   The upward spiral of well-placed subsidies in facilitating increased government services and reduced tax rates

The Compromise Position

Why is it that the compromise does not do better than either the liberal or the conservative position? It should do better in order to explain why compromises are usually adopted. The compromise can do better if it taxes the rich and the poor, but does not do so in such a way as to add up to as much tax as the liberal alternative alone or the conservative alternative alone. And likewise on the spending side. Thus we would not want a split right down the middle.

Instead, we would say the compromise position taxes the rich somewhere between the liberal position on taxing the rich and the conservative position on taxing the rich. It is kept a little closer to the conservative position in order to get adopted and, likewise, it is kept a little closer to the liberal position on taxing the poor in order to get adopted. It compromises by undertaxing the rich slightly to make the conservatives happy, but not going so far as the conservatives would. It undertaxes the poor slightly to make the liberals happy, but does not go so far as the liberals would.

Similarly, on cutting down on the military, such spending could stand between liberals and conservatives. Likewise, cutting domestic spending could be somewhere around the middle. By knocking a little off each of those compromise relation scores, the compromise position comes out the winner among the traditional positions. The compromise does not have to be exactly in the middle on both defense and domestic spending, so long as conservatives come out ahead on one (probably defense) and liberals on the other (probably domestic spending).

Table 1.2   Dealing with the deficit (improved perspective)

Criteria / Alternatives	C Goal Defense and investment	L Goal Domestic policies, consumption	N Total (neutral weights)	L Total (liberal weights)	C Total (conservative weights)
C Alternative Reduce domestic spending, increase taxes on poor	4	2	12	10	14*
L Alternative Reduce defense spending, increase taxes on rich	2	4	12	14*	10
N Alternative Reduce both types of spending, increase taxes on both	3	3	12	12	12
SOS Alternative Increase spending, reduce taxes	5	5	20	20**	20**

Notes:
1. A fuller statement of the conservative goal might be (a) to have a strong national defense, and (b) to stimulate investment through low taxes on the relatively rich. A fuller statement of the liberal goal might be (a) to have strong domestic policies like education and housing, and (b) to stimulate consumption through low taxes on the relatively poor.
2. The SOS involves a reduction of taxes in the form of tax breaks designed to stimulate greater productivity. Likewise, the SOS involves an increase in spending in the form of well-placed subsidies designed to stimulate greater productivity. The increased productivity means an increased gross national product, which means an increased base on which to apply the national tax rate. Thus the tax rate can drop and still bring in increased tax revenue and thereby have more money available for government spending, including defense, domestic policies, deficit reduction and more well-placed subsidies.
3. A single asterisk (here and throughout the volume) indicates the alternative that wins on either the conservative totals or the liberal totals before considering the SOS alternative.

Thus the compromise position is the best of those three traditional choices, but only just. It is like the least of three evils or undesirable positions. Liberals would not consider the liberal position to be an evil, but it is an evil if it reduces spending to the point where defense is jeopardized. Likewise, conservatives would not consider the conservative position to be evil, but it is if it reduces domestic spending to the point where housing, shelter, education, pollution and other domestic policies are jeopardized. It is not necessary to say that liberals, conservatives and compromisers are evil in any absolute sense. It is just necessary to recognize that, by definition and by realistic analysis, they are not as good at working for an SOS.

This is a very general example because increased government spending affects every public policy problem. It is also very general because it puts systematic policy analysis in a favorable key position and it deals with positive incentives and the importance of productivity.

National Economic Growth

The Win–Win Productivity Cycle

What follows is an attempt to draw together a lot of ideas that deal with economic social development in developing nations. The ideas are also applicable to industrial nations since all nations are in the process of developing and of seeking economic growth. Figure 1.2 is a cyclical diagram that begins with productivity causes, moves on to socioeconomic effects, economic indicators and poverty reduction, and recycles back to economic indicators, socioeconomic effects and productivity causes.

The diagram could be drawn as a big circle with each of the four clusters as smaller circles orbiting the center. That is more difficult to draw. More importantly, both a circles model and the present rectangles model lack three-dimensionality: the circles and rectangles should be like an infinitely winding staircase, with each turn bringing us to a higher level in terms of global quality of life. A well-drawn staircase might even show the world going up the staircase at a faster-and-faster rate. This indicates an exponential or geometrical progression in the sense that each new development (especially technological development) may lead to two or more other developments.

This kind of progression has the potential for leading to great progress, unless the new technologies are destructive, like nuclear bombs, and are not restrained. The best restraint, however, may be the mutual benefit that comes from nations buying, selling and investing in each other. Mutual destruction is not likely to occur during rising prosperity, especially prosperity that depends on peaceful mutual interaction.

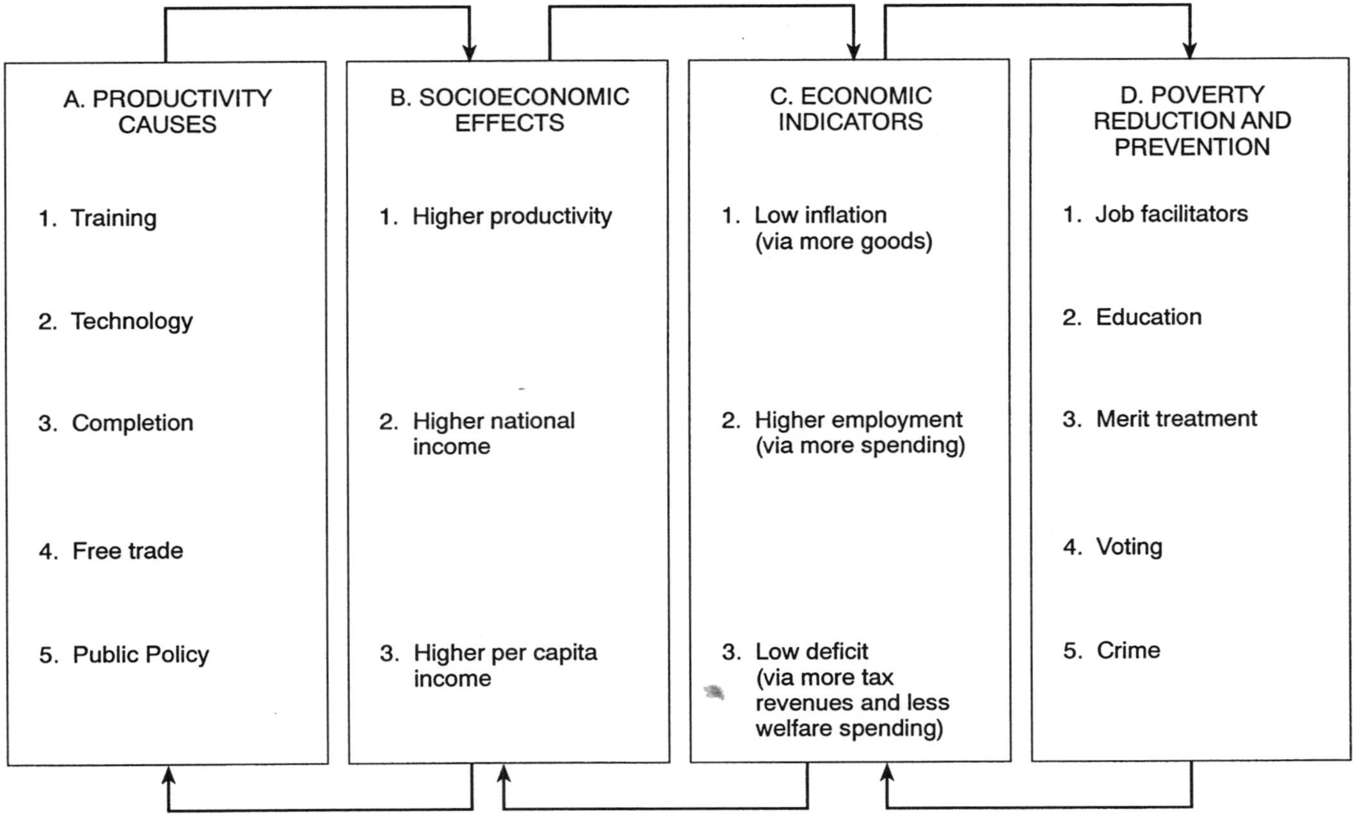

A. PRODUCTIVITY CAUSES

1. Training
2. Technology
3. Completion
4. Free trade
5. Public Policy

B. SOCIOECONOMIC EFFECTS

1. Higher productivity
2. Higher national income
3. Higher per capita income

C. ECONOMIC INDICATORS

1. Low inflation (via more goods)
2. Higher employment (via more spending)
3. Low deficit (via more tax revenues and less welfare spending)

D. POVERTY REDUCTION AND PREVENTION

1. Job facilitators
2. Education
3. Merit treatment
4. Voting
5. Crime

Figure 1.2   The win–win productivity cycle

Productivity causes   The first productivity cause listed in somewhat random order is training. It is important to note that the items within each cluster are cyclical, reciprocal or interactive, as well as the relations among the four clusters of ideas or variables. For example, the training is mainly designed to teach people how to use the new technologies. Competition can be used in contracting out the training. Free trade is relevant to retraining workers who may have been displaced as a result of US consumers having access to less expensive products. Public policy can affect the other four items, as well as the other three clusters.

As regards *training*, we are talking about post-college adult training, as contrasted to pre-adult education, which is part of cluster D. The best or most productive adult training is on-the-job training; the trainee already has a job, but needs training to retain it, or to move up to a better job in the same firm. Perhaps the best way to stimulate such training is a nationwide payroll tax which is 100 per cent refundable to all business firms who use the money for new training and technologies. This leaves the decision making to the individual firms, rather than to a Ministry of International Trade and Industry. Training vouchers can also be given to individuals so as to further decentralize the decision making. Such a voucher system can include the total labor force and even the total adult population. Doing so enables unemployed people to become more productive, but also productive people to become even more productive, to the benefit of all.

As regards *technology*, this is sometimes a two-part problem. One part involves talking about how to develop new technologies, including new energy forms and cures for cancer. The other part involves talking about how to disperse existing technologies. Nobel Prize innovation is mainly for industrial countries. Dispersion is for both industrial and developing countries. The United States does a lot of innovating in its universities, but Japanese and other Asian industries may be faster in adopting US ideas than American industry, including ideas about more productive management methods. Developing countries can have lights, telephones and polio vaccines without having a local Edison, Bell or Salk. What may be especially needed to encourage dispersion is a public policy that requires licensing of new inventions in return for profitable royalties. This is in contrast to the present system of monopolistic patents as rewards for inventions. Patent monopolies may be used to restrict sales in order to get high prices. Royalties encourage sales in order to get high profits. Also relevant to stimulating new technologies is providing grants, rewards and tax breaks to encourage the invention or implementation of new technologies and sometimes new business firms to invent or implement them.

As for domestic *competition* (in contrast to free trade which is international competition), it is unfortunate from the perspective of economic growth that the two most relevant industries are frequently organized as arrogant monopolies in virtually all countries. These industries control the sale of electricity and of communication based on the telephone. Both electricity and telephoning (including Internet communication) are essential to all businesses (and increasingly essential in Internet telephoning). For years electricity and telephone companies have argued that they are natural monopolies, because it would be unnatural to build parallel electricity or telephone lines. Businesses now realize that electricity and telephone companies can be required to license their line at profitable rentals. Doing so brings in competition and thereby stimulates economic growth. Requiring the licensing of a phone network is far more meaningful than breaking a big phone company into regional monopolies.

As for *free trade*, this means reciprocal lowering or eliminating of tariffs on all goods. It should also mean allowing the business firms of all countries to sell electricity, telephone services, domestic airplane services and other services in the United States and elsewhere. This brings down prices and brings up quality through competition. This includes prices to business firms that are buying raw materials for processing or merchandise for resale. US Steel is now able to compete internationally and domestically by being a leading reseller of Japanese steel. US Steel now favors free trade, rather than restrictive tariffs. Free trade may also include the movement of workers to the places where the jobs are and the movement of ideas everywhere.

One of the most important roles for *public policy* in stimulating productivity is to provide job facilitators for workers who are displaced as a result of technology 'downsizing', new competition, free trade, immigration, defense conversion, employing the elderly, employing minorities, employing women and other factors that increase productivity but simultaneously cause some or much worker displacement, dislocation or disruption. These job facilitators appear under cluster D of the productivity cycle. In addition to facilitating jobs for displaced workers, public policy should be stimulating training, technology, competition and free trade, as mentioned above. Those four elements correspond to social, technology, economic and international policy, respectively. Social policy also includes education equity and merit treatment, which appear in cluster D. Technology policy also includes pollution reduction, transport and health policy, which are also relevant to productivity. Economic policy includes inflation and unemployment, shown in cluster C, and facilitating more productive labor–management relations. International policy also includes promoting peace and human rights through international organizations and America's economic influence. Political policy relates to facilitating political participation, which appears in cluster D. Legal policy relates to crime reduction (also in cluster D).

Socioeconomic effects   Higher productivity is the most obvious socioeconomic effect of the productivity causes, including training, technology, competition, free trade and appropriate public policy. All five productivity causes are capable of enabling workers to produce more or better goods or services for a given unit of time or money than they could before. If, for five hours of time or $5 in wages, a given worker produced ten widgets, he or she should now be able to produce, say, 11 widgets, or a 10 per cent increase.

A given labor force of 100 workers, who were formerly producing 50 widgets collectively, should now be producing 55 widgets. If widgets are worth $1 apiece, the GNP has just gone from $50 to $55. We are assuming that the extra five widgets can be sold. Otherwise, they generally would not have been produced. We could also assume for the sake of simplicity that the cost of training, technology or other expenses were incurred in the previous time period. A better assumption would be that those costs are income to other people in the present economy, and thus are also part of the gross national product. If we want to emphasize the output, we call it *gross national product*. If we want to emphasize the income, we call it *national income*. For our purposes, and for all practical purposes, they are the same, especially if we are assuming one economy, which the world is.

If the gross national income goes up as a result of the increased productivity of the labor force, then *per capital income* logically goes up, since it is just national income divided by the number of people in the population. This assumes that the population does not increase faster than the national income. That assumption is being satisfied in most countries of the world, including China, where the national income has recently increased by 13 per cent and the birthrate is being reduced (1) by placing more value on female babies, (2) by providing jobs rather than supportive children for the elderly, (3) by lowering the child mortality rate, and (4) by enabling more rural children to go to college. The per capita income can be increased by either raising the national income or lowering the population. It is easier to raise the national income, which may also have the effect of creating an urban middle class that has fewer children. Raising the per capita income has a strong relation to improvement of the *quality of life*. This goal is presumably what society and public policy exist for.

*Economic indicators   The combination of the productivity causes and the socioeconomic effects of higher productivity can lead to *low or lower inflation*. Inflation generally involves too many dollars chasing too few goods. The chase for those goods drives prices up, to the detriment of people on relatively fixed incomes, businesses buying raw materials or merchandise where the higher prices cannot be easily passed on, and virtually all businesses if the inflation includes a rise in the interest rate or the price of money which is needed for business expansion and current business. Traditionally, inflation has been fought by decreasing the supply of money, mainly through the deliberate raising of interest rates. The effect has been to hurt business expansion and current business, which has in turn created increased unemployment. That kind of cure for inflation has often been worse than the disease.

An alternative approach is to increase the quantity of goods available so that there will not be so many dollars chasing so few goods. The quantity of goods available is increased if productivity is increased. Higher productivity also means that, if wages go up, those wage increases are not inflationary because the employers are getting more for their money as a result of the increased productivity. The increased productivity and the higher national income may also enable consumers to be better able to afford the higher prices. The increased productivity may also mean higher quality of goods. Thus people will be getting more for their money. An example would be where the price of a gallon of milk goes up 10 per cent, but its durability and the healthfulness go up 50 per cent.

The combination of the productivity causes and the socioeconomic effects can also simultaneously lead to *high or higher employment*. This happens as a result of the increase in gross national spending. Gross national product translates into national income almost by definition. National income also translates into spending almost by definition, since the only things that one can do with income are to consume, to invest or the equivalent of putting the income under one's mattress. Either consumption or investment creates income and jobs for other people. Both have multiplier effects since $10 given to Joe for goods or services mean that Joe is likely to give the $10 to Sam, Pete or the local bank for goods, services or deposit. The same $10 thus serves as income for many people, business firms and investment outlets. More importantly, that increased spending from the increased income means increased jobs. If people have been living on $20 000 a year and they are now making $22 000, they may eat in a restaurant more often, make a down payment on a new car, or get something fixed. That may mean a new job or overtime work for a restaurant worker, a car manufacturer or a plumber.

With this process happening millions of times, we may see a substantial percentage increase in jobs available. We may even see employment for people who were previously not counted in the labor force, such as the elderly, the unemployed who are no longer seeking jobs, the disabled and mothers of pre-school children. We may see part-time and seasonal people having real jobs. We may also see people taking jobs that come closer to their aptitudes and interests. The magic of all this increased employment is that it comes from higher productivity. At first glance, one would think that anything that enables one person to do the job of two people would make for massive unemployment. The opposite is true if the one person adds more to the GNP than the two people formerly did. That increment to national income logically means more jobs, as we have reasoned above.

One empirical proof is that, within the past generation, the United States has moved to the high technology of the computer revolution and yet the labor force has greatly increased, rather than decreased. The increased employment has not affected everybody. There is now long-term unemployment in coal mining and steel manufacturing communities and those making some automobiles, and in other industries that have been especially affected by productivity 'downsizing', competition, free trade and other displacement factors for which job facilitators are strongly needed.

Perhaps the most magic is in what all this does to the *national government deficit*. The deficit by definition means that there has been more government spending than income. A high present and accumulated deficit is generally undesirable for at least four reasons. First, it puts upward pressure on interest rates to have the government competing with the private sector to borrow money. Second, it inhibits the government's ability to spend to increase productivity. Third, it creates a nation of people who make a living wholly or partly by clipping coupons on government bonds, rather than doing more productive activities. Fourth, a high deficit may decrease the ability of a developing nation to borrow expansion capital from other nations. The US government is an exception to that effect, because it can borrow from its own people and others on the basis of its high future anticipated income.

The traditional solution to the deficit has been to reduce spending, increase taxes, or both. Conservatives like to talk about (1) reducing spending on the HEW categories of health, education and welfare, and (2) increasing consumption taxes such as a value-added tax or a national sales tax. Liberals like to talk about (1) reducing spending on defense and (2) increasing income taxes, especially at the higher levels. There are, however, big political obstacles to reducing most spending and to increasing most taxes. Our productivity cycle model envisages some opposite activities: increasing government spending by way of vouchers or other subsidies for training, technology, competition and international trade; and having more tax breaks to stimulate training, technology, competition and international trade. Both these increases in spending and the decreases in taxes are designed to increase productivity.

The increased productivity, the accompanying higher national income and the higher per capita income result in a decreased deficit, in two ways. First, if the national income goes up substantially, federal tax revenue also goes up substantially, since federal revenue is mainly individual and corporate income taxes. If those tax sources go up as a result of increased national productivity or for whatever other reason, the deficit is likely to go down. Second, if most individuals have a higher per capita income and jobs, there will be less government welfare spending, which, at the federal level, is almost one-third of the total spending, with about a third being for defense and another third for paying interest on the national debt. Welfare spending may be reduced in many spending categories as a result of increased employment and prosperity. That includes public aid, public housing, food stamps and Medicaid; it also includes welfare or government support for the elderly, who may also find employment.

Poverty reduction and prevention The original title of cluster D in Figure 1.2 was 'Poverty Reduction'. This has been changed to 'Poverty Reduction and Prevention'. Preventing middle-class people from falling into poverty may be easier than raising them back into the middle class after they have become impoverished, possibly for years. This should be a major difference between the Computer Revolution of the 21st century and the Industrial Revolution of the 19th century. In the Industrial Revolution, many artisans, farmers and their children became factory workers, coal miners or unemployed slum dwellers. Some of them were embittered by what Marx referred to as the bourgeoisie becoming the proletariat. They or their descendants became part of the angry fascists or communists of western and eastern Europe.

The Computer Revolution and contemporary globalization have the potential for generating great productivity and prosperity. They also have the potential for generating among many people more unemployment and anger than the Industrial Revolution produced. This is so because so many poverty-generating displacement factors are operating simultaneously throughout the world, including productivity 'downsizing', free trade, defense conversion and immigration. It also includes employing many groups of people who were not formerly competing so much for the available jobs, such as women, minorities, the disabled and the elderly. A key object of an anti-poverty program should be to smooth the transition of displaced workers to other, possibly better, jobs, as well as to provide for the transition of the previously poor toward middle-class status.

Being poor in this context relates partly to individual income. However, it is not possible to say that being poor means having less than a certain income or being below a certain income percentile in one's nation. One can live better on a low income in some places in the world than in others. Being in the bottom ten percentile in a wealthy nation may be better than being in the top ten percentile in an impoverished nation. Poverty should be measured in terms of food, shelter, clothing and medical care. A person or family is impoverished if they cannot afford (1) enough food to avoid all forms of malnutrition, (2) enough housing not to freeze in the winter time, (3) enough clothing to satisfy minimum cultural standards of dignity, and (4) enough medical care for all members of the family to have better than a 50 per cent probability of living to age 60. The fourth point illustrates how our standards keep moving up, since living to age 40 would have been considered good in medieval times, even by royalty.

Sometimes employment and education are included in the definition of poverty. Both employment and education are important for preventing poverty and for rising out of poverty, but they are not part of the definition. They are causes and, to some extent, effects of poverty. More importantly, they are policy variables subject to deliberate improvements through governmental decision making. As regards employment of displaced workers or people in the culture of poverty, there are a number of *job facilitators* that have been shown to be reasonably effective, provided that the nation or community is willing to make a worthwhile investment. These job facilitators include the following.

1   Contracting out to employment services to find jobs for the unemployed on a commission basis. This means the job finder gets a substantial amount of money from the government after the worker has been on the job for three months. And even more of a commission after the worker has been on the job for six months. Such a commission arrangement provides the job finder with an incentive to determine the worker's aptitudes and interests so that the worker will not quit or be fired before the commission is paid.

2   Wage vouchers that are given by the government to the unemployed to supplement what an employer can afford to pay. In return for being able to cash in the wage voucher, the employer must agree to hire unemployed people and provide them with on-the-job training. The worker must agree to perform the work and pass the training within six months when the vouchers end.

3   Vouchers can also be given for training that involves going to school, obtaining daycare services and moving to a new city. These vouchers systems cost money. They may, however, soon more than pay for themselves if the worker gets off some forms of public aid, pays taxes and buys more goods and services with the multiplier effects that such buying has. These employed workers may also refrain from anti-social activities and become better role models for their children and grandchildren.

4   The most important job facilitators are probably the list of productivity causes (cluster A), the socioeconomic effects (Cluster B) and the eco-

nomic indicators (Cluster C). They provide an expanding economy with more jobs widely available to displaced workers and the chronically unemployed, regardless of the reasons for being displaced or unemployed.

The second item under poverty reduction and prevention is *education*. In this context, we are talking about elementary and secondary education, since adult training has already been discussed. There are two big problems in providing better education for low-income children or children in families whose real incomes are falling contrary to general trends. The first problem is lack of money for the local schools. Low-income communities throughout the world are generally not able to raise sufficient local funds to provide adequate school buildings and teachers. There is a big need for more allocation of national or federal tax money to local education. It is not politically feasible to expect rich communities in a province to provide much support for the low-income communities. It is more politically feasible for the national government to do so. The funding as of 1998 could come from channeling defense expenditures into local education expenditures. Defense expenditures are still at near-Cold War levels in most countries, but there is no longer actual or potential warlike conflict between capitalism and communism. The height of the Cold War may have been when Russia was sending missiles to Cuba in the warlike early 1960s, but the US defense budget is now twice as high in the peaceable later 1990s. Another advantage of federal funding is that the money could be used to provide differential salary incentives to teach in the impoverished schools. That is something local school boards have been unable to do because of the power exercised over the local school boards by local unions and senior teachers.

The second big problem in providing better education for low-income children is the need to bring those children more into contact with middle-class children who are above the poverty line, as defined in terms of food, shelter, clothing, medical care or income. The Coleman Report of the 1960s found great variation across school districts in terms of the probability of the average student going on to college or high school. Of the total variation, about 20 per cent can be explained by differences in school facilities, 30 per cent in terms of differences in the salaries and experience of teachers and 50 per cent in terms of the middle-class nature of the interacting students. Having low-income students interact more with middle-income students means they are indirectly interacting with the middle-class parents of those students, who encourage their children to think in terms of getting more education and qualifying for middle-class occupations. One of the best ways of promoting that kind of interaction is through housing vouchers, rather than school vouchers. The housing voucher enables the low-income family to move up one concentric circle in the city in which they live, or to move from an impoverished rural area to a livable urban area. Doing so increases the inter-class interaction, to the benefit of the low-income children, without pulling down the middle-class children, so long as they are not overwhelmed. Middle-class families can also be encouraged to move into low-income areas that are close to urban employment by being sold condominium housing in sheltered communities. The developers of such communities (who receive free government land) are required to set aside about 25 per cent of the condos for low-income families, and all children attend the same community public school.

The third item under poverty reduction and prevention is *merit treatment*. This refers to the fact that poverty is frequently based on discrimination that relates to race, religion or ancestral nationality. Merit treatment does not refer to giving preferences to redress past discrimination; it refers here to treating people on the basis of their individual merit, but with an outreach training program for those who are potentially well-qualified, but who cannot meet high reasonable standards of employment or college admission. More specifically, this kind of outreach training means that applicants with low-income backgrounds who almost pass qualifying tests are invited to participate in a semester-long training program to better prepare them for the test, the job or the education. Low income in this context means that their elementary and secondary schools had per capita expenditures substantially below the national average. If they fail to qualify after the training program, they are channeled elsewhere. Such an outreach training program increases the actual merit of those with high potential merit that has not probably been adequately nurtured, as indicated by the objective criterion of the per capita education expenditures.

As for the *voting* item, this refers to the fact that low-income people need to be empowered to shift more for themselves and be less dependent on public aid systems. Both conservatives and liberals use concepts like empowerment and power to the people. Conservatives sometimes use such concepts in an overly paternalistic way; liberals sometimes use such concepts in an unnecessarily frightening revolutionary way. Both sides are likely to hold that enfranchising poor people (at least in theory) is a good thing for society and especially democracy. In the context of voting, that means making it easier for qualified low-income people to vote as a minimum form of political participation. They are frequently in effect disenfranchised because they find it more difficult to register in advance than middle-class people. A simple solution is to allow for registration at the time of voting, as is done in some countries and states. Low-income people also find it difficult to lose time from work in order to vote. A simple solution is to make election day a holiday, as some countries do, or at least to hold major elections on Sunday or over a number of days. One should also be allowed to vote at one's home precinct, workplace precinct or any other precinct, so long as one passes the test of not having previously been exposed to a container of invisible ink while voting. If more low-income people participate in politics and voting, more public policies will be adopted that relate to the kind of job facilitators, education and merit treatment discussed above.

The fifth item under poverty reduction and prevention is *crime*. Being poor may be a key factor in engaging in street crimes like mugging and burglary, as contrasted to middle-class crimes like embezzlement and swindling. Here we are concerned not with how poverty causes crime, but rather with how crime causes poverty, especially drug-related criminal activity. As with the other four anti-poverty policy variables, we are talking about ways in which anti-crime improvements can be made that will result in poverty reduction and prevention. A big factor in inner city poverty in cities throughout the world (especially the United States) is the highly negative influence of drugs such as derivatives of opium and cocaine on productivity. The availability of such drugs can turn a potentially productive person into a drug addict or, worse, into a drug dealer who creates other drug addicts.

One solution might be to medicalize the drug problem. This means that drug addicts are considered sick people, rather than criminals guilty of possession or sale to get money to buy drugs. It also means that such addicts would be treated under whatever national health care exists by being given a 'phase-out' prescription that gets lower in dosage each month. If they stay on prescription opium or cocaine forever, as diabetics stay on insulin, this is still an improvement on the criminal drug market in a number of ways.

1 One improvement is that drug dealers would have no incentives to give low-income 10-year-olds free samples, because they would be just creating patients for the health care service, not new paying customers.
2 Another improvement is that almost 70 per cent of all the muggings and burglaries would end, since that is the percentage of muggings and burglaries that are committed by drug addicts seeking money to buy drugs.
3 Likewise, almost 70 per cent of the murders in the United States and some other countries are drug-related, meaning that they are committed by drug dealers fighting for control, or committed by addicts in a bungled mugging or burglary.
4 Another benefit, especially to some developing countries, would be the lessening of the corruption of police and government officials by wealthy drug dealers.

5   A further benefit is the tremendous saving in prison costs, court costs, police costs and other costs that are part of the criminalizing of drug addiction, as contrasted to the relatively low cost involved in medicalizing drug addiction and the high benefits mentioned above.

Some Concluding Ideas

As a concluding thought, one might first mention the *cyclical or reciprocal nature* of the productivity cycle referred to at the beginning of this section. This means that not only do the productivity causes produce desirable socioeconomic effects, but those effects also favorably feed back to the causes. For example, spending for training and technology produces higher productivity and higher national income. That means more federal revenue to spend on training and technology. Likewise, spending on job facilitators, education and outreach training can lead to more and better employment. That leads to more income for everybody through the multiplier process. This in turn means more tax revenue at the same or lower tax rates to pay for more job facilitators, education and outreach training. This productivity cycle is even better than a perpetual motion machine, which tends to run at a constant speed. The productivity cycle keeps speeding up at an exploding rate, as previously mentioned.

Another concluding thought is to mention the *win–win or super-optimizing nature* of this kind of productivity cycle. For example, low inflation and high employment have traditionally been considered somewhat inconsistent. Conservatives like both low inflation and high employment, but they like low inflation better since inflation tends to eat up their relative wealth. Liberals also like both, but they like high employment better because that is more important to the worker constituency that liberals usually have. Conservatives traditionally advocate manipulating the money supply to deal with the business cycle. That means high interest rates in time of inflation and low interest rates in time of unemployment. This policy is not meaningful if inflation and unemployment occur simultaneously. Also it is not politically feasible to cut most spending or to raise most taxes. Increasing real productivity and thereby increasing real GNP can, however, simultaneously lower inflation and increase employment, as previously described. That is a win–win outcome in which both conservatives and liberals can rejoice. It is part of the empirical reality of 1998.

Another example of win–win policy making that is built into the productivity cycle is the idea of lowering the deficit through more tax revenues as a result of higher national income due to greater productivity. That higher national income means more tax revenue for conservative defense expenditures and more for liberal health, education and welfare. That is a win–win in itself. The cycle also provides a win–win by allowing for a reduction in tax rates, since total tax revenue is increasing as a result of the tax base or national income growing bigger. That could allow for reductions in capital gains taxes to please conservatives and a reduction in income taxes on the poor to please liberals, by raising the standard deduction and the amount allowed for family member exemptions. Such a set of outcomes might be better than the best that both the conservatives and the liberals might otherwise hope for. In that sense, being better than one's best initial expectations is a super-optimum solution.

In an earlier draft of this chapter the cycle was referred to as 'the productivity cycle'. As a result of perceiving these win–win aspects, we have now changed it to 'the win–win productivity cycle'. What may be needed now, among other things, is more elaboration and implementation of these win–win ideas in the context of both developing and industrial nations. The 21st century could be a win–win century. New technologies, when adopted, are providing for higher national income like an expanding pie which provides bigger slices for rich and poor, men and women, colored and white, rural and urban, developing nations and industrial, and for other categories of people who were formerly in a win–lose tradeoff conflict, which frequently became lose–lose, rather than win–win.

2 Third Party Benefactor and Well-placed Incentives

Housing for the Poor

On the problem of providing housing for the poor, Table 2.1 shows four alternative policies and four criteria. In light of the scores of the policies on the goals, the condominium arrangement seems best for existing government-owned public housing. That policy, is, however, resisted partly because the present public housing management does not want to become the employee of the tenants.

In view of the scores of the policies on the goals, the rent supplements seem best for proving housing for the poor outside of government-owned public housing projects. The policy is, however, resisted partly because it means appropriating new federal funds. The program of home ownership for the poor might have been effectively administered if the intermediary were HUD (Department of Housing and Urban Development) employees who have no commission incentive to de-emphasize maintenance costs or to bribe property assessors as part of repeated foreclosure schemes with the federal government covering the mortgages.

One could add the policy of doing nothing to provide housing for the poor. Such a policy at first glance looks good with regard to the burden on the taxpayer. It could, however, result in unacceptable slum living conditions which could be an ever greater burden on the taxpayer than helping to provide affordable housing.

Housing for the poor is an example in which the private sector has been reasonably effective, efficient and equitable, in comparison to public administration. In this context, public housing means government-owned and government-operated housing projects for the poor. Private housing means giving rent subsidies to the private sector to enable the private sector to provide housing for low-income tenants.

On the matter of *effectiveness*, public housing has been a failure compared to rent supplement programs. In terms of quantity of housing made

47

Table 2.1 Evaluating policies for providing housing for the poor

Criteria / Alternatives	L Goal Decent housing for poor	C Goal Stimulate housing developmt	N Goal Reduce tax costs	L Goal equity: race & class	N Total (neutral weights)	L Total (liberal weights)	C Total (conservative weights)
C Alternative Marketplace	1	4	4	2	22	21	23*
L Alternative Large-scale public housing	3.1	3	1	2	18.2	20.3	16.1
N Alternative Low-rise PH, condos & home ownership	4	3.5	2	4	27	31.5*	22.5
SOS Alternative Rent supplements & skills upgrade	5	5	2	5	34	35**	25**

Notes:
1. The former liberal alternative of large-scale public housing is being abandoned by liberals largely because such housing segregates poor people and maybe poor black people, unlike scattered site or low-rise housing.
2. A single asterisk indicates the alternative that wins on either the conservative totals or the liberal totals before considering the SOS alternative.

available, there has been little increased public housing in the United States since about 1970. In fact, there have been some dramatic decreases, such as literally blowing up the Pruitt-Igoe public housing homes in St Louis. They were considered bankrupt in the sense of consistently costing more to maintain than the monetary or non-monetary benefits could justify. On the other hand, the private sector is willing to make available almost unlimited housing to the poor, as long as poor people with rent supplements can pay the rent.

On the matter of *efficiency*, public housing projects have been extremely expensive per dwelling unit. They were originally designed to save money by being high-rise, which decreases land costs and enables every floor to also be a ceiling, with many common walls. The lack of more individualized dwelling units, however, has led to a lack of a sense of ownership or even possession. That has led to vandalism and the failure to report it. Rent supplements, on the other hand, save money in such ways as (1) avoiding the initial building cost by using existing housing stock, (2) encouraging better care of the property, thereby lowering maintenance costs that might otherwise require higher rent supplements, and (3) increasing pride and ambition which lowers the cost of welfare and crime.

On the matter of *equity*, public housing has resulted in discrimination against poor whites and segregation of poor blacks. Whites have in effect been discriminated against a result of public housing projects being located disproportionately in black neighborhoods where the projects have frequently become all black. Rent supplements, on the other hand, are as available to poor whites as they are to poor blacks. Also important is the fact that rent supplements can easily lead to racial and class integration, whereas big housing projects are not easily absorbed in white or middle-class neighborhoods.

Public housing also does poorly on the political values of public participation, predictable rules and procedural due process in view of the way authoritarian and arbitrary public housing projects have traditionally been managed. This is in contrast to the greater dignity associated with rent supplements. The rent supplement program also serves as a liberal symbol if doing something important for the poor, while also being a conservative symbol of the meaningful of private sector property.

It is relevant to note that, although rent supplements are an example of good private administration of a societal function, this is not the case with the mortgage supplement program of the early 1970s. That program involved the federal government making funds available for poor people to buy homes through private real estate agents, rather than through HUD employees or other public administrators. The privately administered program became a scandal, worse than used car fraud or the Medicare–

Medicaid frauds. Real estate agents failed to inform low-income buyers of the maintenance costs of bad heating, plumbing and electrical systems. Trying to meet those costs frequently interfered with meeting even the low mortgage payments. As a result, foreclosures were frequent, analogous to used car repossessions, but with the federal government making good on whatever was owned. The greed factor became so great that it was not enough to collect two or three times the money owed on the same house through foreclosures. Assessors were bribed to inflate the value of the houses to further increase what was collected. The program was soon abandoned even though it began with strong liberal and conservative support, and might have succeeded if it had been administered by salaried government employees, rather than by private real estate agents operating on commissions.

Food Prices

An SOS Spreadsheet Perspective

High farm prices is the conservative alternative in the context of pricing food in China, and low prices is the liberal alternative (Table 2.2). The liberal weights involve a 3 for urban desires, a 1 for rural desires and a 2 for all the other goals. With the liberal weights, the SOS wins 76 to 48 for all the other alternatives. We then go back and put in the conservative weights. The conservative weights give a 2 to all the neutral goals just as liberal weights do, but they move in opposite directions on urban and rural desires. For the conservative in the context, rural desires get a 3 rather than a 1, and urban desires get a 1 rather than a 3. The SOS is a winner even with the conservative weights, although now the high prices do better than they did before, but still not as well as the SOS.

The neutral perspective is not to give everything a weight of 1, but rather a weight of 2. If the neutrals gave everything a weight of 1, they would be giving neutral goals less weight than either the liberals or the conservatives give them. Thus the neutral picture is that rural desires get a weight of 2, and so do urban desires. To the neutral, everything gets a weight of 2. The SOS wins with the neutral weights too. It is super-optimum, because it is out in front over both the conservative and liberal alternatives using both the conservative and liberal weights. It also wins over the compromise. The SOS involves the farmers getting better than high prices and the urbanites paying lower than low prices, with the government providing a supplement like the minimum wage supplement, provided that administrative feasibility is satisfied.

Table 2.2 Pricing food in China and elsewhere

Criteria / Alternatives	C Goal Rural Well being	L Goal Urban Well being	N Goal Admin. feasibility	N Goal Improve farming methods	N Goal Increase exports	N Goal Import technology	N Goal Increase GNP	N Goal Political feasibility	N Total Neutral weights	L Total Liberal weights	C Total Conservative weights
C Alternative High price	5	1	3	4	4	4	4	1	52 (18)	48 (14)	56* (22)
L Alternative Low price	1	5	3	2	2	2	2	5	44 (18)	48* (22)	40 (14)
N Alternative Compromise	3	3	3	3	3	3	3	3	48 (18)	48 (18)	48 (18)
S Alternative Price supplement	5.1	5.1	3	5	5	5	5	5	76.4 (26.4)	76.4** (26.4)	76.4** (26.4)

Note: The intermediate totals in parentheses are based on the first three goals. The bottom line totals are based on all the goals, including the indirect effects of the alternatives.

51

Administrative feasibility involves the use of food stamps. They are given to urban food buyers. They cannot be easily counterfeited. Food buyers give them to retailers, who in turn give them to wholesalers, who in turn give them to farmers, who turn them in for reimbursement. Criterion 8 just involves political feasibility. There should be a separate criterion for administrative feasibility.

Of special importance is the fact that no farmer gets the supplement unless he agrees to adopt more modern farming methods. Otherwise, it is just a handout for subsidizing inefficient farming. As a result of adopting more modern farming methods, productivity goes up. Food becomes available for export. Foreign exchange is then acquired for importing new technology. The new technology increases GNP and everybody is better off, including the taxpayers who pay the supplement. They are better off because, with the increased GNP, the government could even reduce taxes if it wanted to do so. It could reduce taxes below a 20 per cent level and still have more tax revenue if the GNP base has increased substantially.

An Economics Perspective*

The food price has long been a big problem in China. Since the foundation of the People's Republic of China, the government, influenced by the Soviet economic model, had adopted the policy of extremely low prices for agricultural products and high prices for industrial products. That means there was a big gap between the price of industrial products and that of agricultural products. The farmers paid a high 'tax rate' through the form of a low selling price. For this reason the farmers got little profit from agricultural production, which in turn meant the farmers had not enough financial input in farming. This led to a shortage of agricultural products, as shown in Figure 2.1.

At the low price of p_0, farmers were only willing to produce and sell agricultural products at the quantity of q_0. If the price were settled by market, the equilibrium quantity would be q_1, the price would be p_1, and Δq, which is the gap between q_1 and q_0, would be the shortage. The urban people want from agriculture an abundance of farm food products at reasonable low cost, while the farmers wish to sell their products at a price as high as possible. This is the conflict met by the government in the agricultural policy-making process, the solution to which can be used as an example of a super-optimum one.

---

*   This section on the Chinese food prices problem is written by Tong Daochi of the People's University of China. He also inspired the basic idea of applying super-optimizing to the food-pricing problem.

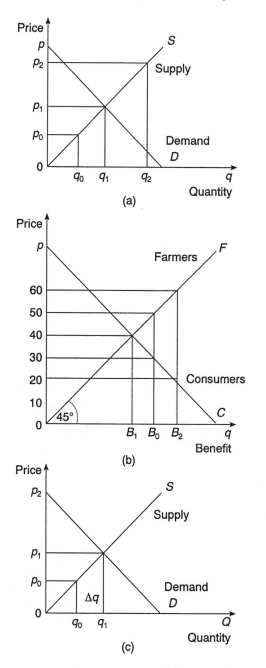

Figure 2.1   An economics perspective on the food pricing SOS

We give the grain price as an example. The producers wish to sell at the price of 50 fen per kilogram ($1 = 3.78 yuan = 378 fen), while the highest price acceptable to the consumers is 30 fen per kilogram, as Figure 2.1 shows. The line $C'C$ indicates that, along with the decreasing of the grain price, it will cost the consumers less to buy the grain. That is to say, the consumers' benefit will increase. The line OF illustrates that the higher the price of the grain the farmers sell, the more benefit they will get from it, and vice versa. If the price at which the farmers sell their products is 50 fen per kilogram, and the price at which consumers buy is 30 fen per kilogram, both sides can get the benefit of B_0. The compromise price would be 40 fen per kilogram, at which the consumers or the farmers might get the benefit of B_1. It might be a loss for both consumers and farmers. (As Figure 2.1(b) indicates, $B_1 > B_0$.) It is a loss to farmers if the 50 fen per kilogram is the minimum price for them to cover the cost of the production. The 40 fen per kilogram is a loss to consumers if the 30 fen per kilogram is the maximum price that they can afford to pay at their present wages.

A super-optimum solution to this problem might involve the price at which the farmers sell their products being raised to 60 fen per kilogram, but simultaneously requiring consumers to pay only 20 fen per kilogram. The 40 fen difference would be paid by the government through the food price subsidies: the government collectively buys the agricultural products from farmers at the price of 60 fen per kilogram, then sells them to urban people at the price of 20 fen per kilogram. In this situation, as Figure 2.1(b) shows, the benefit that the consumers or the farmers might get increases from B_1 to B_2, and B_2 is higher than B_0, which indicates that, through the government subsidies, both the consumers and farmers can get greater benefit than their best expectation.

But what can the third party benefactor, the government, get from this program? It seems that the subsidies will increase the government expenditure and deficit, but the fact is that the government might come out ahead. This is so by virtue of the following.

1 The increase in the supply of agricultural products. This is shown in Figure 2.1(c). If the new price p_2 is higher than the original price p_0 and the equilibrium price p_1, the supply of the agricultural products will increase from q_0 to q_2. This not only will resolve the shortage problem, but may also make the country a food exporter.
2 The increase of farming inputs to the land by farmers. This in turn will reduce the government investment in agriculture.
3 The decrease in the inflation rate. This is very important for the economic reform and development of China.

In fact, the beginning of the economic reform of China came in the rural area in the late 1970s, with the adoption of the Family-Contract-Responsibility-System in agricultural production and the increase in the price of the agricultural products that the government bought from farmers. From 1980 to 1984, the quantity of crops produced reached the highest point in Chinese history, but, since 1985, agricultural economic growth has stagnated. The reasons may involve many aspects, but one of the important factors leading the rural economy to this situation is the increase in the price of the industrial products that are used in farming, such as farm machinery, seeds, fuels and pesticides. The benefit that farmers got from the rise in the price of agricultural products has been absorbed by the increase in the cost of the agribusiness input. In order to change this situation, the government has taken the decision to increase such farming inputs to increase food output. New agricultural policies were made and implemented in the 1990s.

A Reaction to the Food Pricing SOS

A social scientist from the World Bank has commented orally on this analysis. He said he could not accept the idea of a food supplement that would make both the rural farmers and the urban workers simultaneously better off in developing countries. The reason he gave was the following. The example said that the farmers in China wanted 20 cents per pound for rice and the workers wanted to pay only 10 cents per pound. A compromise would have been 15 cents per pound. The food supplement would have paid the farmers 21 cents per pound and the workers would have had to pay only nine cents per pound. The social scientist objected on the grounds that he had recently been to China and the price of rice was not what I said it was.

The chairman of the panel told him that the exact prices might be an irrelevant consideration: he should just view this as a hypothetical problem to see the big picture with regard to the idea of a third party benefactor making both sides come out better. The chairman also suggested that, instead of 20 cents per pound for rice, he just use algebraic symbols and that maybe he would see what was happening better. That did not seem to help. The problem was that this international organization has spent large amounts of money trying to come up with solutions for exactly this kind of problem. The social scientist's mind apparently was so narrowly focused that he refused to recognize any kind of solution that he had not thought of or that other people at his institution had not thought of. Therefore he clutched at whatever straw he could find to argue that this was not a solution.

The moral of the story is not to provide any straws. One has to be careful about the details, even if the details are irrelevant. For instance, the correct figure is $200 per week (instead of $800 per month) for the subscription fulfillment and related costs of the Policy Studies Organization. Which figure one uses makes no difference at all in comparing a set of alternative proposals. Nevertheless, someone like this international executive will say we cannot accept this analysis because the correct figure is really $200 per week and not $800 per month. Similarly, the correct figure for a pound of rice in China as of 20 July 1989, when the presentation was made, was actually about 12 cents per pound. I said it was somewhere between 10 and 20 cents, implying that it was 15 cents. If an intelligent international executive could say that that destroys the whole idea of super-optimum solutions, then less intelligent, less knowledgeable people might be even more likely to find a defense mechanism. Such a mechanism enables them to avoid explicitly or implicitly admitting that they might have been scooped on a solution. It also avoids allowing the opposition side to come out ahead regardless how well one's side comes out ahead.

Raising Faculty Salaries without Raising Taxes

This example was developed at People's University and Beijing University especially by Professor King Chow and a graduate student named Lu Junwei. The example involves the dispute between the government and university professors in China over faculty salaries. The professors have been seeking a salary of approximately 300 yuan for a certain length of time. The government has been willing to give, at the most, 200 yuan. The object is to come up with a way in which the faculty members could be paid more than 300 yuan, but where the government would be able to pay even less than 200 yuan.

The solution developed by Professor Chow, Mr Lu, and others, is to institute a system of low-level tuition throughout the Chinese universities while simultaneously increasing the number of eligible students. The money obtained could be used to pay faculty salary increases without having to draw upon the government's limited resources. Provision could be made for low-income students to receive scholarships or loans, especially loans that would be forgiven if the students go into fields of work that are in short supply. The result would be salaries higher than 300 yuan for the faculty, with a possible reduction of the government's contribution to less than 200 yuan. The result would also be more people receiving a college education, to the benefit of national productivity, which in turn would bring in increased national income and more government revenue (see Table 2.3).

This is an example of a super-optimum solution where everyone comes out ahead. The low faculty salaries have also been a point of antagonism between the government and graduate students who anticipate becoming

Table 2.3 Evaluating policies concerning Chinese faculty salaries

Criteria / Alternatives	L Goal Attract faculty	C Goal Reduce cost of government	L Goal Equity to students	N Goal More educated population	N Goal Increase GNP	N Goal Political feasibility	N Total (neutral weights)	L Total (liberal weights)	C Total (conservative weights)
L Alternative Faculty demand	4	2	3	4	4	2	38 (18)	43 (23)*	33 (13)
C Alternative Government offer	2	4	3	2	2	4	34 (18)	35 (19)	33 (17)*
N Alternative Compromise	3	3	3	3	3	3	36 (18)	39 (21)	33 (15)
SOS Alternative Tuition and scholarships	5	5	4	5	5	5	58 (28)	62** (32)	54** (24)

Notes:
1. For those who prefer numbers to words, the faculty demand can be thought of as 300 monetary units, the government offer as only 200 units and the compromise as 250 units.
2. The super-optimum solution consists of the government paying the faculty 190 monetary units, but the faculty receiving 310 monetary units. The difference comes from establishing a low-tuition system to replace the current zero tuition. The low-tuition system would provide for scholarships and other forms of student aid for those students who cannot afford the tuition. The SOS would also allow for larger student enrollment without lowering admission standards.
3. The intermediate totals in parentheses are based on the first three goals. The totals not in parentheses are based on all six goals, including the indirect effects of the alternatives.

professors, especially when sellers of orange pop and cucumbers can make more in a few days than a university faculty member makes in a month.

The Chinese faculty salaries problem thus illustrates a number of broader aspects of public policy evaluation. First, having a third party benefactor is a useful way of arriving at super-optimum solutions, but the third party benefactor does not have to be the government. This is especially so when the government is one of the two main parties. In this particular case, the third party benefactor was in effect the students paying for tuition.

Second, it is important to consider the side-effects of an SOS solution on the gross national product. Those side-effects include (1) the multiplier effect which occurs as a result of increased income causing increased income for numerous other people via a chain of spending; (2) the compound interest effect which results from an increase in the base to which next year's growth rates are applied, similar to getting compound interest on interest; (3) the intergenerational effect as a result of improving parental role models; (4) the taxpaying feedback effect due to increased GNP generating more tax money and subsidy money, even if the tax rate is constant or lowered; (5) the export surplus effect which occurs via a productivity surplus that is available for export to obtain new capital goods and technologies which further increase productivity; and (6) the welfare reduction effect whereby the prosperity of increased GNP means less of a burden on the government to provide for unemployment compensation, public aid, public housing, food stamps, Medicaid and other forms of welfare. These six points emphasize the upward spiral benefits of investing in human resources and new technologies to increase GNP.

The importance of considering equity and not just effectiveness and efficiency in evaluating alternative public policies is a third aspect. It is ironic that equity may be more highly considered in an affluent capitalistic society than in a hard-pressed Marxist society, even though Marxism in theory is supposed to be more sensitive to the spread of benefits and costs across economic classes and ethnic groups.

Inflation in Russia

As part of the transition from a communist economy to a free marketplace, a key problem is the inflation which is likely to occur. It occurs for a number of reasons. First is the lifting of price controls which provide for artificially low prices on essentials like food, shelter and clothing. The better approach is food stamps, rent supplements or subsidies, rather than price controls.

A second reason is the shortages of goods, at least until the private sector can replace the production of the public sector. This may require subsidies to enable would-be entrepreneurs to get started, especially if competition among producers is desired.

There is also the tendency on the part of the government to print money in order to meet government payrolls and other expenditures. That tendency is stimulated by the loss of income due to the government turning over income-producing activities to the private sector. In theory, the remedy is to establish new taxes and raise old ones. In practice, one of the prices of democracy is effective public resistance to being taxed. The long-run solution is to increase the GNP through well-placed subsidies. Doing this increases the tax base so that relatively low tax rates can bring in more revenue.

Alternatives and Goals

Some of these ideas are incorporated in Table 2.4. The conservative *alternative* in Russia is to maintain the command economy of price control as much as possible. The liberal position is to establish a free marketplace with a 'hands-off' policy by the government. The compromise position is the in-

Table 2.4   Inflation and Russia, starting 1992

Criteria / Alternatives	C Goal Fast stop to inflation C=3 N=2 L=1	L Goal Fast move to free enterprise C=1 N=2 L=3	N Total (neutral weights)	L Total (liberal weights)	C Total (conservative weights)
C Alternative Command economy (price control)	4	2	12	10	14*
L Alternative Free marketplace ('Hands-Off')	2	4	12	14*	10
N Alternative Indexing interest rates, less spending, more taxing	3	3	12	12	12
SOS Alternative Raise GNP fast by well-placed incentives	≥3.5	≥3.5	≥12	≥14**	≥14**

Note: The SOS incentive are designed to stimulate: (1) better marketing, (2) more competition and (3) more equitable distribution through vouchers for food, clothes and housing.

dexing of wages to cushion the effects of inflation, manipulating interest rates, as with the American Federal Reserve system, and decreasing government spending while increasing taxes in accordance with Keynesian theory. Indexing is objected to in Russia on the grounds that it encourages inflation. Raising interest rates does not mean much as regards reducing inflation in Russia if people are not driving up prices with borrowed money. Reducing government spending and increasing taxes may be even more difficult in Russia than it is in the United States. This is so because of the need for well-placed government spending as part of the transition and because the people may be more resistant to being burdened with new taxes than to having old taxes raised.

The key conservative *goal* is to put a fast stop to inflation. The key liberal goal is to facilitate a fast move to free enterprise. On stopping inflation, price controls in a command economy can do that better in the short run than in a free marketplace, especially one that has both a shortage of goods and a shortage of competitive producers and sellers. On a fast move to free enterprise, a 'hands-off' policy by the government promotes that almost by definition, although not necessarily through competitive free enterprise. A command economy interferes with free enterprise almost by definition, but that partly depends on what the economy commands.

A Three-part SOS

A super-optimum solution involves raising GNP fast by use of well-placed incentives. This means incentives that relate to better marketing, more competition and more equitable distribution. On the matter of *marketing* relative to production, the Russian economy is not doing so badly in producing food, housing, clothing and other essentials, but the products are not getting to the consumers the way they should be. Food is rotting in the fields for lack of adequate storage and transport facilities. A key reason in the past for spoilage was low controlled prices. Food that is getting out of the fields to the cities may then rot in warehouses for lack of a well-organized retailing system. Communist Russia drove out a high percentage of its retail businessmen in the early years and drove out their sons and daughters in more recent years. Communist Russia as of 1917 was comparable to medieval Spain in 1492, driving out the Arab, Jewish and other merchants. Both countries went downhill thereafter. Russia, however, is in a position, through well-placed subsidies (including training subsidies), to stimulate a new entrepreneurial class.

On the matter of more *competition*, it was an enriching experience to hear one of the leaders of the Communist Party of the Soviet Union speak at a conference at the Russian Academy of Sciences on the need for a competitive free market. His position was that the Communist Party had no objection as of 1990 to private ownership and operation of the means of production and distribution. They did, however, object to putting those facilities into the hands of national, regional and local monopolists. In that sense, the Communist Party was preaching a doctrine of competitive capitalism more akin to Adam Smith than either Marxist-Leninists or American conservatives. Both Marx and Lenin objected to monopolies, but thought that government ownership would show sensitivity to workers and consumers that private monopolies do not. That was a bit naive in view of the abuse of workers by such government-owned entities as the Polish steel mills, or the abuse of consumers by such government-owned entities as public power companies. Likewise, American conservatives tend to be quite supportive of monopolistic power companies, as opposed to the competitive system of the New Deal whereby the Tennessee Valley Authority and other publicly owned power companies would serve as competitive yardsticks.

It is one thing to say that competition is desirable. It is another thing to bring it about. It does not occur through natural forces or invisible hands, as indicated by the increasing monopolization of the American economy through business mergers. Nor does it occur through antitrust penalties, since both conservatives and liberal governments are reluctant to break up what they consider to be efficient big businesses using economies of scale. The Japanese Ministry of International Trade and Industry (MITI) may have an ideal modern approach of combining privatization with competition. The MITI gives subsidies to Japanese firms in such industries as automobiles, electronics and computers. It does so in such a way as to guarantee multiple Japanese firms in all those industries, rather than a single monopolistic giant or two or three oligopolistic giants. Well-placed subsidies in Russia could deliberately encourage the development of competing firms. Such competition results in lower prices, better-quality goods and better workplaces to attract workers.

The third area for well-placed subsidies is guaranteed *more equitable distribution*. Private enterprise is not likely to want to provide an unprofitable mail service to isolated rural families. The publicly owned post office is willing to do so. A private enterprise, though, would also be willing to do so with a well-placed equity subsidy, assuming that society feels that there should be a rural mail service. That is more efficient than forcing the price of postage below a profitable level across the country, causing private mail delivery and other enterprises to want to sell out to the government. It makes more sense in terms of prices that operate within the laws of supply and demand to let the price of food and housing rise or fall in accordance with those forces. Food stamps and rent vouchers can be provided for those who otherwise would not eat or would go homeless.

Tabular or Spreadsheet Analysis

Thus, with a system of well-placed incentives to improve marketing, competition and equitable distribution, the Russian economy could reduce inflation, especially inflation that is due to shortages of goods and monopolistic pricing. The effect may not be as great in the short run as price control, but it avoids black markets and is better in the long run. Likewise, such a system of incentives can move the economy fast toward free enterprise, especially competitive free enterprise that the public will accept and even welcome. The effect on free enterprise may not be as great in the short run as a total 'hands-off' policy, but the incentives system avoids the unfree system in the long run of monopolistic control with inflated prices.

Table 2.4 illustrate how the super-optimum alternative can be a loser on every goal and still be an overall winner. Being that kind of a loser means not coming out in first place on any of the goals, but generally running contrary to the tradeoff idea that, if an alternative does well on some goals, it must do less well on other goals. All we need are alternatives that are generally on the positive side on a 1–5 scale, which means doing better than a 3. Such an alternative is then likely to score higher on the liberal totals than the liberal alternative, which does poorly on the conservative goals. The SOS alternative is also likely to score higher on the conservative totals than the conservative alternative, which does poorly on the liberal goals.

Overall conclusions can be derived from this analysis in terms of the substance of what is involved in the transition from socialism to capitalism in Russia and eastern Europe. Do not go to the opposite extreme of adopting a form of capitalism that the capitalistic United States would consider to be a move too far in a right-wing conservative direction. The American federal government owns lots of land, especially in the western United States. It would be virtually unthinkable in American politics for the federal government to give the land away to private business, or even to sell a place like Yosemite National Park for private commercial development. It is not unthinkable, though, for the federal government to lease federal land for grazing, farming or other development. It is likewise not unthinkable to award franchises to private entrepreneurs to sell products in Yosemite National Park.

The American federal government even (and maybe especially) during the conservative Reagan administration did not have a 'hands-off' policy regarding the American economy. Reagan sought to make use of well-placed subsidies in the form of enterprise zones to attract business firms to the inner cities, and housing vouchers as a way of providing equity in the housing market.

Do not go to the so-called 'middle way' that is associated with places like Sweden or the mixed economies of western Europe. It may provide the worst of both possible worlds. That means the relative unproductivity of socialism and the relative inequity of capitalism. The socialistic countries are also in a position to decide between the two basic alternatives by winding up with the best of both possible worlds. That means retaining the equities and social sensitivities of government ownership, while having the high productivity that is associated with profit-seeking entrepreneurial capitalism. It would be difficult to find a better example of compromising versus super-optimizing than the current debate over socialism versus capitalism.

Well-placed Incentives and Governmental Investments

Public policy is often defined in a highly general way that makes it virtually synonymous with government decisions or with what government does. Sometimes public policy is defined in terms of the results of those decisions, thereby emphasizing the allocations of things of value which the government makes, or who gets what as a result of government decisions. The purpose of this section is to view public policy, not in terms of its form or its effects, but more in terms of its potential. In that sense, public policy can be viewed as incentives for encouraging socially desired behavior. In the context of developing countries, public policy can be viewed as incentives for societal development and improvement.

An appropriate way to show the potential incentives roles of public policy is to go through a varied list of social problems and to discuss each one in terms of public policy incentives for lessening the social problems. The list should be chosen in a roughly random way so as not to appear to be slanted in the direction of making the potential of public policy look good. The *Encyclopedia of Policy Studies* has chapters on 22 specific policy problems divided into five sections dealing with (1) political problems, (2) economic problems, (3) sociology–psychology problems, (4) urban–regional planning problems, and (5) natural science–engineering problems. These problems exist in both developed and developing areas, although not necessarily in the same form. We can take two problems from each section to illustrate public policy as incentives for societal development or for lessening social problems.

Before getting into the specific social problems, one should note that public policy has the potential for encouraging socially desired behavior by working through five different related approaches:

1   increasing the benefits of doing right,
2   decreasing the costs of doing right,
3   increasing the costs of doing wrong,
4   decreasing the benefits of doing wrong, and

5   increasing the probability that the benefits and costs will occur.

This checklist logically leads to such questions as to who are the doers, and what benefits and costs are involved. The answers depend on the specific subject matters to which we now turn.

Problems with a Political Science Emphasis

Perhaps the most basic problem for a developing country or area is to encourage good government in the sense of competent, dedicated people and in the sense of stimulating innovative, useful ideas for dealing with social problems. Using the five-part checklist, public policy can encourage competency and diversity by such means as the following:

1   increasing the compensation of meritorious government workers,
2   decreasing the communication costs of people with innovative ideas by providing them with access to mass media,
3   increasing the possibility of removal or demotion from government of those who do not satisfy competency standards,
4   confiscating the gains of people in government who corruptly benefit from wrongdoing, and
5   decreasing the risks of 'whistle blowers' who report wrongdoing and providing bonuses for those who report rightdoing.

The realm of political science is sometimes divided into internal and external government problems. External or foreign policy tends to be dominated by problems of how to encourage peaceful interaction on the part of other countries, especially neighboring countries. Relevant public policy incentives in that regard might include the following:

1   increasing the benefits of mutual trade by developing agreements to benefit from each other's specialties;
2   decreasing the costs of mutual trade by lowering barriers in the form of tariffs, quotas, complicated customs arrangements and other restrictions;
3   increasing the cost of wrongdoing by developing internationally imposed penalties;
4   decreasing the benefits of wrongdoing by emphasizing that aggressive interaction will result in the acquisition of nothing of value by virtue of policies that provide for destruction of oil wells and other resources if necessary;
5   detection systems to determine that wrongdoing is occurring or is being prepared for.

Problems with an Economics Emphasis

At the macroeconomics level, public policy is primarily concerned with decreasing unemployment and inflation, or increasing employment opportunities and price stability. Devices such as manipulation of the money supply or taxing–spending differences are not so meaningful if unemployment and inflation are increasing simultaneously. An economy can also become distorted by trying to order business firms not to raise prices justifiably or by trying to order unemployed workers into certain jobs. An incentives approach might include such devices as the following:

1 tax incentives to business firms and labor unions for keeping prices and wages down; also monetary incentives to employers to hire the unemployed and monetary incentives to the unemployed to accept training and jobs;
2 decreasing the costs of finding jobs and workers through better information systems;
3 increasing the costs of violating price–wage guidelines and work incentives by withdrawing benefits and (in rare cases) by applying fines and other negative penalties;
4 confiscating the benefits of price–wage violations by imposing special taxes on the gains;
5 more accurate information on prices, wages and unemployment in order to allocate the benefits and costs more effectively.

At the microeconomics level, public policy is concerned with relations between business and consumers, labor and other business firms. Those subjects have been traditionally dealt with through economic regulation as manifested in such US government agencies as the Federal Trade Commission, the National Labor Relations Board and the Anti-Trust Division of the Department of Justice. An incentives approach might be substantially more effective in either a developed country or a developing country, including such devices as:

1 providing tax incentives to business firms to develop better relations with consumers, labor and other businesses;
2 decreasing the costs of such activities by providing appropriate government subsidies;
3 increasing the penalties where the lives or safety of people are jeopardized, as with dangerous products and working conditions;
4 confiscating the gains that come from violating guidelines concerning consumer protection, worker protection and the protection of a competitive environment;

5   hotline systems for facilitating the reporting of wrongdoing, and award systems for encouraging the reporting of rightdoing.

Problems with a Sociology–Psychology Emphasis

In the realm of social problems, poverty may be the most serious one for both developing and developed countries. That problem, however, is closely related to the macroeconomic problem of providing job opportunities briefly discussed above. Other key social problems include crime and ethnic group relations. On the matter of crime, the incentives approach might involve doing things like the following.

1   The main benefit of complying with the law should be that doing so gives one access to opportunities that are denied to law violators. This means that legitimate career opportunities must be provided to those who would otherwise turn to crime.
2   One cost of doing right may be a loss of prestige among youthful gang members who consider criminal behavior an indicator of toughness. There is a need for working to redirect such peer group values so that toughness can be displayed in more constructive ways.
3   The costs of doing wrong can include negative incentives of longer prison sentences, but it may be more meaningful to emphasize the withdrawal of career opportunities which would otherwise be available.
4   Provisions should be made for facilitating the confiscation of the property gains of criminal wrongdoing, and decreasing the vulnerability of the targets of crime to lessen the benefits obtained.
5   The probability of arrest and conviction can be increased partly through more professionalism among law enforcement personnel.

On the matter of relations among races, religions and other ethnic groups, the incentives approach can encourage more equitable treatment on the basis of individual merit through such means as the following:

1   tax incentives to employers, schools, landlords and others who deal with racial minorities to seek out well-qualified minority members more actively;
2   decreasing the costs of such affirmative action by having better information systems directed toward both the suppliers of opportunities and the minority members who are interested in advancing themselves;
3   increased penalties for racial discrimination, including the publicizing of the convicted discriminators as a deterrent to others;
4   confiscating gains from discriminating in the payment of wages or the provision of housing;

5   periodic reporting of affirmative action activities so that benefits and penalties can be appropriately allocated.

Problems with an Urban–Regional Planning Emphasis

The social problems most closely associated with urban–regional planning are housing and environmental protection. The housing field is one of inadequate provision of decent housing for the poor and the lower middle class. Incentives to lessen that social problem might include the following.

1   Tax incentives and subsidies to building contractors to construct more housing, especially for low-income tenants or owners. On the demand rather than supply side, there may be a need for rent supplements to enable low-income tenants to afford what is available.
2   One of the costs of renting to poor people may be the extra maintenance expense, which could be reduced by educating tenants in property maintenance and by giving them more of a stake in the housing through equity arrangements, or at least representation in the decision making.
3   Increasing the costs of wrongdoing could include penalties imposed on landlords who do not provide housing that satisfies minimum decency levels, and also penalties imposed on tenants who are destructive or negligent.
4   Decreasing the benefits which landlords receive who illegally provide sub-standard housing by having them pay rebates, or having their property subject to attachment to cover the benefits they have wrongfully received.
5   Encouraging tenants to report both good and bad behaviour on the part of landlords, and encouraging tenants to report vandalism on the part of fellow tenants and others.

As for environmental protection, that is an area in which there has been substantial experimentation with a variety of incentives, including the following:

1   providing tax incentives designed to encourage adopting pollution-reduction devices by business firms and municipal agencies; such incentives can include pollution taxes which are levied in proportion to the amount of polluting done;
2   subsidies designed to reduce the cost of expensive retrofitting and new facilities;
3   penalties other than fines for wrongdoing, such as publicizing brand-name wrongdoers, facilitating damage suits by people suffering environ-

mental injuries, the withdrawal of benefits, and (as a last resort) injunctions that close polluting firms;
4   confiscating the profits made as a result of not introducing required pollution controls;
5   better pollution monitoring systems and bounties for reporting pollution violations, plus enforcement agencies that do nothing but pollution enforcement.

Problems with a Natural Science or Engineering Emphasis

A key problem among engineering-related problems is how to encourage the development of new energy sources and the conservation of existing energy. Relevant incentives include the following.

1   Increasing the benefits of doing right by making tax reductions for adopting energy-saving devices like improved insulation, special thermostats and coal-burning furnaces. Offering government purchase guarantees as an incentive to develop a feasible electric car.
2   Decreasing costs of doing right by providing municipal governments with subsidies in order to reduce their costs of energy-relevant enforcement of housing and building codes.
3   Increasing the costs of doing wrong by publicizing the petrol consumption qualities of different cars. Also charging vehicle taxes in proportion to petrol consumption.
4   Decreasing the prestige benefits of driving fuel-guzzling cars by making small-car driving a manifestation of patriotism.
5   Compiling data on the characteristics of alternative energy sources and energy-saving devices so as to allocate better the rewards, penalties and other incentives.

Energy policy is mainly a physical science problem. The key biological science problem in public policy is how to encourage better health care on the part of both providers and recipients. This is an especially important problem in developing societies, where there is generally more concern for biological survival than in more developed societies. Relevant incentives might include the following.

1   Health care providers can be subsidized to provide low-cost care on a mass basis; recipients can be given cash incentives to submit to vaccinations and birth control.
2   The cost to health care insurers can be reduced per insured person by requiring universal public participation.

3 The cost of wrongdoing can be increased by requiring higher health care insurance premiums for people who are at fault in having bad health records, such as smokers or those who have excessive cholesterol rates.
4 Sometimes infant formulas are diluted in developing countries in order to make the formula go further. That would not be a benefit if there were no need for it as a result of adequate provision of infant milk and food supplements.
5 There is a need for better record keeping concerning the quantity, quality and prices of the health care providers and concerning the health of individuals so that public policy can better address the positive and negative incentives.

A third problem concerns science and technology. This is an especially important problem because technological innovation has large multiplier effects by virtue of its spillover into providing job opportunities, better products and workplaces, less expensive housing, anti-pollution devices and other high-technology means of dealing with social problems. Applying the checklist here might involve noting the following.

1 Government subsidies may be especially important for technological innovation because private capital may not be available in sufficient quantities and investors may not be so willing to wait for risky returns.
2 There are wasteful costs in reinventing the wheel, which means public policy should strive to inform those who can benefit from new technologies as to what is available.
3 Penalties can be imposed upon firms such as car manufacturers or steel mills that do not modernize. The penalties can at least consist of not being provided with bail-out money or tariffs if they are threatened by more modern competition.
4 As for decreasing the benefits of doing wrong by not adopting new innovations, there are few benefits with the exception of not having to adapt or retool.
5 There is a need for more coordination in the allocation of subsidy benefits and tax incentives for technological innovation which may necessitate having a coordinating agency like the Japanese Ministry for International Trade and Investment.

Some Conclusions

The incentives approach to public policy should be supplemented by a structures approach whereby public policy is viewed as also providing social structures that encourage socially desired behavior. For example, one can decrease crime through the above-mentioned incentives which cause people to choose right from wrong when faced with a decision dilemma. However, it would be better to structure social relations so that people are seldom faced with such decision dilemmas. Gun control is an example of such structuring. If gun control does effectively remove a large quantity of guns from circulation, the likelihood is less that an individual will be faced with deciding whether or not to shoot someone. On a broader level of structuring, one might note that, if people have been socialized into considering killing other people as a virtually unthinkable activity, they will also seldom, if ever, face a decision dilemma of whether or not to kill someone; it would not enter their minds to even entertain the dilemma, let alone decide in favor of the wrongdoing position. One can also appropriately structure relations in dealing with other social problems, as well as crime.

The incentives approach to public policy is as applicable to a socialist government as to a capitalist government. The key difference is that, under a socialist government, the incentives are generally directed toward government managers rather than private entrepreneurs. In the field of environmental protection, for example, the Soviet Union is faced with the same problem of getting factory managers to adopt anti-pollution devices as the United States. Under either system, factory managers have been traditionally rewarded in terms of the demand for their products and the lowness of their production costs. Adopting anti-pollution devices does not increase demand/income or reduce expenses. In fact, it increases expenses. Thus either economic system requires public policy incentives to get relevant decision makers to operate contrary to the traditional reward system by adopting expensive anti-pollution equipment.

The incentives approach is applicable to developing areas in either developing or developed countries. The essence of the incentives approach is manipulating the benefits and costs of rightdoing and wrongdoing in order to encourage socially desired behavior. That includes the kinds of changes that are needed in order to develop a developing area in a desirable way. The development of such areas may especially mean providing incentives for internal or external capital and innovators. It also generally or often means providing for good government, foreign policy, unemployment/inflation, economic regulation, crime control, ethnic relations, housing, environmental protection and energy.

If public policy is important in providing these kinds of developmental incentive, then public policy studies are also important. Policy studies are largely the study of how to make public policy more effective and efficient. Thus the question of how policy studies can be useful to developing areas is closely related to questions of how public policy can be useful. One can perhaps conclude that policy studies can be most useful by further exploring the ways in which public policy can provide incentives for societal development and improvement.

Notes

On the third party benefactor, especially in the context of the government intervening to reduce class conflict and ethnic conflict in housing and other urban problems, see Butler (1981), Sternlieb and Listokin (1981), Salamon (1989), Bawden and Skidmore (1989) and Ball *et al.* (1988). Also see Nagel (1994, 1997, 1998) and Nagel and Mills (1993).

Public policy evaluation in the context of developing areas is discussed in Freeman *et al.* (1980), Little and Mirrleesin (1974) and Schwartz and Berney (1977).

For other material dealing with public policy from an incentives perspective, see Blumstein (1978), Mitnick (1980), Tornatzky (1980), Hamilton *et al.* (1984) and Nagel (1984).

3 SOS Allocation by Expanding the Budget

The General Method

Here we are discussing what is involved in win–win analysis. The conservative allocation has to be exceeded, and the liberal allocation also has to be exceeded simultaneously. That information is summarized in Table 3.1. The key items are labelled X and Y. X is the amount of dollars that would be allocated to the conservative budget category or categories if the conservatives had their way. Y is the amount of dollars that would be allocated to the liberal budget category or categories if the liberals had their way. The object is to develop useful and realistic ways of enabling both the conservatives and the liberals to have their way simultaneously.

Table 3.1 tells us that the conservatives will be getting more than their best expectations if the police are allocated $113. It also tells us that the liberals will be getting more their best expectations if the courts are allocated more than $129. Thus the problem reduces to finding ways whereby the police can be allocated $113 and the courts can be allocated $130. That means finding $43 more than the initial budget constraint. This satisfies the idea of useful information since it makes clear that we do not need a budget of $500 or $800 to exceed the best expectations of both sides. Also we will not be able to do it with a budget of only $210, $200 or less than $200, unless we increase the relation scores, which will be discussed later, under the second SOS allocation approach, in Chapter 12.

Substantive Ideas

To be a meaningful SOS allocation, the recommendation must also be realistic. That means doing a Policy/Goal Percentaging (P/G%) analysis to determine the alternative or combination of alternatives that can raise the

Table 3.1   The SOS allocation based on increasing the budget

Goals / Budget categories	C Goal Crime reduction	L Goal Fair procedure	N Alloc. Wts =2.2	C Alloc. Wts =3.1	L Alloc. Wts = 1.3	SOS Alloc.
C Item				(X)		X+1
$ Police	2	1	$92	$112	$71	$113
	(67%)	(25%)	(46%)	(55%)	(35%)	(46%)
L Item					(Y)	Y+1
$ Courts	1	3	108	88	129	130
	(33%)	(75%)	(54%)	(44%)	(65%)	(54%)
Totals	3	2	$200	$200	$200	$243
	(100%)	(100%)	(100%)	(100%)	(100%)	(100%)

Notes:
1. Each allocation is arrived at by (a) multiplying the percentages in the goal columns by the neutral, conservative or liberal weights, (b) summing across the products, (c) dividing the sum by the total of the appropriate weights to obtain a weighted average allocation percentage, and (d) multiplying the total budget of $200 by that allocation percentage.
2. The super-optimum budget is $243 since that is the minimum amount which will allow for a bigger allocation than the best expectations of both the conservatives ($112 + $1 to the police) and the liberals ($129 + $1 to the courts).
3. The next step would be to analyze various ways of increasing the budget from $200 to $243, and then taking the best combination of those in light of various criteria.

additional $43. There are a number of possible alternatives of a general nature. First, the legislature could be convinced to appropriate additional funds in view of the importance of the goals to be achieved and the positive marginal rate of return from investing in each of the budget categories.

Second, the executive agency or agencies that are above the police and the courts should be convinced that, from within the total that they sub-allocate, more should be assigned to the police and the courts in view of the same considerations that might be presented to the legislature. Those considerations might differ if the legislature is a Democratic Congress and the executive agency is a Republican White House.

Third, funds can be raised through income-generating activities of the courts and the police themselves. This is a well-known alternative in higher education, where state universities' budget requests are turned down by the state legislature and by the state board of higher education. For a start, the police and courts could charge higher fees for some of their services, in the way that state universities charge more for tuition, especially to wealthier students, to cover scholarships for low-income students. The courts could charge higher fees for corporate litigation. The police could conceivably provide, for special fees, special services that would be the equivalent of private security work. That could run into political feasibility problems, given the frequent unwillingness of private enterprise to tolerate what could be stimulating competition.

Another analogous activity would be seeking contributions. There is no reason why the courts cannot write to all lawyers in the jurisdiction asking for voluntary contributions or even involuntary contributions. The lawyers can be asked to pay a practice fee for making use of the court facilities. The fee could be based on various levels of earnings. The police do currently ask for contributions for various police pension activities. This can border on intimidation, especially if it is associated with receiving a bumper sticker that the contributor expects to constitute an exemption from some traffic tickets.

Fifth, universities raise large amount of money through grants from foundations. Courts and police forces could so something similar. This would serve two purposes: it would bring in money and it would stimulate innovative thinking on the part of courts and police forces as to how they could do a better job with regard to fair procedure and crime reduction so that some foundation would be willing to fund the experiment and implementation.

Sixth, a big source of internal funding at universities is the taxing of academic and non-academic employees by postponing raises or having ceilings on raises, or offering non-monetary fringe benefits such as free education for faculty and staff children. Manipulating salaries in order to deal with a $43 shortfall would not bring in additional income, it would only reduce expenses. What might be needed is the equivalent of passing the hat or selling savings bonds or stamps among the employees to borrow money from them in anticipation that it will be repaid in better times. The internal loan would probably have to be paid back in cash because the traditional services provided by courts and police are like an entitlement, unlike the optional right to go tuition-free to the university where one's parents teach.

Finally, the idea of procuring loans internally from the people who work in the system also suggests the idea of taking out loans externally. It would not be appropriate for the police force to be borrowing from the syndicate. The police force and the courts, however, could be authorized to issue government bonds just as any government agency could be authorized to do so. There might be plenty of takers if the bonds provided for the usual tax exemption, which is a key factor enabling rich lenders to have large incomes without paying income tax.

One thing that is especially needed is for someone to make a thorough survey, combined with creative brainstorming, of all the devices that various government agencies use to supplement their main source of income, which is legislative appropriations filtered through higher-level executive agencies. The Reagan administration, for example, experimented with a variety of user fees. It might be interesting to know more about the good and bad experiences with these fees. This is an area where different government agencies can learn from each other, such as learning from the income-raising methods of state universities. It is also an area in which there may be many analogs between private sector institutions and government institutions on ways to raise income where one is basically providing a not-for-profit service and not selling merchandise.

The key idea in this context is the importance of thinking beyond the traditional allocation analysis which tends to take a budget constraint as a given and talks in terms of how to allocate between the budget categories within that dollar amount. One does not want to go to the opposite extreme and totally ignore budget constraints, which is the equivalent of ignoring economic and political feasibility. The SOS analysis based on increasing the budget emphasizes expanding the budget just enough to be able to arrive at an SOS allocation where conservative and liberal best expectations are exceeded, rather than where each viewpoint gets an infinite, excessive or unrealistic amount. This provides a meaningful target to aim at. Also of high importance is the fact that the SOS and P/G% analysis provide a meaningful way of analyzing how to meet that target.

Decision-aiding Software

One can, for example, take seven alternatives just mentioned and insert them into a P/G% data file called +17%INC. The reason for this title is that $34 is a 17 per cent increase on the $200 income. This file name emphasizes the target we are seeking. One can then insert a variety of relevant goals such as those that were mentioned in discussing the seven alternatives. The goals or criteria for judging among the alternatives might include the following:

1   an estimated probability figure indicating the likelihood of a particular alternative being able to generate the 17 per cent needed;
2   an estimate of the dollar cost of pursuing each alternative;
3   a 1–5 score on a political or legal feasibility variable, since some of these alternatives may require political or legal authorization, which may or may not be forthcoming;
4   in seeking to clarify one's criteria, it is often helpful to think in terms of checklists that include effectiveness, efficiency, equity, public participa-

tion, predictability and procedural due process – the three Es associated with economics, and the three Ps associated with political science;

5   the best way of raising the 17 per cent income increase is not an SOS problem in itself, although it is relevant to one kind of SOS solution. Thinking along SOS lines of conservative and liberal goals and alternatives may, however, be helpful. On the matter of increasing court fees, for example, conservatives might advocate charging something for the services of the public defender or a jury trial. Liberals might advocate charging for resolving large contract disputes or other relatively big business controversies. This reveals important criteria regarding the equitable spread of the benefits and costs of raising the 17 per cent income increase.

The above list of alternatives and goals is rather abstract, since the problem presented in Table 3.1 does not involve a specific place, time and set of factual circumstances. If we had those details, it would be even easier to come up with more and better alternatives and criteria than when one is working with abstractions that border on the symbolic logic of Xs and Ys. In this context, the real world is more suggestive than abstract methodology is, but both together are better than either alone.

PART II
MORE EFFICIENCY IN
ACHIEVING GOALS

4   Setting Higher Goals

The Artificial Labor Shortage

A critical issue for many countries is labor shortage. Redefining goals to meet new levels is another SOS application. In Hong Kong, for example, the labor shortage was such a problem, which was approached from a very traditional perspective. One alternative was to import additional labor. All this would have required was simply to stop arresting people who were seeking to cross the borders from all directions. These included the Vietnamese boat people, the people from the Chinese mainland, Filipinos and even some people (although not many) from English-speaking countries such as Australia, Britain and India. Most English-speaking people were rather cautious about settling or staying in Hong Kong, given that it became a Chinese province in 1997. (See Table 4.1.)

Profit opportunities create a dilemma that paralyzes decision making. The choice is one between retaining the labor shortage, and thereby missing opportunities to make Hong Kong even more prosperous than it is, and allowing labor in, and thereby diluting the population of Hong Kong. This is partly a racist matter, but it is also a legitimate concern, for education and welfare are expensive. Immigrants, however, may be particularly ambitious people who in the long run will pay more than their share of taxes. This may be especially true of the Vietnamese boat people, although coming by boat from Vietnam to Hong Kong is easier than boating to other countries and not much more difficult than crossing the border from Mexico to Texas. They are, however, giving up whatever they had in Vietnam.

The SOS was simply to redefine the labor force, thereby overcoming the limits of the traditional definition. Redefining the labor force means recognizing all the potential labor. There is then a labor surplus.

Since the above suggestions were made for a super-optimum solution to the alleged labor shortage problem in Hong Kong, the former British colony has become part of mainland China. The suggestions are still valid that all major sides would be more likely to consider themselves winners if Hong Kong were to lead the world in fully employing its adult population. Such a

Table 4.1   The Hong Kong labor problem

Criteria / Alternatives	C Goal Reduce taxpayer burden	L Goal Increase quantity of labor	L Goal Increase quality of labor	N Total (neutral weights)	L Total (liberal weights)	C Total (conservative weights)
C Alternative Keep as is	3	3	3	24	24	24*
L Alternative Import labour	4	5	2	24	26*	22

SOS Alternative
  Increase labour
  force
	3	4	3	28	28**	28**

SOS Alternative Upgrade labour	2	3	5	28	30**	26**

program could aid the transition to new jobs for people who are displaced by productivity 'downsizing', free trade, defense conversion and immigration, and would give jobs to women and jobs to others who have been previously discriminated against. These are worldwide problems as we enter the 21st century.

The Parliamentary Alternative and New Constitutional Rights

This is the fundamental political science dispute between parliamentary and presidential governments, which is applicable to all countries. (See Table 4.2.)

The Alternatives

The conservative position is generally to support presidential government because it gives greater stability, which conservatives like. The liberal position is to support parliamentary government largely because it is more responsive and liberals have traditionally been more interested in responsiveness, at least with regard to economic issues (although not necessarily with regard to civil liberties issues). The neutral position is to try to find a middle position, which is not so easy. One can make it easier to remove the president through impeachment, but that has never been done. One can try to give parliamentary government more stability by saying that it takes a two-thirds vote to bring down the prime minister rather than a mere majority vote, but that has never been done. One can have a presidential government

Table 4.2 Presidential versus parliamentary government

Criteria / Alternatives	C Goal Continuity	L Goal Responsiveness	N Total (neutral weights)	L Total (liberal weights)	C Total (conservative weights)
C Alternative Presidential government	4	2	12	10	14*
L Alternative Parliamentary government	2	4	12	14*	10
N Alternative Compromise	3	3	12	12	12
SOS Alternative Right to continuous economic growth & right to upgraded work	5	5	20	20**	20**

with short terms and no provision for re-election to get more responsiveness. One can likewise have long terms for members of parliament in order to get more stability.

The Goals

The conservative goal should be referred to as continuity, not stability. Stability sounds like stagnation. Continuity implies growth, but smooth growth rather than jerky growth. Continuity can imply change, but change in accordance with some kind of predictability based on previously developed trends. The key liberal goal is responsiveness, which is broad enough to include more than just electoral responsiveness. This could be an example of raising one's goals so as to broaden the notion of responsiveness, like broadening the notion of unemployment, and also broadening the notion of continuity.

The Super-optimum Solution

The SOS is to say that it is not especially important whether one has a chief executive who is chosen directly by the people or indirectly by the people through the Parliament. What is needed is a constitutional or statutory commitment on the part of the chief executive and the government in general to responsiveness and stability.

Responsiveness   A responsiveness is required that goes beyond merely reading the public opinion polls in order to get re-elected. Responsiveness in the traditional political context has meant that it is easy to throw the government out of power. That is more a process designed to bring about responsiveness than responsiveness itself. Responsiveness should mean such things as the government being sensitive to people who are displaced as a result of new technologies or reduced tariffs: that is, the government is responsive to their need for new jobs. A government is much more responsive if it sees to it that displaced workers find new jobs even though the president is a president for life and cannot be thrown out of office than would be a government in which the prime minister can be replaced by 10 per cent of the Parliament saying they want to get rid of him. Responsiveness should mean that, when people are hurting, the government does something about it other than changing prime ministers.

Stability   On the matter of stability, we do not want stability. We want continuity. We want continuous growth. Growth is change, not stability. We want statutes and constitutional provisions that will require the government, regardless of whether it consists of Republicans or Democrats, to engage in policies that guarantee about 6 per cent growth per year. We do have a 1946 Employment Act and a 1970 Humphrey-Hawkins Act that say unemployment should not get above 3 per cent, or that inflation should not get above 3 per cent. Such laws mean nothing because they provide no provision for enforcement. Worse, they provide no provision to achieve those goals. They are akin to Canute asking the waves to stop, which can be done by the Army Corps of Engineers building appropriate dams, but not simply by issuing a 'there shalt not be' statement.

A Pair of Constitutional Provisions

The SOS thus would be a set of statutes or a pair of statutes (or, better yet, a pair of constitutional provisions).

Continuous economic growth   The SOS would require 6 per cent a year continuous growth. That is a minimum. There is nothing wrong with doing better than that, even if growth is jerky – one year 10 per cent, another year 6 per cent, another year 12 per cent. This sounds very unstable, but neither conservatives nor liberals would object to that kind of instability. Nobody is likely to object to having their income highly unstable, with one year $1 million, the next year $20 million. When people talk about instability they mean jumping from positive to negative, or positive to zero, but not from very high positive to positive and back.

Upgrading skills   The second statute or constitutional right is an obligation to displaced workers that they will be retrained and/or relocated. This is like two new constitutional rights. Traditional constitutional rights have related to free speech, equal protection and due process. Modern constitutional rights have related to social security, a minimum wage, a safe workplace and, more recently, clean air. What we are proposing is a constitutional right to economic growth and to be relocated if one is a displaced worker. The word 'relocated' sounds too much like moving a person from one city to another. We are also talking about upgrading skills so one can get a better job without moving to another city. Instead of talking about the right to relocation, we should talk about the right to upgraded work. It is not 'the right to work', a phrase which has been ruined by people who use it to mean the right not to be in a union. A problem with the concept of the right to upgraded work is that there is nothing in that concept that confines it to displaced workers, although that is not necessarily bad. Perhaps all workers should have a right to upgraded work, but especially those who have no work at all as a result of technological change or tariff reductions. If there were really a meaningful right to economic growth and upgraded work, that kind of SOS would score highly on continuity. To emphasize this, we need to talk about continuous economic growth. The upgraded work part especially relates to responsiveness.

Making Rights Meaningful

A key point is that these rights are not made meaningful by merely being stated in statutes or constitutions. Nor are they made meaningful by saying that someone who feels he has been denied one of those rights can sue Congress or the president. They are made meaningful by the establishment of institutions like the Ministry of International Trade and Industry that has a mandate, a budget, personnel and sub-units that are meaningfully relevant to promoting continuous economic growth. One could establish a separate government agency to enforce the right to upgraded work. The rights become meaningful when you have institutions in place to enforce them, not just words in place in a statute or a constitution. The courts cannot enforce them. It requires specialized administrative agencies. The courts can enforce due process by reversing convictions that violate due process. The courts can enforce free speech and equal protection by issuing injunctions ordering the police to cease interfering with speakers or marchers, or ordering the schools to cease operating segregated classrooms. The courts have no power to award well-directed subsidies or tax breaks which are needed for economic growth and upgraded work. That requires appropriate administrative agencies.

Voting Rights in South Africa

Alternatives, Goals and Relations

The conservative *alternative* has been to deny blacks the right to vote. The extreme left-wing alternative of some of the Pan-Africans has been to deny whites the right to vote, or even to expel them from the country, meaning to deny that they have any right to even live in South Africa. The middling position is that of one person, one vote, although that could be considered a left-wing position since the blacks would dominate. (See Table 4.3.)

The black *goal* is basically for blacks to be better off. The white goal is not necessarily for whites to be better off than they are at present, but at least not to be much worse off.

The conservative position and the more extreme left-wing position would *result* in a kind of super-malimum position where both blacks and whites would be worse off. The only way the conservatives could succeed in keeping blacks from having the right to vote any longer would be through a system of repression even greater than they have attempted in the past. The country would be in a state of continuous guerrilla warfare, with no safeguards against being bombed or murdered. There would be no foreign business, or not much that would want to be located there. Much domestic business would leave. If the extreme blacks had their way and all the whites were driven out, the result would be somewhat similar, in that there would be a lack of foreign investment. Much domestic business would leave, voluntarily or involuntarily.

Developing an SOS

The *object* is to develop a system in which none of those bad things happens, meaning (1) that foreign investment does not shy away from South Africa, but substantially increases, (2) that businesses within South Africa stay there and even expand to hire more people an provide more job opportunities, and (3) that violence ends, as contrasted to merely being temporarily suspended, as the situation is now, while people wait to see what will happen.

As mentioned above, merely providing one person with one vote is not a middle-of-the-road compromise since it would greatly favor blacks who are the overwhelming majority. A true compromise would provide institutional constraints on pure majoritarian rule. Three devices are proposed. First, partition the country into states like the United States, especially as of 1789, when there were 13 states. There would be basically four states in South Africa: the Cape provinces, Natal, Transvaal and the Orange Free State.

Table 4.3 Voting rights in South Africa

Criteria / Alternatives	C Goal Whites well off C=3 N=2 L=1	L Goal Blacks well off C=1 N=2 L=3	N Total (neutral weights)	L Total (liberal weights)	C Total (conservative weights)
C Alternative Only whites vote	4?[4]	2	12	10	14*
L Alternative Only blacks vote, or majority rule without minority safeguards	2	4?[5]	12	14*	10
N₁ Alternative[1] Bill of Rights	3	3	12	12	12
N₂ Alternative[2] US Constitution	3	3	12	12	12
SOS Alternative[3] Economic rights	>3.5	>3.5	>14	>14	>14

Notes:
1　Neutral alternative 1 is minority safeguards such as free speech, equal treatment and due process.
2　Neutral alternative 2 is minority safeguards such as senate, electoral college and special majorities to pass or amend.
3　The SOS alternative includes economic growth and upgraded skills combined with neutral alternative 1 and some neutral alternative 2.
4　There is a question mark next to the 4 in column 1 because it is questionable whether and to what extent whites will be well off if only whites voted. Under such circumstances there might be continuing and increasing vengeful terrorism, sabotage and vandalism directed against whites by angry disenfranchised blacks. There might also be continuing worldwide boycotts on exports, imports, sports participation and other negative reactions from countries.
5　There is a question mark next to the 4 in column 2 because it is questionable whether and to what extent blacks would be well off if only blacks voted. There would probably be much greater loss of non-black domestic and international capital than there has been. President Mandela has tried hard to make such capital feel welcome and comfortable.

Eight senators, however, would be too few to run the country. The United States Senate has 100 senators based on 50 states. Maybe the new South Africa could have at least five senators per state, so there would be a total of 20 senators. But the blacks could not run the Senate any more than the north could run the US Senate. The white states would have the power to prevent even ordinary legislation from being passed but especially any legislation that requires a two-thirds vote, such as the approval of treaties or appointments, and any amendments to the constitution would require a three-quarters vote.

Second, everything that has been proposed is exactly what was adopted in the United States in the constitution. There would be separation of powers, federalism and judicial review, everything designed to enable a minority of states to prevent the majority from exercising the power that its numbers give it. The South African constitution could have an electoral college in which the president would be chosen on the basis of how many senators each state has, which would have nothing to do with how many people they have, since every state would have the same number of senators. They would have a supreme court that would have the power to declare unconstitutional legislation that interferes with property rights and the state's rights, all of which would be code words for white people's rights.

Third, it is ironic that those who want to preserve white power in South Africa choose as their model the American constitution, including the Bill of Rights. They are all of a sudden very much in favor of minority rights because they are the minority. Here the word 'minority' means numerical minority, not lack of power.

A super-optimum solution would have to involve something that would be the equivalent of an internal economic union. It would have to involve a system whereby white business interests would have an environment in which they could prosper, and blacks would have job opportunities accompanied by merit criteria and affirmative action with preferences for people who cannot satisfy a minimum competence level. Basically, it means going directly to what it is that each side wants to achieve by way of increased voting power and concentrating on how to do more than guarantee that, regardless of the voting rights. It means elevating certain economic rights to a higher status than the status of federalism, separation of powers and the other constitutional issues.

Relevant SOS Reasoning

The key way out is to emphasize both blacks and whites being much better off economically as a result of SOS thinking. That is, political power is directed toward economic well-being for each group. It is important in modern times to get away from the goal of stagnant stability and to move more toward the goal of continuous economic growth. It is also important to get away from the idea that a responsive government is one that easily collapses when public opinion changes, and to move toward the idea that public policy helps people upgrade their skills in response to changing times and technologies, especially by providing potential trainees and trainers with subsidies and vouchers.

Three questions may be put to revolutionary South African blacks:

1   What is going to happen to the whites? This is an implicitly racist question that shows rather biased sensitivity to what is going to happen to the whites, but not what is going to happen to the blacks, who may be in bad shape as a result of white flight, loss of investment and other socioeconomic disruptions.
2   How can whites and blacks be encouraged to make concessions? This is the traditional compromise position, which is better than civil war.
3   How can both blacks and whites be enabled to be better off than their best expectations? This is the SOS position. The SOS dispute resolution activity is one that we are getting increasingly involved with. Past and current thinking emphasize dividing the national pie or income among blacks and whites in proportion to their numbers, needs or contributions. The SOS solution emphasizes expanding the pie through economic growth brought on by expanded training and technologies. With such an expanded pie each side could wind up with more than its previous best expectations. Such solutions are becoming increasingly possible as a result of improved technologies and public policy.

Since the above suggestions for a super-optimum solution to the voting rights problems in South Africa were made, apartheid has ended. The suggestion is still valid that all major sides would be more likely to consider themselves winners if South Africa were to lead the world in establishing an effective constitutional right to economic growth and upgraded skills. These new rights could be associated with the 21st century, just as economic rights concerning wages, hours, child labor, safe workplaces, consumer rights and environmental rights were associated with the 20th century, and the rights of free speech, freedom of religion, merit treatment and fair procedures were associated with the 19th century. It might also be noted that, as of 1998, South Africa is still struggling for the most productive balance or super-optimum solution between the rights of different groups, including blacks versus blacks and whites versus whites, not just blacks versus whites.

High Goals in General

Doing Better than the Best

One of President Carter's mottos was 'Why not the best?'. President Kennedy used to say, when people questioned his high goals, that it was better to aim higher and only get halfway there than to aim not so high and get all the way there. Achieving the optimum is considered to be a high goal, although that partly depends on how the optimum is defined. However, the optimum, or at least what is customarily considered to be the optimum, may not be high enough.

The purpose of this chapter is to pursue that thought in the context of public policy problems, especially policy problems that are as fundamental as unemployment and inflation. If unemployment and inflation can both be reduced to close to zero, then the economy, almost by definition, is in a state of high prosperity. Such prosperity leads to improvements in all other problem areas, such as poverty, discrimination, crime and ill-health. It can also have positive effects on conditions of consumers, farmers, labor, the environment, housing and education, as well as civil liberties and international peace.

In addition to talking about doing better than the optimum on unemployment and inflation, this chapter also discusses doing better than the optimum on crime reduction and other social indicators. It is also concerned with general means for achieving the goals, including an incentives growth perspective, and addresses the question whether it is better to set one's goals not so high and fully achieve them, or to seek to achieve more than the optimum and not get all the way there.

Doing Better than the Optimum on Unemployment

Optimum unemployment can be defined as having no more than 3 per cent of the labor force out of work. If the figure goes below 3 per cent, there may be insufficient movement upward from less appropriate to more appropriate jobs. The Humphrey–Hawkins legislation specifies 4 per cent as the target figure. One could, however, talk about unemployment that is below 0 per cent or better than 0 per cent. 'Below 0 per cent' and 'better than 0 per cent' both mean that many people who were formerly not counted as unemployed now have jobs, as explained below.

For example, suppose there are 25 people in a society and ten are in the labor force. Of the ten in the labor force, two are unemployed, giving a 20 per cent unemployment figure. If a job is found for one of the two unemployed workers, then we have 10 per cent unemployment. If both formerly unemployed workers are employed and there is no new unemployment, then we have 0 per cent unemployment.

Getting credit for adding to the labor force   If we expand the labor force, the unemployment figure is recalculated using a new base or denominator. Thus, if we improve the real or perceived job opportunities so that four of the 15 people who were not in the labor force now become job seekers, then unemployment will go up to 4/14 or 29 per cent. In other words, the unemployment figure as a social indicator in effect penalizes expanding the labor force. This may be an important defect in so important a social indicator.

Perhaps it might make more sense to say that putting to work someone who was formerly outside the labor force should be counted as partly offsetting one person who is already in the labor force but unemployed. Suppose we find jobs for all four of those new additions to the labor force. One could then say that unemployment has now dropped to 2/14 or 14 per cent from the figure of 20 per cent. Thus adding people to the labor force and finding jobs for them does reduce the unemployment figure, even if the previously unemployed people are not found jobs.

One could say that 0/14 in this context is better than 0/10, even if they both represent 0 per cent unemployment. Is 2/14 worse than, equal to, or better than 0/10? The answer is 'equal to' if finding jobs for four people formerly outside the labor force is worth as much to society as finding jobs for two unemployed people who were already in the labor force. In other words, the answer to the question depends on the tradeoff between employing unemployed people 'outside' and 'in' the labor force. A two to one tradeoff seems reasonable.

A well-employed society should have a combination of a low percentage of unemployed people (as determined by the quantity of unemployed divided by the total labor force) and a high percentage of the total adult population in the labor force. Thus a society of 25 people is not doing so well on employment opportunities if it has 18 adults and only 10 are in the labor force, while another society of 25 people with 18 adults has 14 in the labor force. In other words, we need to place more emphasis on bringing more people into the labor force who are willing to work and capable of working. That includes older people, disabled people and single parents receiving public aid. Older people often have skills that could still be applied, especially in a white-collar society. Disabled people and public aid parents can often be trained to qualify for profitable and satisfying jobs. The public aid parents may also need daycare services. Training and daycare involve tax expenditures, but the investment may be worthwhile if public aid expenses are reduced even more than the tax expenditure.

In the unemployment context, doing better than the optimum means seeking not only to get unemployment down close to about 3 per cent or 4 per cent, but also seeking to get the percentage of the labor force up close to maybe 80 per cent or 90 per cent of the adult population. In an optimizing society, virtually every adult should be provided with sufficient job opportunities, job training and related services so that virtually every adult will be constructively employed.

Getting credit for lessening underemployment   Doing better than the optimum in the employment context should also include having an expanding economy such that anyone who wants to take on a second job can do so. Thus we need to emphasize a third measure which addresses the extent to which employed people are fully employed. There are really two measures. One relates to the percentage of employed people who work full-time. If only six out of ten people in the labor force have at least full-time employment, we have a less well-employed society than if the figure were nine out of ten. Full-time employment can be defined as working 40 hours a week, although the standard as to what constitutes full-time employment has, over the years, involved a reduction in the number of hours. It is appropriate to reduce the number of hours as society becomes more productive and people can produce more output in fewer hours and thus receive more salary or wages for fewer hours of work.

The other measure of full employment could relate to the percentage of people who would like to have a second job who do have a second job. Suppose all ten people are employed 40 hours a week, but four of them would like to work more, but there is no more work available for them. That is a less satisfactory situation than all four being able to obtain extra work, or only three seeking extra employment.

It is more important to employ unemployed people in the labor force than to provide more employment to those who already have a part-time, seasonal or full-time job. If the desirability tradeoff is two to one for unemployed in the labor force versus unemployed outside the labor force, the desirability tradeoff is probably about three to one for finding jobs for the *un*employed in the labor force versus the *under*employed. A more precise measure might consider the degree of underemployment for each worker.

A summary index   Thus we now have an expanded concept of doing better than the optimum of 3 per cent or 4 per cent unemployment which includes the following:

1   providing jobs for older people,
2   providing jobs for disabled people,
3   providing jobs for single parent public aid recipients,
4   providing jobs for others outside the labor force, including those who might otherwise be discouraged or depressed about finding jobs,
5   providing full-time jobs for those who are only working part-time or on seasonal jobs,
6   providing second jobs for those who want them,
7   providing jobs for those who are already part of the labor force but are totally unemployed.

Category 7 has traditionally been the only category of jobless people counted as unemployed. By obtaining jobs for the other six categories as well as category 7, we are doing better than the traditional optimum.

All these ideas can be incorporated into a new index of employment in accordance with the formula, $E = (F + P/3)/(L + A/2)$, where

E = employment index;

F = number of fully employed people in the economy (six people in our hypothetical economy); if it feels more realistic, add 'million' after all these numbers: the society may be hypothetical, but the arithmetic is accurate and the percentage of people employed roughly corresponds to most economies of the world;

P = number of people partly employed (two people in the economy);

L = number of people in the labor force (ten people);

A = number of able-bodied people who are not in the labor force – that is, who are not actively seeking jobs (eight additional people).

This means the denominator of the index is $10 + 8/2$, or 14. The numerator is $6 + 2/3$, or 6.67. Thus the employment index is 6.67/14, or 48 per cent. This is in contrast to the traditional unemployment percentage which would be 2/10, or 20 per cent, with a complement of 100 per cent – 20 per cent, or 80 per cent.

The above formula has the following advantages over the traditional unemployment percentage.

1   It emphasizes the more positive goal of seeking high employment, rather than the more negative goal of seeking low unemployment.
2   The denominator considers both people in the labor force and also able-bodied people outside the labor force at the two to one tradeoff mentioned above.
3   The numerator considers both people partly employed and those fully employed at the three to one tradeoff mentioned above. Partly employed could include those who are fully employed, but who are seeking additional work.
4   This index enables a society in effect to do better than 0 per cent unemployment or 100 per cent employment by fully employing people and by finding jobs for able-bodied people not counted in the labor force.

Both the employment index and the traditional unemployment percentage are incapable of going below 0 per cent or above 100 per cent. This is so under the employment index because one cannot employ more than all the people in the labor force plus all the able-bodied people not in the labor force. We could redefine the index in order to allow for improvements in the employment picture that would exceed 100 per cent. Doing so would mean using last year's labor force base or denominator, but this year's employed people or numerator. For example, suppose that last year, or in the last time period, the denominator was 14 people and the numerator was 6.67. Suppose further that ten more people were added to the labor force for whom jobs were found. That would cause the numerator to go up to 16.67, and the employment index to go up to 16.67/14, or 119 per cent. This is in contrast to adding the ten newly employed people to both the numerator and the denominator. That would give an employment index of 16.67/24, or 70 per cent, which seems more meaningful.

Along related lines, one could subtract one unemployed person from the traditional unemployment percentage for every newly employed person who is brought into the labor force. With enough subtractions one could go below 0 per cent unemployment, but that would hide the fact that there are still some unemployed people in the labor force. One can recognize, however, that 0 per cent unemployment with more people brought into the labor force and fewer *under*employed people is better than 0 per cent unemployment with lots of discouraged people outside the active labor force and lots of underemployed people within it. Thus it is possible to do better than 0 per cent unemployed without getting into the conceptual problems of a negative percentage.

Doing Better than the Optimum on Inflation

Doing the optimum with regard to inflation can, for many countries, be defined as staying below double-digit inflation. In the United States, 3 per cent inflation might be considered optimum. Getting below 3 per cent could be considered undesirable from the point of view of the long-term desirability of improved wages, products and national income. However, one could talk about inflation that is below 0 per cent or better than 0 per cent while still having improved real wages, products and national income.

For example, suppose last year a type of worker cost $10 an hour, and this year the cost is $15 an hour. That sounds like 50 per cent inflation, as determined by calculating ($15 – $10)/$10. In order for wages (as the price of labor) to go up only 3 per cent, those workers would have to receive a wage increase (in light of these calculations) of only 30¢. To have negative inflation, the workers would have to take a reduction in their $10 wage. This is the traditional way of calculating inflation. It can be applied to any specific price, average price or set of prices.

Getting credit for increased quantitative benefits Suppose, however, those same workers become more productive, so that they are producing $30 worth of goods in the second year, whereas they were only producing $12 worth of goods in the first year. That means the benefit/cost ratio for the first year was $12/$10, or 120 per cent. The benefit/cost ratio for the second year was $30/$15 or 200 per cent. Thus the benefit/cost ratio rose 80 percentage points from last year to this year. That is a more meaningful figure than just noting that the cost rose 50 per cent from $10 to $15 from last year to this year. It is unbalanced to look only at costs without looking at benefits, or to look only at benefits without looking at costs.

In light of these considerations, we can have a form of negative inflation or disinflation if benefit/cost ratios go up, even if costs do not go down. Calculating benefit/cost ratios is more difficult than simply calculating costs. In this context, however, we are not necessarily talking about subjective benefits, but instead mainly about units of production. That is not such a difficult indicator to measure. It is relatively easy to measure bushels per acre, cars produced, or gallons of milk produced by cows or bottling plants. To determine the benefit/cost ratio for various products or industries, one divides the total production by the total cost bill for the year. Estimates may be necessary where different products are attributable to the same costs. However, it is better to use imperfect estimates of a correct measure (like benefit/cost ratios) than perfect estimates of a wrong measure (like price increases which ignore increases or decreases in benefits).

Getting credit for increased qualitative benefits One could extend this analysis still further by talking about benefits in a qualitative as well as a quantitative sense. For example, suppose a milk-producing firm produced 50 gallons of milk last year at a wage bill or total cost of $100. That is a benefit/cost ratio of 50/$100, or 1/2, or 0.50. Suppose this year it produces 80 gallons of milk through new technology at a cost of $120. That is a benefit/cost ratio of 80/$120 or 0.67. Suppose further that this year's milk has a new quality that enables it to last twice as long without going sour. There should be some way of considering that improved benefit in the numerator of the benefit/cost ratio.

The best way might be to talk, not in terms of 80 gallons of milk, but in terms of the new market price. That price should be higher if people are willing to spend more for longer-lasting milk. Maybe the old price was $2 a gallon, and the new price is $2.50 a gallon. This means the old benefit/cost ratio expressed in dollars was (50×2)/$100, or $100/$100, or 1.0. The new benefit/cost ratio is (80×$2.50)/$120, or $200/$120, or 1.67. This further means that the benefit/cost ratio rose from 1.00 to 1.67, which is a 67 per cent rise, even though the cost of producing milk went up.

To be more precise, one would have to adjust the price increase of $2.00 to $2.50 for inflation. Thus, if prices in general are up 10 per cent, then only 90 per cent of that incremental $0.50, or $0.45, can be attributed to improved quality. Some of the $0.50 increment might also be due to favorable changes in consumer tastes, reduction in the supply of the product or manipulated prices. These factors, though, tend to explain price changes over a longer time period, rather than just from one year to the next. There is no question that measuring improvements in qualitative benefits is more difficult than measuring quantitative benefits. Again, however, it is better to try to estimate the increase in qualitative benefits than to ignore them completely.

A summary index   How might one pull these ideas together to create a new summary index of benefits received per dollar spent? The new index could be called the national B/C index, analagous to the National Employment Index discussed above. The index would divide benefits by costs so as to emphasize the more positive goal of seeking higher benefits relative to costs, rather than the more negative goal of seeking lower costs relative to benefits.

The total national cost is approximately the same as the total national income plus what is spent outside the United States. The quantitative benefits in the numerator could not meaningfully lump together a variety of products like cars, staplers, oranges and so on. Instead, we could use a basket of products in the way that the Department of Labor determines the Consumer Price Index (CPI). Suppose the basket consists of cars, staplers and oranges. To calculate the benefit/cost ratio from one year to the next would involve determining the average car price for cars in general or for a specific type of car for last year and this year. Doing so would also involve determining such things as (1) improved mileage in the average car from last year to this year, (2) improved or worsened durability, and (3) improved safety. Each of these criteria could be roughly measured in percentage terms, so that we might obtain three percentages such as +10 per cent, +6 per cent and +2 per cent. If we treat each criterion equally, the average improvement in benefits is 6 per cent. If the average cost goes up 3 per cent, the benefits have improved twice as much as costs have worsened. That gives us a 2.00 score on the B/C index, although it could be called an index of change in benefits/change in costs.

Some benefits are more important than others. Consumer surveys could be made to determine relative weights. For example, consumers might consider improved mileage to be twice as important as improved durability or safety, especially when fuel prices are high. If mileage receives a relative weight of two and durability and safety a relative weight of one apiece, then the components of the B/C index would be 10 per cent + 10 per cent + 6 per cent + 2 per cent divided by four, instead of 10 per cent + 6 per cent + 2 per cent divided by three. The new B/C index would be 7 per cent, rather than 6 per cent. Weights could also be assigned to cars versus staplers versus oranges. That is no different from the present assigning of weights to the products in the shopping basket from which the consumer price index is now calculated. The national B/C index would thus be a weighted average somewhat like the consumer price index.

The advantages of the B/C index over the CPI include the following.

1 People prefer scoring in which a high score is desirable to scoring in which a low score is desirable, although one could work with the complement of the traditional inflation index.
2 The B/C index considers improvements or worsening in benefits, not just changes in costs.
3 The B/C index can be treated as a measure of national productivity, and thereby encourage more sensitivity to national productivity.
4 A special B/C index could be developed just for the cost of labor. It would involve dividing the changes in the current labor productivity index by changes in wage costs.
5 The B/C index is capable of going over 100 per cent if the percentage change in benefits is greater than the percentage change in cost.

The fact that the B/C index can go over 100 per cent is analogous to having negative inflation. A decrease in costs from $4 to $2 with benefits remaining constant at $12 is the equivalent of an increase in benefits from $12 to $24 with costs remaining constant at $4 or rising slightly. Thus we obtain the equivalent of negative inflation or disinflation, not by concentrating on trying to get prices down, but rather by concentrating more meaningfully on trying to get benefits up.

Doing Better then the Optimum on Crime Reduction

Presidential administrations seem to think they are doing well on crime if the crime rate does not increase. That is a rather unambitious standard. It means that, if crime is rampant at 90 crimes per 100 people per year, that standard has been met so long as crime does not move up to 91 crimes per 100 people. Even asking for a 10 per cent reduction seems unambitious, since that would only mean going down from 90 crimes to 9 crimes fewer, or 81 crimes. An ambitious goal, analogous to getting unemployment and inflation below 0 per cent, would involve getting crime below zero crimes per 100 people. That raises two questions: how is it conceptually possible, and how is it empirically possible?

On the matter of being conceptually possible, suppose we have a society with 100 people. Last year, 20 of them were victims of crime. For the sake of simplicity, let us assume the crimes were all equally severe, although a more sophisticated method would weight the crimes in terms of the maximum or average sentence given to those who are convicted of each type of crime. Suppose further that another society or year also had 100 people and 20 crimes, but an additional 15 people were victims of negligence or other forms of civil wrongdoing. Suppose also that the second society had another 10 people who were fired from their jobs or lost their licenses for job wrongdoing. Clearly the first society would be the more desirable society to live in. Likewise, if both societies had zero crime, but the second society had a number of instances of civil wrongdoing and bad job performance, the first society would in effect be doing better than zero crime on a broadened wrongdoing index. This index includes civil wrongs (like negligently but non-criminally running over a pedestrian) and bad job performance (like negligently making lamps that electrocute people). These are wrongs that we want to reduce, even if they are not crimes. We likewise want to reduce the unemployment of elderly people, even if they are not counted as unemployed.

Considering civil wrongdoing   We need an index broader than a crime index or crime indexes to measure wrongdoing in the United States and elsewhere. There has possibly been too much emphasis on crime as a form of wrongdoing and too little emphasis on other important forms of wrongdoing. Crime indexes can be broadened by including white-collar crimes as well as street crimes. White-collar crimes include violations of the laws that relate to embezzlement, consumer fraud, antitrust, safe workplaces, environmental protection, discrimination, housing codes and fair labor standards, provided that the law allows for fines and/or jail sentences. If the law only allows for injunctions or damages paid to victims, it is a matter of civil wrongdoing. Having composite wrongdoing indexes also allows for keeping separate count on different kinds of wrongs, since reducing them may require different methods.

One could measure civil wrongdoing by gathering data on all court and administrative proceedings in which a defendant has been found liable or a defendant has agreed to pay damages or to cease and desist without being found liable. Our society has collectively decided that criminal wrongdoing is more serious than civil wrongdoing. Therefore each crime committed should receive about two or three times as much weight as each civil wrong, other things held constant. A more sophisticated measure would talk in terms of degrees of civil wrongs, as measured by the average amount of damages awarded.

Considering job wrongdoing If we are going to have a comprehensive wrongdoing index (WDI), it should also include job wrongdoing as an important form of wrongdoing in a society that is seeking to be productive and efficient. Job wrongdoing does not simply mean working slowly or inaccurately within a permissible range. It means performing poorly enough to be fired if one is an employee, or to have one's license suspended or removed if one is a professional person or in a licensed business. Being laid off because business is bad is not the same as being fired because of bad individual behavior. A more precise index would consider the relative severity of different kinds of firings. Employer wrongdoing is a form of civil wrongdoing if it is subject to damages or an injunction.

If the Department of Labor can gather information on employment on a city-by-city basis every month, it should be able to gather information on firings on at least a national basis, although it would be preferable to do so on a state-by-state basis. That kind of information is relevant to paying unemployment compensation, since fired employees are not entitled to compensation. Gathering statistics on firings and license suspensions or removals could be useful to studies designed to determine how to increase the competency of employees, professionals and business firms. One could study variations across time periods, places, type of occupations, individuals and other units of analysis to obtain useful insights.

A summary index Thus we have now converted the concept of getting crime down into the concept of getting wrongdoing down, where wrongdoing is substantially broader than just criminal wrongdoing. These ideas can be summarized in the following wrongdoing index: $WDI = 3(CRW/POP) + 2(CVW/POP) +)FLW/L)$, where

WDI = wrongdoing index,
CRW = criminal wrongdoing (from FBI crime reports),
POP = national population (from census data),
CVW = civil wrongdoing (from statistics of courts and administrative agencies),
FLW = firings and license withdrawals (to be gathered by the Department of Labor),
L = total labor force (also a Department of Labor figure).

To take partially into consideration the relative severity of criminal wrongdoing, civil wrongdoing and firings, we give these measures weights of 3, 2 and 1, respectively. Sometimes the same act, such as stealing from a client, may be a crime, a cause for civil action and grounds for suspension of one's license. That is a form of triple counting which may or may not be justified by the severity of the act. The best way to calculate relative severity would be to talk in terms of types of crimes, with each type having a different severity depending on the average sentence. Likewise, one could measure degrees of severity among civil wrongs, depending on the average damages awarded. Firings and license withdrawals could be measured for each type of occupation in terms of how many dollars the average occupation holder is likely to be losing. One could then talk in terms of three separate wrongdoing indexes. These could be combined together rather grossly with the 3–2–1 weighting, or by using more sophisticated methods for putting all the sub-types of wrongdoing on a commensurate monetary or non-monetary scale.

We divide criminal and civil wrongdoing by the national population in order to talk in terms of wrongdoing per capita. We divide instances of firings and license withdrawals by the size of the labor force in order to obtain an analogous ratio. If we subtract the number of firings and license withdrawals from the size of the labor force, we obtain a measure of the number of people in the labor force who are doing reasonably correctly or well on their jobs. However, there is no figure from which we can subtract the number of crimes in order to determine the number of compliances. We have no way of knowing how many opportunities people had to commit crimes in which they refrained from doing so. The same is true of civil wrongdoing. We could determine the percentage of people who have been convicted of a crime over the past year and likewise the percentage of people who have not been convicted of a crime. The latter percentage would be a rough measure of rightdoing, although it refers to people rather than to acts.

The best way to convert the wrongdoing index (WDI) into a rightdoing index (RDI) is to calculate the complement – the way 7 per cent unemployment can be expressed as 93 per cent employment. More specifically, if crimes per capita is 2 per cent, civil wrongs per capita is 4 per cent, and firings and license withdrawals is 5 per cent, the sum of those three percentages is 11 per cent and the complement or rightdoing index is 89 per cent. To calculate a weighted rightdoing index using the 3–2–1 weighting system, the three products would be 3 times 2 per cent, plus 2 times 4 per cent, and plus 1 times 5 per cent, for a total of 19 per cent. We would then divide the 19 per cent by the sum of the weights to get a weighted average percentage. That means 19 per cent divided by 6 which is 3.17 per cent. Subtracting that figure from 100 per cent gives a rightdoing index of about 97 per cent. A rightdoing index emphasizes the positive, but the wrongdoing index may be easier to grasp. The important point is that both broadly include civil and job wrongdoing, as well as criminal wrongdoing.

We could then subtract the number of crimes or the CRW figure from the number of crimes solved. The subtraction would yield the number of unsolved crimes. Doing so would in effect be saying that only unsolved crimes are a form of wrongdoing, which would not be true. The victim of a solved crime is just as much a victim as the victim of an unsolved crime, although the victim of a solved crime might feel better later. Solved crimes are better than unsolved crimes for obtaining (1) victim compensation and maybe consolation, (2) deterrence of the individual defendant from committing other crimes, and (3) deterrence of other potential wrongdoers from committing similar crimes. Nevertheless, the distinction between solved and unsolved crimes seems best left to indexes designed to judge the efficiency of the police or the criminal justice system, rather than the desirability of the society.

There is no analogous way of talking about civil wrongs reported versus civil wrongs solved. The way we know about civil wrongs is through the records of civil courts and administrative agencies. We would, however, only want to use records showing injunctions issued and damages awarded, not merely complaints filed. The filing of a civil complaint is roughly the equivalent of the reporting of a crime. Merely filing a civil complaint, though, does not indicate that a civil wrong has been committed. Likewise the firings and dismissals tend to be confirmations of wrongdoing, in contrast to allegations of misbehavior.

Other Fields of Public Policy

Every field of public policy lends itself to thinking along the lines just presented. All policy problems are thus capable of being conceived as having a level of achievement that would traditionally be considered optimum. They also have a level of achievement that can be considered as doing better than the optimum. Table 4.4 summarizes some of the possibilities.

The arrangement is in roughly random order. It is difficult and unnecessary to try to arrange major policy problems in order of importance. One could offer something in favor of every problem being the most important problem. They are all essential to the smooth functioning of a society and to general societal happiness.

Economic problems Inflation and unemployment policy have already been discussed. Consumer policy is closely related to inflation policy, just as labor policy is closely related to unemployment, poverty and discrimination. Consumer policy, though, also illustrates well the distinction between traditional optimums which emphasize removing obvious wrongs, while neglecting the less obvious. The obvious wrongs tend to be sins of commission like consumer fraud, which involves active deception. The less obvious wrongs tend to be sins of omission or failures to take affirmative action, such as

Table 4.4   Doing better than the optimum

Policy problem	An optimum society	A better than optimum society
A *Economic problems*		
Unemployment	Zero unemployment	The optimum plus a higher percentage of adults in the labor force and fully employed
Inflation	Zero inflation	The optimum plus increased benefits for prices paid
Consumer	Zero fraud	The optimum plus giving useful information
B *Political problems*		
World peace	Zero casualties	The optimum plus world cooperation
Free speech	Zero interference	The optimum plus providing a supportive atmosphere for innovative ideas
Government	Zero waste and corruption	The optimum plus creativity, popular participation, equity and due process
C *Social problems*		
Crime	Zero crime	The optimum plus zero civil wrongdoing and job wrongdoing
Poverty and discrimination	Zero poverty and discrimination	The optimum productive job satisfaction
D *Science problems*		
Education	Zero functional illiteracy	The optimum rising to one's maximum, with broadness and inquisitiveness in education
Health	Zero non-aging diseases	The optimum health robustness and greater longevity
Environment	Zero pollution	The optimum plus reclamation and renewal

failing to supply consumers with useful information that could enable them to be more rational consumers.

Political problems   Having world peace as measured by zero war casualties would be wonderful. That is true of the achievement level in the middle column, labeled 'An optimum society' for every policy problem in Table 4.4. If, however, there are two time periods and both have zero war casualties, the better time period would be the one that has more world cooperation. That includes cooperation regarding unemployment, inflation, crime, free speech, poverty, discrimination, health, environment, education, consumer policy and government institutions. The specialized agencies of the United Nations, such as the World Health Organization, the International Labor Organization and the United Nations Economic, Social and Cultural Organization, strive to achieve these cooperation goals.

The United States has a reasonably good record on not interfering with freedom of speech. The main exceptions are where another constitutional right is in conflict, such as (1) due process in criminal proceedings requiring avoidance of prejudicial pre-trial newspaper publicity, (2) equal treatment under the law requiring some restrictions on campaign expenditures, and (3) the right to privacy requiring restrained newspaper reporting on the private lives of non-public figures. One could measure the degree of free speech by looking at the number of people held in jail for activities that are critical of the government or other institutions. Getting a score of zero on such interference, however, may not be enough. A society deserves a higher score on free speech if, in addition to non-interference, it provides a supportive atmosphere for innovative ideas. That can include (1) requiring radio, television and other mass media to be willing to sell time to groups critical of society's institutions, (2) requiring the mass media to give free time to all major candidates if they give free time to any one candidate for office, and (3) making inexpensive cable television time available to fringe groups who would otherwise not be able to buy time to communicate their ideas.

An important policy problem is the problem of improvements needed in the structures and procedures for policy formation and implementation. This can be considered a meta-problem since it cuts across all the specific problems, although so do free speech, education, unemployment, poverty and still other problems. The Reagan administration conducted a strong campaign against waste and corruption in government. It would be fine if all waste, corruption and other forms of inefficiency were eliminated. Again, however, that ignores the sins of omission whereby the government operates wastefully and ineffectively because it is not encouraging creativity with regard to developing new ideas for dealing better with public policy problems. One could also say that, if two societies are equally devoid of waste and corruption, the better society is the one that stimulates more popular participation in government activities, more equity and fairness in the distribution of benefits and costs, and more due process in enabling those who have been wrongly denied benefits or subjected to costs to defend themselves with witnesses, cross-examination and counsel.

Social problems   In the 1960s, there was talk about eliminating the poverty gap by spending $15 billion to bring every poor family up to the line separating being poor from not being poor. That line was roughly estimated at $4000 a year for a family of four as of 1965. The price now is much higher. The important point, though, is that poverty means more than just being below an annual income level. If poor families were brought up to that level, they would be better off. If, however, they still have high unemployment, low education and dead-end jobs, they are not likely to have the happiness that goes with having middle-class employment opportunities. Thus going beyond the optimum of zero poverty means having an economy and education system whereby everyone can have access to a job that provides productive job satisfaction. In a super-ideal world, everyone would enjoy their productive jobs so much that they would continue at their jobs even if they were to become independently wealthy and would no longer need to work for the income.

Closely related to poverty is the policy problem of discrimination. In the 1960s, legislation was passed at the national, state and local levels providing for fair employment, open housing, public accommodation and other rights against discriminatory treatment. If there were 100 per cent compliance, we would then have a form of zero discrimination. The absence of such racial and related discrimination in the housing field, for example, does not sufficiently help blacks if their incomes are so low that they cannot afford decent non-discriminatory housing. What is needed to make non-discrimination more meaningful is the economic ability and education to be able to take advantage of fair opportunities in employment, consumer rights and other activities.

On the matter of goals for educational policy, the United States and most countries would be pleased to achieve 100 per cent functional literacy or zero functional illiteracy. Literacy means being able to read and write at a bare minimum level. Functional literacy means being able to read and write sufficiently to be able to complete job applications and to carry on the reading and writing aspects of a normal job. A goal that is better than that optimum would be to have zero functional illiteracy and have everyone rise to their maximum educational achievement level. One could also seek to achieve higher-quality standards in education. The standards might include the kind of broadness which is tested for in the National Educational Assessment Program. Educational quality could also include stimulating a high level of inquisitiveness, as contrasted to rote learning of facts and doctrines.

Science policy problems   On the matter of health policy, a society might be considered as operating at the optimum if governmental programs have succeeded in stimulating the development and distribution of cures and vaccines for all non-aging or non-degenerative diseases. Merely not having diseases is an excellent societal condition. It is even better, though, to have a society without diseases plus a high degree of robust health. This manifests itself in people being energetic and mentally healthy, which may also involve productive job satisfaction. Also on the matter of health, we may be reaching the point where there will be no need to tolerate even aging diseases like cancer, heart disease and diabetes. The time may come when modern genetics will make it possible to change the genes of people not yet conceived so as to adjust their biological clocks. Doing so will mean growing to adulthood, but not into old age. People would still die as a result of accidents, although a super-optimum society would have a minimum of accidents as a form of civil wrongdoing. Many people now say they would not want to live indefinitely, but that is probably a 'sour grapes' attitude, since living indefinitely is not currently available. People are probably no more likely to commit suicide at age 300 than they would now at age 30.

As for environmental protection, one might consider conditions as being optimal if there were no pollution regarding air, water, solid waste, noise, radiation or other forms of pollution. That would be fine. The absence of air pollution, however, might make urban and rural slums more visible. What is also needed is more reclamation and conservation of land that has been ruined or damaged by strip mining, erosion, overgrazing and other forms of bad land use. What is also needed is more urban and rural renewal of buildings and other man-made structures, but in such a way as to minimize the disruption to the present occupants.

General Means of Achieving the Goals

The purpose of this section is not to discuss in detail how to achieve low unemployment, low inflation or low crime rates, or how to get below zero per cent or above 100 per cent on any specific social indicator. Rather, the purpose is to talk on a relatively high level of generality about ways in which such high goals can be achieved.

An incentives perspective   All policy problems can be viewed as problems that involve encouraging socially desired behavior. A good checklist for generating ideas on the way public policy can encourage socially desired behavior is to think in terms of (1) increasing the benefits of doing right, (2) decreasing the costs of doing right, (3) increasing the costs of doing wrong, (4) decreasing the benefits of doing wrong, and (5) increasing the probability that the benefits and costs will occur.

Each specific problem might involve a five-pronged approach with the above framework. The five prongs or policies are listed and described in Chapter 2, under 'Problems with an Economics Emphasis'.

1   Tax incentives to business firms and labor unions for keeping prices and wages down. Also monetary incentives to employers to hire the unemployed and monetary incentives to the unemployed to accept training and jobs.
2   Decreasing the costs of finding jobs and workers through better information systems.
3   Increasing the costs of violating price–wage guidelines and work incentives by withdrawing benefits and (in rare cases) by imposing fines and other negative penalties.
4   Confiscating the benefits of price–wage violations by special taxes on the gains.
5   More accurate information on prices, wages and unemployment in order to allocate the benefits and costs more effectively.

As a second example of this kind of perspective, we might look at crime reduction. A five-pronged approach would also be especially appropriate here. The five prongs or policies are listed and described in Chapter 2 under 'Problems with a Sociology–Psychology Emphasis'.

1   The main benefit of complying with the law should be that doing so gives one access to opportunities that are denied to law violators. This means that legitimate career opportunities must be provided to those who would otherwise turn to crime.
2   One cost of doing right may be a loss of prestige among youthful gang members who consider criminal behavior an indicator of toughness. There is a need for working to redirect such peer values so that toughness can be displayed in more constructive ways.
3   The costs of doing wrong can include negative incentives of long prison sentences, but it may be more meaningful to emphasize the withdrawal of career opportunities which would otherwise be available.
4   Provisions should be made for facilitating the confiscation of the property gains of criminal wrongdoing, and decreasing the vulnerability of the targets of crime to lessen the benefits obtained.

5   The probability of arrest and conviction can be increased partly through more professionalism among law enforcement personnel.

One could apply this kind of analysis to all 11 policy problems in Table 4.4, as well as other more specific policy problems. One might consider such an approach to be an optimum set of procedures for optimizing societal goals. One can, however, do better than the optimum with regard to procedure as well as substance. Doing better in this context means not having situations occur where people need to be stimulated to do the right thing or deterred from doing the wrong thing. There are two ways to arrange for such situations never to occur, by making them either physically or mentally impossible.

An example of making wrongdoing physically impossible is not allowing cars to be sold that can go faster than a certain speed limit, such as 55 miles per hour, except in short spurts. Then there is much less need to have a system of punishments for doing wrong or a system designed to determine who the wrongdoers are. Another example is prohibiting the manufacture of certain kinds of aerosol cans that do great harm to the ozone in the environment. Still another example would be prohibiting the existence of nuclear breeder reactors to supply energy in view of their likelihood of leading to the production of bomb-grade plutonium.

An example of making certain kinds of wrongdoing mentally impossible, or close to it, relates to murder, robbery, burglary and other street crimes among most middle-class people. When affronted in a store, on a bus or elsewhere, the average person never thinks of the possibility of pulling a gun or going home and getting one in order to kill the person who has insulted him. It is an unthinkable thought. Likewise, when driving late at night and observing a convenience store or a petrol station that is open, with no customers around, the average person never thinks of robbing the place. It is as unthinkable as flapping one's arms to fly to an appointment when one is late. The reason murder and robbery are unthinkable is not that they are physically impossible or because of a fear of the penalties, but because for most people their socialization has been such that those thoughts are not within the realm of one's normal thinking.

A society operating at the optimum or above it on various policy problems can thus be defined as a society which distributes benefits and costs in such a way as to encourage socially desired behavior with regard to unemployment, inflation, crime and other social problems, but which also does as much as possible to make undesirable behavior impossible and/or unthinkable.

A growth perspective   In discussing the general means for achieving the super-optimum goals, one must recognize that those means are going to cost large amounts of money for appropriate subsidies, tax breaks and some forms of regulation. A super-optimum perspective tends to be optimistic in setting goals and in believing that the means can be found for achieving them. This is not, however, a naive optimism, but rather one that is based on what is realistically possible, especially if one proceeds with a positive orientation.

A growth perspective implies that the funding to support the achievement of the super-optimum goals will come mainly from growth of the economy, rather than from a redistribution of wealth. In fact, a redistribution from the rich to the poor may interfere with economic growth by unduly reducing incentives to save, invest and even work as hard or as well as one otherwise would, regardless of whether one is rich or poor. Likewise, a redistribution from the poor to the rich through regressive taxes and investment incentives could also interfere with economic growth and public morale.

A growth perspective tends to be endorsed by both conservatives (who favor supply-side economics and Reaganomics) and by liberals (who favor industrial policy and economic planning). They even tend to agree that the main means to economic growth is tax breaks and subsidies, although they may disagree as to exactly what form they should take. President Reagan originally put considerable faith in the idea of a 30 per cent across-the-board tax cut to stimulate the economy. The economy was not very well stimulated, partly because of conflicting tight-money policies to reduce inflation, but also because tax cuts with no strings attached may tend to wind up disproportionately in real estate, luxury goods and higher executive salaries. Gary Hart had indicated a willingness to provide tax breaks to business much higher than 30 per cent, provided that the tax breaks were only given if the money used was for modernizing industrial practices, giving on-the-job training or other productivity-improving activities.

Some of the costs could be covered by improving the US defense capability at a lower cost by concentrating more on weapons systems which are more effective and efficient. That may mean more emphasis on Trident submarines and low-flying cruise missiles, and less emphasis on easily destroyed B-1 bombers, aircraft carriers and MX missile silos. It may also mean more realistic defensive systems, such as a radar and laser-firing system for destroying enemy nuclear submarines, rather than a 'star wars' system for supposedly destroying all incoming enemy missiles. Making defense expenditures more effective and efficient and thereby reducing their numbers makes more sense, in contrast to increasing questionable defense expenditures by taking from on-the-job programs and subsidies for technological innovation and implementation. It is no coincidence that the United States and the Soviet Union ranked lowest among the industrial nations on productivity growth since about 1980, and highest among the industrial nations on defense expenditures.

On the matter of bipartisan growth, both conservatives and liberals also tend to endorse the idea of more systematic governmental decision making in order to achieve economic growth. Conservatives consider such decision making to be a form of bringing good business practice to government. Liberals consider it to be a form of economic planning. Systematic governmental decision making manifests itself in using contemporary methods of benefit/cost analysis (1) to choose among discrete alternatives, (2) to choose under conditions of risk, (3) to choose where doing too much or too little is undesirable, and (4) to allocate scarce resources in light of given goals and relations.

Relations Between High Societal Goals and Societal Happiness

One might question whether it is socially desirable to set societal goals substantially higher than one is likely to achieve. The same question might be raised concerning individual goals. Some people say that it is better to set one's goals low and achieve them than it is to set one's goals high and not achieve them. They further argue that happiness is not measured by achievement, but by the size of the gap between goals and achievement.

This philosophy of minimizing the gap has many defects. Carried to its logical extreme, we should all have as our goals in life to be no more than winos, bag people and other forms of derelicts: it would be difficult to fail if we set our sights so low. This is sometimes referred to as happiness by 'downward comparisons'. It is epitomized in the idea of telling people who have no shoes that they should be glad to have feet. People who are severely disabled or economically destitute would thus be told how happy or satisfied they should be just to be alive.

Actually, it would be quite difficult for most people to achieve the goal of being a derelict. Most people have been socialized into having much higher goals. It might thus be impossible for them to bring their goals drastically down without becoming very unhappy. Doing so would result in a gap between expectations and achievement. Those who do not like a downward comparisons approach to obtaining happiness sometimes reject it on the grounds that it is morally undesirable. A firmer basis would be to show through logical reasoning and empirical data that downward comparisons do not bring as much happiness as upward achievement.

One might be happy with low goals if everyone else also had low goals. If, however, an individual or a country is highly unusual in having low goals, the individual or country is going to be unhappy unless it can isolate itself from being aware of how well others are doing. This is consistent with the findings reported by Michalos about the importance of deprivation relative to one's reference group. In feudal times, people may have been happy to get through the day without bubonic plague, starvation or being caught in the middle of a feudal war. In modern times, people expect a lot more regarding public policy toward health, poverty and violent death than did people in the dark ages. This is consistent with the idea that one's goals become higher as one's capabilities become greater.

Suppose one person has a goal of earning $100 000 a year, or of producing $100 000 worth of useful goods a year, whichever sounds better. Suppose that person, however, is capable of achieving only $50 000 a year. Suppose further that another person only has in mind to achieve $10 000 a year in the same society and fully succeeds. Not many people would rather be the 'successful' $10 000 a year person than the 'unsuccessful' $50 000 a year person. In other words, people judge others and themselves in terms of what they achieve more than, or as well as, by the gap between goals and achievement. The gap between goals and achievement may also be quite important to happiness, as Michalos indicates.

The person who has a $100 000 goal is more likely to achieve in his or her field at the $50 000 level than a person who has only a $50 000 level. There seems to be a natural tendency not to fully achieve goals. This is so because goals are like incentives that stimulate further effort, especially when they are just out of reach, like the carrot that hangs in front of the donkey to make the donkey move forward. This point is in effect saying that high goals are desirable because they stimulate greater productivity and creativity and thereby benefit society, even if individuals with high goals are not happy. Thus high societal goals can be justified pragmatically.

Contrary to the position which recommends setting one's goals low or 'realistically' to achieve happiness, there are numerous examples of people who are saddened by having achieved their goals and having lost the excitement of the pursuit. One does not have to be Alexander the Great to want new things to conquer. Business people and others sometimes say that getting an uncontrollable flood of mail is bad, but much worse is getting no mail at all. In other words, people like to have something in their boxes to be done. They do not like having nothing to do as a result of having achieved their goals. What this point is saying in effect is that there is a hill-shaped relation between happiness as an effect and the goals–achievement gap as a cause. That means happiness is low if the gap is either very small or very large. The gap theory people tend to overemphasize the right side of the hill-shaped curve, where happiness goes down as the gap becomes bigger, rather than the left side of the hill-shaped curve, where happiness goes down as the gap becomes smaller. The optimum gap is somewhere in the middle.

In management by objectives, it is considered much better to have 50 per cent achievement on a big objective than 100 per cent achievement on a small objective. For example, on a 0 to 100 scale, if a big objective is scored

90, then 50 per cent achievement would be worth 45 points. A specific small objective might be scored five, and 100 per cent success would receive the full five points. Thus, in this example, 50 per cent success on a 90-point objective would be nine times as worthy as 100 per cent success on a five-point objective. One might object to this on the grounds that saying a 45-point achievement is better or more worthy than a five-point achievement is not the same as saying that it produces more happiness. One might further argue that there is an implied assumption that achievement is good or worthy for society regardless of the personal happiness of the achiever. That assumption may be true, but what is really being argued is that achievement brings both personal happiness and societal happiness, and that achievement is encouraged by having high but realistically attainable goals.

Applying the same kind of reasoning to societal goals as is expressed in the above points, one can say that no goals are too high so long as they are physically possible. Even what is physically possible may be subject to change. It is thus socially desirable for a society to be an optimizing society, or one that is seeking to achieve the optimum or the super-optimum on various social indicators. That is true with regard to public policies concerning unemployment, inflation, crime, world peace, free speech, poverty, discrimination, health, environment, education, consumers and government structures/procedures. It is hoped that this chapter will stimulate further ideas along the lines of doing better than the optimum, with regard both to what it means and how to do it.

Notes

On raising goals above what is considered the best, see Etzioni (1988), Raskin (1986), Clark (1989) and Nagel (1989). On goal setting and measurement in policy analysis, see Alberts (1970), Dorfman (1964), Cook (1986) and Nagel (1984). On national social indicators, see MacRae (1986), Carley (1981) and Gilmartin *et al.* (1979).

On measuring and reducing unemployment, see Bailey (1950), Duggan (1985), Ginzberg (1963) and Baumer and Van Horn (1985). An even more ambitious notion of being fully employed might take into consideration job satisfaction. This would mean that, if two societies are fully employed in the full sense of the summary index, the society in which 80 per cent of the people report being pleased with their jobs is a better employed society than a second society with a lower than 80 per cent job satisfaction rate. One could thus discount or multiply the employment figure by the job satisfaction percentage in each society. An ideal society might be defined partly as one in which the people so enjoy their work that they would continue doing it even if they were to become independently wealthy as a result of receiving a large inheritance or winning a lottery.

On measuring and reducing inflation, see Prentice (1981), Eckstein (1983), Slawson (1981) and Peretz (1983).

On measuring and reducing crime, see Walker (1985), Sheley (1985) and the President's Commission on Law Enforcement (1967).

On an incentive growth perspective, see Magaziner and Reich (1982), Etzioni (1983), Roberts (1984) and Canto *et al.* (1983).

5   Decreasing the Causes of the Conflict

Capital Punishment

A continuing issue in state government is the nature of the penalty for murder (see Table 5.1).

Points Favoring Capital Punishment

1   It probably deters some murder, but not much, given the other relevant factors such as the monetary or emotional benefits perceived at the time of committing a murder and the perception of the low probability of being executed.
2   It sets a good example with regard to society's concern for deterring murder.
3   It represents total incapacitation of the defendant in the sense of not being able to recommit one's crime.
4   Rehabilitation does not seem to be very effective in the criminal justice system, although maybe more so with one-time murderers than with chronic robbers, burglars, sex offenders and so on.
5   It saves the expense of incarceration.
6   Public opinion is about evenly divided and fluctuates, with the majority in favour in the United States in the 1980s and 1990s.
7   It may receive some support from conservative interests who welcome an emphasis on violent crimes to distract attention from business crimes.
8   At the present time it is considered constitutional, provided that capital punishment laws are precisely written but allow for flexibility to consider specific circumstances.

Points Disfavoring Capital Punishment

1   It may encourage some murder by cheapening the value of life.
2   It tends to be disproportionately inflicted upon minorities and the poor.
3   It leads to due process violations with regard to convicting the innocent since there generally are no eye witnesses, or at least victim witnesses in murder cases.
4   It wastes society's resources in obtaining executions.
5   Public opinion is about evenly divided and fluctuates, with the majority opposed to capital punishment in the 1960s and early 1970s.
6   It distracts attraction from more widespread civil liberties violations such as excessive use of pre-trial detention.
7   Its constitutionality is questionable under the cruel and unusual punishment laws: it is cruel if it does not substantially deter; it is unusual if it is a matter of chance whether it is to be imposed, and it is a rare phenomenon.

Murder Reduction via SOS

Given the opposing viewpoints, that may appear irreconcilable, a combination of the following would be acceptable to both views:

1   gun control,
2   drug medicalization (treating addicts as people who are sick),
3   reducing violence socialization by fostering peaceful resolution of disputes during childhood,
4   resolving the drug problem by taking away the profit and attendant violence through provision of free, medically prescribed drugs to addicts under a phase-out plan.

Chinese Population Control

Ideology and Technocracy

In the 1970s, the People's Republic of China was seeking to resolve public policy problems largely by consulting the *ideological* writings of Karl Marx, Mao Zedong and their interpreters. In the 1980s, government agencies in China were seeking to become more professional by way of the introduction of personnel management, financial administration and other bureaucratic ideas from the West, some of which are actually a throwback to Confucian bureaucracy.

Table 5.1 Evaluating the policy of capital punishment

Criteria / Alternatives	C Goal Less crime & murder	L Goal Separate innocent & reduce executions	N Goal Lower tax costs	L Goal Less discrim. against blacks & poor	C Goal Anti-murder symbol	N Total (neutral weights)	L Total (liberal weights)	C Total (conservative weights)
C Alternative CP for all murders	3.1	1	2.5	2	5	27.2	22.1	32.3*
L Alternative No CP	2.9	4	3.5	3.5	2	31.8	34.4*	29.2
N Alternative CP for special murders; special procedures	3	4	3	3	3	32	33	31
SOS Alternative Reduce murder by gun control, drug medicalization, socialization	5	4.5	2	4	4	39	38.5**	39.5**

Notes:
1 'Anti-murder symbol' refers to the idea that even capital punishment does not reduce murder: it puts society on record as being strongly opposed to murder. Those who are opposed to capital punishment sarcastically say that, by providing for executions, society is indicating that it is so opposed to murder that it is willing even to murder to show its opposition.
2 The neutral alternative refers to allowing for capital punishment but only for special types of murder such as mass murder, murdering of police officers, murder while one is under life imprisonment, or murder of children. The neutral alternative also refers to special procedures such as requiring jury approval for the execution, or requiring separate juries to decide on the guilt question and the capital punishment question if the defendant is found guilty.

Thus ideology became offset by *technocracy*. What we were seeing may fit the classic Hegelian and Marxist dialectic of thesis, antithesis and synthesis. Ideology represented the prevailing thesis in the 1970s, whereby population control might be analyzed by reading Marx and Mao. Technocracy represented the antithesis in the 1980s, whereby population control might be analyzed by reading biological literature.

The 1990s represented a super-optimum synthesis of the best, not the worst, of both possible worlds, drawing upon the idea of having *goal-oriented values* from the ideological thesis, as contrasted to rejecting values as being unscientific or not objective. Values and goals may be quite objective in the sense of being provable means to higher goals, or in the sense of proving that certain alternatives are more capable of achieving the goals than others.

The 1990s also drew upon the idea of *empirical proof* based on observable consequences, rather than the ideological labels of socialism or capitalism. It is empirical proof that also makes sense in terms of deductive consistency with what else is known about the world, rather than mindless technical 'number-crunching' with no thought about how the results might fit common sense. Being technical does not necessarily mean being effective in getting the job done efficiently and equitably, which is what should really count in governmental decision making.

The kind of *synthesis* here is a synthesis of goals to be achieved (the ideological element) and systematic methods for determining which alternative or alternatives most achieve those goals (the technical element). The true dialectic is dynamic not only in the sense that a thesis leads to an antithesis which leads to a higher level synthesis. It is also dynamic in the sense that a synthesis does not stagnate, but becomes a subsequent thesis to be resynthesized by a new antithesis into a still higher level of analysis.

There may be policy evaluation methods that are even more effective, efficient and equitable. These are the methods that are hinted at in various places in this section where *super-optimum solutions* are explicitly or implicitly mentioned.

Alternatives, Goals and Relations as Inputs

Table 5.2 can be used to illustrate what is meant by super-optimizing policy analysis where all major viewpoints can come out ahead of their best initial expectations. The table addresses excess population, rather than the population problem. This is so because most of China's so-called 'population problem' does not relate to a surplus of people, but rather to a shortage of production. Some of the population problem (at least in the short run) may, however, relate to a strain on China's current resources that can be lessened by reducing the number of consumers.

Table 5.2 Super-optimizing analysis applied to the China excess population problem

Criteria / Alternatives	C Goal Small families	L Goal Reproductive freedom	N Total (neutral weights)	L Total (liberal weights)	C Total (conservative weights)
C Alternative Strict one-child policy	4	2	12	10	14*
L Alternative Flexible on family size	2	4	12	14*	10
N Alternative One child, with exceptions allowed	3	3	12	12	12
SOS Alternative Reduce causes of excess children	5	5	20	20**	20**

Notes:
1. Relevant causes of excess children in the Chinese population context include:
    (a) the need for adult children to care for their elderly parents, which could be better handled through social security and/or jobs for the elderly;
    (b) the need for extra children to allow for child mortality, which could be better handled through better child health care;
    (c) the need for male children in view of their greater value, which could be better handled through providing more opportunities for females;
    (d) the fact that rural parents have not traditionally been so concerned about the cost of sending their children to college because they were not as likely to go to college. That cause can be partly overcome through a more vigorous program of recruiting rural children to college with scholarships, literature and high school pep talks.
2. It is not a super-optimum solution to provide monetary rewards and penalties in this context because:
    (a) the monetary rewards for having fewer children enable a family to then have more children;
    (b) the monetary punishments for having more children stimulate a family to have still more children to provide offsetting income;
    (c) the monetary rewards and punishments are made meaningless by the simultaneous policies which are increasing prosperity in rural China.

The *alternatives* are listed in the rows. The conservative alternatives (in the sense of being the most regulatory) is to try to enforce a strict one-child policy. The liberal alternative (in the sense of allowing the most freedom) is to be completely flexible on family size. This is also possibly most in conformity with Marxist ideology, which tends to view population control as a capitalistic idea designed either to increase the population of the poor (in order to have a reserve army of unemployed people) or to decrease the population of the poor (out of fear that the poor will overwhelm the middle class). These two Marxist views tend to nullify each other, possibly leading one to the conclusion that there is no Marxist view on population policy. The compromise position between conservative regulation and liberal freedom is to have a one-child policy, but with various exceptions such as allowing a second child if the first is a daughter, or allowing a second child among rural but not urban people.

One of the key *goals* is small families, given the tremendous burden on the Chinese economy and government service of a billion people reproducing at a rate greater than one child per family. Even one child per family would mean substantial short-run population growth. This would occur because people are living longer in China. We may simplify the arithmetic by saying that, if the 500 million males marry the 500 million females and have one child apiece within the next few years, the population will go from a billion to 1.5 billion. This increase of half a billion is more people than every country of the world currently has, with the exception of China and India. The rich may not get richer, but the highly populated get even more highly populated. The second key goal is reproductive freedom. Even the conservatives recognize that interfering with reproductive freedom makes for a lot of antagonism toward the government. Thus both goals are endorsed by both conservatives and liberals in China, but Chinese conservatives place relatively more emphasis on small families, and Chinese liberals place relatively more emphasis on reproductive freedom.

The *relations* between the alternatives and the goals are shown on a 1–5 scale, where 5 means highly conducive to the goal, 4 means mildly conducive, 3 means neither conducive nor adverse, 2 means mildly adverse, and 1 means highly adverse to the goal. We have here a classic tradeoff. A strict one-child policy is good on small families, but bad on reproductive freedom. Flexibility on family size is good on reproductive freedom, but bad on small families. The compromise alternative is middling on both, like compromises in general. This compromise is better than the worst on both small families and reproductive freedom. It is clearly not better than the best expectations on either goal.

Finding a Super-optimum Package of Policies

In many public policy problems, the super-optimum solution involves well-placed subsidies and tax breaks. Well-placed *tax breaks* are meaningless in a communist society. Under communism, people do not do much direct paying of taxes (especially income taxes) the way they do in western societies.

(Instead the government is supported by paying people less than they are worth in their government jobs.) The difference is a hidden tax. Thus, if a worker produces in an hour goods worth $10, but is only paid $4, the government has in effect taxed the worker $6 an hour even though the worker pays no income tax. Ironically, this fits well with the Marxist idea of surplus-value exploitation of labor. It is an easy form of tax to collect, but it does not allow for the use of tax breaks as incentives.

China has tried subsidizing small families by giving *monetary rewards* to those who have small families, and *monetary punishments* to those who do not have them. The effect has been almost the opposite of the government's intent. The subsidies to small families have in many instances increased their income, so they can now afford to have more children. Having a monetary punishment or reduced salary may even motivate parents to have an additional child to help bring in more income to offset the reduced salary. Also moving simultaneously toward a more prosperous free market (especially in farm products) has enabled many rural people now to have more children and not be bothered by the withdrawal of subsidies or other monetary punishments.

A kind of super-optimum solution may make a lot more sense for dealing with the Chinese population problem. It could provide small families and reproductive freedom simultaneously. Doing so requires looking to the causes of having additional children and then trying to remove or lessen those causes. One cause is a need to have children who will support parents in their old age. Adopting a more effective social security system helps eliminate or lessen that cause.

Another cause is having additional children as back-up because the death rate is so high among rural Chinese children prior to age 5. Various forms of pediatric public health care, such as giving injections and using effective remedies to prevent life-jeopardizing infant diarrhea and dehydration, can make a big difference.

A third cause is the widespread feeling that female children are worthless in terms of bringing honor to the family. One therefore keeps trying until at least one son is born. That cause can be substantially lessened by the new moves in China toward much greater opportunities for females to become lawyers and doctors and to enter other prestigious occupations. In China, women's liberation has facilitated birth control, whereas in the United States birth control has done more to facilitate women's liberation.

Trying to Commute to and from Manila

The Manila commuting problem is a good example of how people in developed countries may have false stereotypes of policy problems in developing countries being simpler and less urbanized than policy problems in more developing countries. There may be no country in the world that has a worse commuter problem than the Philippines. Commuting is relatively simple in New York, London, Paris, Berlin, Moscow, Tokyo and elsewhere. It is more complicated in the Philippines for a number of reasons.

First, the Philippines has only one really big metropolitan city to which people are flocking, whereas countries like the United States have many such cities: New York, Chicago, Los Angeles and so on.

Second, metropolitan Manila may be bigger in population and area than most other big cities where there are many complaints about the difficulty of commuting. It consists of about five adjacent cities, including Quezon City which is a big city itself.

Third, greatly complicating the commuting problem in Manila is the fact that it is on an island peninsula where the Pacific Ocean is just waiting to flood any attempt to build a subway system. A further complicating matter is the lack of money for an expanded elevated or surface train system.

Fourth, it has been proposed that there should be more vehicles that carry numbers of people to and from work to ease the commuting problem. Washington, DC, for example, makes a big thing of providing special lanes for cars and buses that have more than one passenger, especially as part of a pooling arrangement. The Manila area probably has more small buses per capita than any city in the world. A mass transit system has been developed based on the extended jeep, carrying a dozen or more passengers crowded together.

Fifth, having more jeepneys, small buses and big buses would just further clog the highways and streets into and out of Manila. They would thus worsen the problem and make commuting even more time-consuming.

Sixth, having more bicycles will not ease the Manila commuter problem the way it helps in Beijing. Poor people and middle-class people have too far to travel to make the journey on a bicycle, and they can also ride the jeepney buses for only one peso, which is about a twentieth of an American dollar. Thus it is not cost-effective to buy and ride a bicycle to work. Also, the more influential car drivers would not tolerate giving up an auto lane on each side of the streets to be used by bicycles.

Finally, this commuting phenomenon is not peculiar to the Philippines as a developing country. Many developing countries have a capital city or central city to which rural people are flocking in the search for jobs. The people build whatever shanties they can. The city becomes highly overcrowded, not just relative to the jobs available, but in an absolute sense, given the limited space and the limited technological capabilities of moving people around in that limited space. Thus this problem is more likely to occur in developing countries than in industrial countries, which may have many industrial cities to attract the surplus rural population.

Alternatives

Table 5.3 shows the Manila commuter problem in the context of a decision analysis table or a super-optimizing framework. The conservative alternative (as is often the case) is to leave things as they are, or leave it to the marketplace to change things. Some conservatives like to talk about people buying cities the way they buy products. In that sense, people supposedly vote with their feet by going to Manila. The invisible hand of Adam Smith may eventually cause them to change their votes and go back to the countryside. This runs contrary to the idea that once you have tasted the big city, it is hard to go back to the farm, especially if, as a landless peasant, you have no farm to go back to. Maybe, in the extremely long run, things get so bad in overcrowded cities that medieval diseases return periodically to decimate the population. That, fortunately or unfortunately, is not so likely, given modern public health care.

The liberal solution tends to involve spending big money, but often with no strings attached and with an unduly narrow focus on the immediate problem, rather than the bigger picture. Liberals also tend to project their middle-class New York or Chicago values on to poor people, rural people

Table 5.3 Manila's commuter problem

Criteria Alternatives	L Goal Less time commuting	C Goal Fewer taxes	N Total (neutral weights)	L Total (liberal weights)	C Total (conservative weights)
C Alternative As is	1	4	10	7	13*
L Alternative Mass transit	4	2	12	14*	10
N Alternative Hodge/podge with more jeepneys and buses	2	2.5	9	8.5	9.5
SOS Alternative Suburbs, regional cities, overseas & other employment centers	4.5	4.5	18	18**	18**

and people in developing countries. In this context, it means proposing a New York or Chicago subway or elevated line, or Washington, DC car pooling – alternatives which were mentioned above as not so applicable to Manila, and maybe not so applicable to most developing countries, due to lack of capital. The available capital could probably be better spent on upgrading human skills and machinery for producing goods. It should also be noted that at least some developing countries may be in a good position to act fast, in time to prevent a good deal of urban congestion, rather than try to cure it or have a commuting mess afterwards.

The neutral alternative, as in many situations, tends to involve splitting the difference between conservative expenditures or recommendations and those of the liberals. If the conservatives say spend nothing on mass transit (since it will overburden the taxpayer and may encourage people to move to Manila), and if the liberals say spend many millions, the neutral compromisers try to find a figure in between. Doing so may result in half a train system and may be an example of half a loaf being worse than none. A halfway system could be expensive without adequate incremental benefits. Neutrals also tend to emphasize trying a lot of things simultaneously. In this context, that would mean a few more jeepneys, small buses, big buses, bicycles and subsidized taxis. The result would probably be more congestion and more commuting time wasted, as mentioned above. Building wider highways for the additional vehicles is also unlikely to help. Many of the commuting roads in Manila are already much wider than Chicago's Outer Drive. The ultimate would be to clear out all the buildings, and have nothing but commuting roads.

Goals

As for goals, a key goal is to reduce the tremendous amount of time wasted getting to and from work. Only the richest of Filipinos can afford to live near the central city, or the poorest who set up illegal shanties in whatever alley might be available. The people who live in those shanties frequently do not have jobs to commute to, and neither do the people who live in the rich villas. The working people tend to live substantial distances away, and they may spend as much as two exhausting hours getting into central Manila and then getting out. These hours are literally 'exhausting' because the exhaust fumes are unbelievable owing to the stop-and-go operation of many diesel-fuelled vehicles and propane buses. Many of the drivers and street vendors wear handkerchiefs over their faces.

Delays are also caused by numerous trucks going to and from factories that are in the central city, along with office buildings; a great number of beggars and street vendors interfere with traffic at intersections; a further factor is the large military barracks in the central city that could be used for residential housing. Camp Aguinaldo, which is one of the leading army camps in the Philippines, is in downtown Manila. During the abortive coup against President Aquino, Americans read about soldiers from Camp Aguinaldo invading the Makati business district. Americans might think that the soldiers came as paratroopers. In reality the soldiers simply walked from their barracks down the block into the high-rise buildings. The hot climate further adds to the problem by making the commuting less bearable and causing a lot of overheated cars to stall and block traffic.

The second key goal is to keep the tax burden down. On the matter of tax burden, though, one has to distinguish between the short-run burden and the long-run burden. The long run (if it is not too far away) is more important since it lasts longer. In this context, it may be necessary to spend a lot of money to do something about the problem in order to save a lot of money later from wasted time. More importantly when people in the Manila area are enabled to be more productive and healthy, the gross national product may benefit substantially, thereby increasing the tax base. If that happens then the percentage tax rate can be lowered subsequently and still bring in more money for other projects.

Saving commuting time for workers tends to be a relatively liberal goal, and saving tax money for taxpayers tends to be a relatively conservative goal. As with other SOS analyses, however, both liberals and conservatives endorse time saving and tax saving. It is just a matter of the relative emphasis of liberals compared to conservatives.

Scoring and Totals

In scoring the alternatives, leaving things as they are is terrible for saving commuting time, but it does have a positive relation with short-run tax saving. Spending a lot of money on a train system that would run through developed areas of Manila or on a median strip of widened highways could save commuting time, but it does have a negative relation with short-run tax saving. The neutral compromise is not much help on saving time, although it is not as bad as doing nothing. Likewise, it does have a short-run incremental tax burden, although not a bad as liberal mass-transit expenditures.

Looking at the totals, the conservative alternative comes in first using the conservative weights, with the liberal alternative in third place. Likewise, the liberal alternative comes in first using the liberal weights, with the conservative alternative in third place. The neutral alternative is everybody's second. It is possibly even the second or third choice of the neutrals since the hodgepodge neutral alternative does poorly on both goals, although it is not the worst on both goals. In arriving at a super-optimum solution, the important thing is to find an alternative that exceeds both the liberal and conservative initial best expectations, not necessarily the neutrals'.

The Super-optimum Solution

The super-optimum solution in this context has at least three parts. The first is to build up employment opportunities in the suburbs or outlying parts of Manila. The commuting is highly unbalanced. It is nearly all inward in the morning, starting at about 5 o'clock and it is nearly all outward in the evening, starting at about 3 o'clock. This is unlike the case of American cities, where there is increasing use of suburbs as places for employment opportunities, not just bedrooms. Farmland northwest of Chicago in places like Schaumberg Township now has skyscraper office buildings and low-pollution factories.

As a concrete example, it is amazing that the University of Philippines, which is located in Quezon City, outside Manila, does not have a high-tech area around it. That would take advantage of the fact that the university is the leading university in the Philippines and possibly the leading university in Southeast Asia. Most American universities that have engineering schools attract high-tech employment in their areas. The Philippine government could provide subsidies to create a high-tech employment area around the university. This would make a dent in the commuting problem and set a useful precedent for other subsidized suburban employment. Also important is that it would help subsidize technological innovation and diffusion, which could have broader useful effects on the Philippine economy than would just easing the Manila commuter problem.

The second part of a possible super-optimum solution is subsidizing the development of regional cities throughout the Philippines. Certain cities in the southern provinces of Mindinao and the middle provinces between Manila and Mindinao could be made more attractive to rural people from those provinces as places to migrate to, rather than go to Manila. They could even be made attractive enough possibly to get some people to move from Manila back to those regional cities in their home provinces. This is a kind of subsidization that has been done in the Soviet Union to encourage people to move west. It was also done by the United States to encourage people to move west, although more as a matter of providing people with land for farming in the west, than of providing urban employment opportunities. However, in the 1930s, the Rural Rehabilitation Administration did provide low-interest loans to enable rural people from Oklahoma, Arkansas and elsewhere in the southwest to go to Los Angeles and establish petrol stations and other small businesses or become car mechanics, rather than go to

Chicago, Detroit, Cleveland and New York, as was the case with poor southern blacks and whites.

The third part of the solution might be for the Philippine government to work more actively with a number of other governments that have labor shortages who could hire some of the excess labor in the Manila area and other parts of the Philippines. This might apply to Hong Kong, Singapore, Taiwan, Malaysia, Korea and even Japan. It might be worthwhile for the Philippine government to do more to upgrade labor skills to make this kind of guestworker program more attractive. Those guestworkers also send back lots of money, so boosting the Philippine economy, which may be even more important than relieving the Manila commuter problem. The Philippine government has developed labor-exporting relations with Arab countries on the Persian Gulf. As a result, Philippines Airlines may stop at more Persian Gulf cities than almost any other non-Arab airline. This is another illustration of the need to elevate some of the policy problems of individual countries to a more international or global level.

With this kind of three-part super-optimum solution, commuting time could be substantially reduced, more so than by doing nothing, having a mildly effective train system, or a hodgepodge of miscellaneous vehicles rivaling the evacuation of Dunkirk every morning and evening in Manila. Likewise, this kind of super-optimum solution could not only save taxes in the long run by increasing GNP and the tax base, but it could also help resolve lots of other policy problems besides the Manila commuter problem. An increased GNP through suburban employment, regional cities and overseas employment can do wonders in reducing the problems of crime, poverty and discrimination, and lack of money for education, health care, housing and other public policy expenditures. The SOS does show up in Table 5.3 as being a substantial winner on the liberal, conservative and neutral totals. This includes doing better than the previous liberal and conservative alternatives or expectations even with liberal and conservative weights.

Notes

The literature on removing or decreasing the source of liberal–conservative conflicts includes the literature on dealing with dilemmas. See 'The Dilemma', Chapter 13 in Ruby (1950). The super-optimum solution is related to the idea of escaping from the horns of the dilemma by showing that there are other alternatives, such as an SOS alternative. Traditional reasoning is more associated with taking the dilemma by the horns, whereby one shows that one horn or side is true and the other is false, or one is better than the other, analogous to a win–lose solution. For further details on the example of eliminating or reducing the capital punishment controversy by reducing the murder rate, see Winslow (1977), Walker (1989) and Levine *et al.* (1980). The book by Walker has a kind of super-optimum perspective, showing defects in the conservative and liberal approaches to crime reduction and the need for a new synthesis of what each has to offer of a meaningful nature.

For further details on public policy analysis of China's population problems, see Banister (1987) and Robinson (1991).

6   Redefining the Problem

Trial by Jury

Quite often a highly emotional controversy between liberals and conservatives may be capable of being resolved beyond the best expectations of each side through the approach of redefining the problem. They may be arguing over how to deal with a problem that is really relatively unimportant in terms of achieving their goals, as contrasted to a more important problem on which they might be likely to achieve mutually satisfying agreement. This involves looking beyond a relatively superficial argument to the higher-level goals which are endorsed by both liberals and conservatives, although possibly not to the same relative degree. (See Table 6.1.)

Traditional Alternatives and Goals

A concrete example is the controversy over the size of juries in criminal cases. Liberals argue in favor of preserving the traditional 12-person jury, as contrasted to allowing juries as small as only six people. Liberals view the larger jury as being important for protecting the innocent, since it is more difficult for a prosecutor to convince 12 jurors unanimously of the defendant's guilt than it is to convince six jurors. Liberals may also argue that 12-person juries allow for more public participation, but that seems less important than decreasing convictions, although public participation may sound more acceptable.

Conservatives argue in favor of allowing six-person juries. They view smaller juries as being important for convicting the guilty since it is easier for a prosecutor to convince six jurors unanimously of the defendant's guilt than it is to convince 12 jurors. Conservatives may also argue that six-person juries reduce delay, but that seems less important than increasing convictions, although delay reduction may sound more acceptable.

Liberals in this context are thus especially sensitive as regards avoiding errors of convicting the innocent, although they also want to avoid errors of not convicting the guilty. Conservatives are especially sensitive as regards

Table 6.1   Six-person versus 12-person juries

Alternatives \ Criteria	C Goal Convict the guilty	L Goal Avoid convicting the innocent	N Total (neutral weights)	L Total (liberals weights)	C Total (conservatives weights)
C Alternatives Six-person juries	4	2	12	10	14*
L Alternative 12-person juries	2	4	12	14*	10
N Alternative Between 6 & 12 or unanimity	3	3	12	12	12
S Alternative Videotaping or notetaking	5	5	20	20**	20**

avoiding errors of not convicting the guilty, although they also want to avoid errors of convicting the innocent. So long as the problem is defined in terms of optimum jury size, there is an inherent tradeoff between those two goals. Liberals see any reduction in jury size as sacrificing protection of the innocent, in favor of convicting the guilty. Conservatives see a retention of the 12-person jury as sacrificing the need to convict the guilty, in favor of an undue sensitivity as regards protecting the innocent, whom they tend to see as not being a significant percentage of the defendants who are tried.

An SOS Solution

What may be needed in this policy controversy is to redefine the problem away from the question, 'How many people should be present on a jury in criminal cases?'. A more appropriate definition of the problem in light of what the liberals and conservatives are actually arguing over is the question, 'How can we simultaneously increase the probability of convicting guilty defendants and increase the probability of acquitting innocent defendants?'. There is no inherent tradeoff between these two goals. In fact, there may be no inherent tradeoff between any two goals. By so restating the problem, one's attention is directed toward thinking about what procedural changes could achieve increases on both goals simultaneously, rather than thinking about what is the ideal compromise, middling position or equilibrium between 12-person and six-person juries.

There are some procedural changes that could simultaneously increase goal achievement on both the liberal and conservative goals. They all involve increasing the general accuracy of juries and decreasing the general inaccuracy. One such procedural change would be allowing jurors to take notes. In most US states, they are prohibited from doing so. It is unclear why this prohibition began. One plausible explanation is that, when the jury system was started in about the 1500s in England, few people could read or write. It may have been felt that, if those few jurors who could take notes were allowed to do so, they would dominate jury decision making. A 12-person jury could then in effect become a jury of one or two people who have been making a written record of what those jurors perceived as having occurred. As of the 1990s, virtually all jurors are capable of taking notes and should be allowed to do so. That would improve their accuracy in both convicting the guilty and acquitting the innocent.

Along related lines, an especially useful innovation would be to provide for automatic videotaping of jury trials and bench trials. This is a possible double super-optimum solution. It is super-optimum in the sense that it increases the accuracy of convicting the guilty and acquitting the innocent simultaneously. Quite often in jury deliberations, there is disagreement among the jurors as to what was said by a certain witness, lawyer or the judge. One juror who is especially domineering may say that the witness said the defendant was seen at the scene of the crime at 8am. Other jurors may think it was 8pm. The disagreement can be quickly and accurately resolved with a videotape made by a camcorder that can be played back on any television set with a video playback capability. Otherwise the winning perception is the one held by whichever jurors may have the most aggressive personalities. This could result in either the error of acquitting a guilty person or the error of convicting an innocent person.

The second sense in which the camcorder videotaping is super-optimum is that it decreases costs and increases benefits simultaneously. It is substantially less expensive to videotape a jury trial than it is to pay a stenotypist to try to record verbatim what was said at the trial. The camcorder can be operated by someone who can easily be taught what little is involved. The cost of each tape is nominal and the tape can be reused. The benefits are substantially increased because (1) one gets instant replay, as contrasted to transcribing stenotyping possibly months later, (2) one gets accurate replay, as contrasted to the extensively ad-libbed record that is made by court reporters, (3) one can see facial expressions, (4) one can hear voice connotations, and (5) one can hear two or more people talking at the same time, which often leads to gibberish or missing information in stenotyping notes.

In addition to note taking and videotaping, there are a number of other ways of increasing general jury accuracy. They include allowing jurors to have access to a written copy of the judge's instructions. This helps improve the interpretation of the law by juries, just as note taking and videotaping improve their understanding of the facts. Most states do not provide for written judicial instructions. This also goes back to medieval times, when relatively few people could read. It was felt that those few who could read the judge's instructions would dominate jury decision making, just as those few who could write notes would dominate. The present-day reason for the inertia as regards allowing juries to have written instructions may relate to the fact that the instructions tend to favor safeguards for the innocent. Legal decision makers may be reluctant to do anything that will further increase acquittals and decrease convictions.

Other approaches to improving general juror accuracy that have been adopted in only a minority of states, if any, include the following.

1   Allowing jurors to submit questions to the judge, the lawyers or even the witnesses indirectly through the lawyers. This could clarify factual and legal ambiguities that lead to wrong decisions.
2   Providing a training course for each juror that would last a full day before they were eligible to decide cases. The course could clarify what is involved in conducting a trial, jury deliberation, judicial instructions, various kinds of evidence and other matters. The course could allow jurors to ask questions. It could also have a test at the end to determine whether each juror has a minimum level of understanding of what is involved.
3   The ability to read and write or other educational qualifications could improve the general accuracy of jurors. Such requirements, though, can be subject to abuse, as with southern literacy tests for voting. Such tests enable semi-literate white registrars to disqualify college-educated black applicants on the grounds that they did not like their interpretation of a constitutional clause. Even if the tests are objective, they could bias the composition of juries in favor of middle-class attitudes which favor the prosecution in criminal cases and the defendant insurance companies, for example, in civil cases. Any measure designed to improve accuracy should not unthinkingly change the direction or bias of jury outcomes.
4   Jury accuracy can be improved by having counsel on both sides. American governments at virtually all levels now provide free counsel to indigent defendants in criminal cases, but we do not adequately guarantee counsel to indigent litigants in civil cases where there is no contingency fee involved. The federal Legal Services Corporation in the United States is not sufficiently funded to guarantee counsel to indigent civil litigants, although the result is that they do not litigate or go to trial, rather than go to trial without a lawyer.

Factors Interfering with Adoption

One might ask why such procedures as taking notes and using videotaping have not been adopted already. The key answer with regard to videotaping is that it is a relatively new technology, although audiotaping has been around for some time. The potential for taking meaningful jury notes has been around for at least a hundred years. An important answer may be the overemphasis on tradeoff controversies in discussing jury decision making, such as jury size, the percentage needed to convict, the admissibility of various kinds of evidence, and other controversies in which going one way protects the innocent but facilitates convicting the guilty, and going the other way does the opposite.

Asking why note taking has not been adopted, or why it may be a long time before videotaping is adopted, raises a separate set of SOS problems that have to do with getting SOS solutions adopted after they have been generated. A key problem is simply inertia, especially in the legal system, where there is possibly an overemphasis on preserving the past regardless of the present consequences. There is no system of evaluation that places so much emphasis on prior precedent, rather than present and future benefits and costs.

In any SOS adoption, there may also be problems of vested interests, property and jobs. Changing procedural rules may often change substantive results contrary to powerful interest groups, such as where the procedural change makes it harder or easier for one side to win. For example, having a trial for liability separate from the trial for damages is likely to lead to a much higher percentage of victories for the defendant. The jury under such split trials cannot adjust the damages to take the plaintiff's contributory negligence into consideration. That kind of change in substantive results does not seem to be a factor in allowing note taking or videotaping. Vested property can complicate the adoption of SOS solutions with regard to replacing public housing with rent supplements or moving unemployed coal miners to better jobs. That kind of consideration does not seem to be present here. Vested jobs can be a problem in mutually beneficial international tariff reductions. Videotaping would greatly reduce the need for court reporters, but they may not be a strong enough interest group to block videotaping, and they probably would not object to jurors taking notes.

The Importance of Problem Definition and SOS Awareness

Looking over the points that relate to the adoption of either note taking or videotaping as a super-optimum solution to the problem of increasing both the conviction of the guilty and the acquitting of the innocent, one can draw at least two conclusions. First is that redefining the problem to emphasize simultaneous goal achievement can greatly facilitate the generating of super-optimum solutions. Perhaps as a general matter, one could even start with that approach in seeking to arrive at an SOS solution. It works even with alternatives that are inherently incapable of being combined such as liberals wanting juries that consist of 12 or more people, and conservatives wanting juries that consist of 6 or less people.

Second is the important point that the battle for achieving super-optimum solutions is not won by merely generating policy alternatives that satisfy the definition of an SOS solution. There may be problems of technology, inertia, vested interests, property, and jobs that need to be taken into consideration. The main reason for lack of adoption, however, may be a lack of awareness as to what there is to adopt. Thus, a key conclusion may be the importance of communicating basic ideas as to what is meant by a super-optimum solution, and how one or more super-optimum solutions may be possible in any policy controversy. That kind of communicating is the main purpose of this chapter and this book.

Bilingual Primary Education

The problem here is trilingualism in Philippine primary education. The *alternatives* are (1) only English in the schools, (2) only Filipino in the schools, (3) both English and Filipino. The SOS emphasis is on not what language is used, but what the substance is that is covered. The emphasis is placed on substance that is relevant to national productivity (see Table 6.2). All of these alternatives involve the local dialect as well. There is no way of avoiding that, which is where the third language comes in. As far as ideological orientation is concerned, speaking only English is associated with conservative elites; speaking only Filipino has a left-wing nationalism to it; retaining both is the neutral compromise. The SOS can be referred to as the language of productivity. This is English, but with an emphasis on subject matters that are likely to encourage a work ethic, technical skills, appreciation of science, creativity and efficiency. In college, and later, English can also open doors to textbooks, courses, magazines and other reading, listening and conversing which can facilitate productivity.

The first *goal* is access to the world's literature. The second goal is national unity. While the first goal is basically conservative, the second goal is basically liberal, although not necessarily so.

Thus there are only two goals but they are not easily referred to as a conservative and a liberal goal. There are business conservatives who would like Filipinos to have more access to the English-speaking business world,

Table 6.2   Trilingualism in Philippine education

Goals / Alternatives	Access to world's books	Unity	Totals			
			A Access wgt=3 Unity wgt=2	B Access wgt=1 Unity wgt=3	C Access wgt=1 Unity wgt=1	D Access wgt=3 Unity wgt=3
A Only English	5	4	23	17	9	27
B Only Filipino	2	4	14	14	6	18
C Only local dialect	1	1	5	4	2	6
D Both English and Filipino	4	4	20	16	8	24
SOS Both for productivity	5	5	25	20	10	30

but there are educated leftists who would like Filipinos to have more access to the English-speaking technical world even if that means capitalist American engineers. On the other hand, there are ethnic conservatives who resist what they perceive to be American and Asian cultural imperialism, and likewise leftists who resist the English language because of its association with American economic imperialism. The issue thus makes for somewhat strange bedfellows.

The problem is further complicated by three languages being involved. For the sake of simplicity, we have designated them A, B and C. (D is the compromise of both English and Filipino.)

The A alternative is only English. This is endorsed by conservative business people who would like to have more access to international trade. It is also endorsed by liberal intellectuals who would like to receive more Fulbright grants and to contribute to the literature in their fields.

The B position of only Filipino appeals to cultural conservatives, but also to left-wing nationalists.

The bilingual position comes out neutral, regardless of whether the first and second positions are considered liberal or conservative.

As regards *scoring the relations*, if we call 'only the local dialect' position C, then it comes out to be a totally dominated position since it provides the worst with regard to access to the world's books and the worst with regard to national unity.

In this context, combining English and Filipino should give the benefits of both. It does not, though, because it detracts from learning English and it detracts from learning Filipino. This is like when I tried to learn French with records that played while I slept: I neither learned French nor got any sleep, instead of getting both.

The big problem encountered by the University of the Philippines was deciding how to *assign weights* if the alternatives were not clearly conservative or liberal.

1   The people who take the A position would give a high weight to access to the world's books, and maybe only a weight of 2 to national unity.
2   The people who advocate speaking only Filipino are giving a low weight to access and a high weight to unity.
3   The people who advocate teaching in the local dialect are giving a low weight to access and a low weight to unity. They are giving a high weight to localism, which is why that alternative may not have been used. It is one thing to say that there is no way of stamping out local dialects; it is another thing to say that the national educational system should encourage local dialects by arranging for books and teachers for every local dialect. We may eliminate this alternative as not being rea-

sonable. What we may wind up with, though, is a fairly traditional analysis in terms of the liberal and conservative nature of the alternatives and goals.

4   We could say that the bilingual group is group D, and that it is placing a high weight on both access and unity. It could be referred to both as the D group, and as the neutral group.

With these weights, we can calculate four different *total columns*. The way things are now set up, we are operating independently of liberal and conservative concepts. The example thus serves the useful methodological purpose of showing how that can be done.

Notes

For literature on the problem of jury size, see Zeisel (1971). Mills (1973) and Nagel and Neef (1975).

For studies of the ways in which the general accuracy of juries can be improved with regard to simultaneously increasing the likelihood of convicting the guilty and acquitting the innocent, see Kassin and Wrightsman (1988) and Penrod (1985).

There have been hundreds of studies of jury decision making, but virtually none that are relevant to improving the public policies or legal rules that relate to the general accuracy of juries (see Davis *et al.*, 1977). The typical outcome variable relates to whether the jury will decide in favor of the plaintiff or the defendant, not whether the jury will decide accurately. The typical input variable relates to the background or attitude characteristics of the jurors, not to the legal rules under which they operate, such as prohibitions on note taking or on having written instructions from the judge. It is easier to measure direction of jury decisions, rather than accuracy. It is also more relevant to the interests of psychologists and social scientists (as contrasted to lawyers) to talk about backgrounds and attitudes (rather than legal rules), although the legal rule of jury size fits psychology interests and can be more easily measured than the nature of legal precedents.

7 Increasing Benefits and Decreasing Costs

Another useful perspective to have for generating SOS solutions is to think in terms of reducing costs and increasing benefits simultaneously. Like many of the methods for generating SOS solutions, this may run contrary to conventional thinking. The important considerations, however, are that (1) it works pragmatically as a method for developing SOS solutions, and that (2) SOS solutions where all major viewpoints come out ahead of their best expectations are socially desirable.

Computer-assisted Instruction

Also like many of the methods for generating SOS solutions, this method is best understood with a concrete example followed by more generalized language. Table 7.1 shows the method applied to the problem of some aspects of elementary school education. As for the alternatives, the conservative emphasis in education policy is often on reducing costs including teachers' salaries, as manifested in their opposition to education tax increases, possibly without adequate consideration of the reduced learning benefits. The liberal emphasis is often on increasing the learning experiences of students, possibly without adequately considering the cost in terms of increased salaries. The neutral or compromise position is somewhere between the low salaries for teachers that are associated with conservative taxpayers and the high salaries for teachers that are associated with liberal labor unions. That neutral position is also somewhere between the reduced learning experience that may be associated with low salaries and the increased learning experience that may be associated with high salaries in terms of quantity of salaried teachers as well as average salary per teacher.

As for the goals, conservatives place a relatively high value on the goal of reducing taxes or cutting costs. Liberals place a relatively high value on

Table 7.1   Reducing costs and increasing benefits in education

Criteria / Alternatives	C Goal Fewer taxes (Fewer costs)	L Goal More learning (More benefits)	N Total (neutral weights)	L Total (liberal weights)	C Total (conservative weights)
C Alternative Lower salaries (Reduced learning)	4	2	12	10	14*
L Alternative Increase learning (Higher salaries)	2	4	12	14*	10
N Alternative In between on both dimensions	3	3	12	12	12
SOS Alternative CAI and videotaping	5	5	20	20**	20**

having enriched learning experiences, especially for inner-city children and others who are not so well off. The conservative alternative of conservative salaries does well on the conservative goal, but generally not so well on learning quality and quantity. The liberal alternative of liberal salaries does relatively well on the liberal learning goal, but not so well on the conservative cost-saving goal. The neutral or compromise alternative logically falls between the other two alternatives in terms of its impact on both goals.

One SOS alternative in this context is to make more use of modern technology whereby one can lower the costs, especially of the number of teachers needed while simultaneously increasing many aspects of the learning experience. One kind of technology for doing this is computer-assisted instruction (CAI). Children who love to play computer games are more likely to respond favorably to a game-playing orientation to learning reading, writing, arithmetic, social science, natural science and other subjects. It is more fun than being lectured to, passively reading or being at home pretending to be sick. In the 1990s, computer-assisted instruction now adds coordinated videotapes to the computer software by way of videodisks. This kind of technology is capable of combining the joys of Pac-Man and the Ninja Turtles with *Sesame Street* by combining computer games with television and movies in a useful interactive way. On their own, Pac-Man is not very useful and *Sesame Street* is not very interactive.

Thus, through modern educational technology, one teacher could possibly supervise two or three classrooms working with CAI with or without a video component. That saves two teachers' salaries. It does mean some additional costs for the equipment, but the maintenance costs tend to be rather low for electronic as contrasted to mechanical devices. Software costs are less than book costs, especially if the software is developed by the teachers themselves and widely reproduced. The key consideration is that this kind of thinking can lead to an alternative that will easily win on the liberal totals by virtue of the increased benefits, while holding costs down, and win on the conservative totals by virtue of the reduced costs while at least preserving the learning benefits.

Other Examples

Many other examples could be given. One is shown in Table 7.2 regarding Federal Aviation Administration policy. There the conservative position emphasizes reducing costs to the airlines. The liberal position (relatively speak-

Table 7.2   An SOS analysis of some aspects of Federal Aviation Administration policy

Criteria / Alternatives	N Goal Less taxpayer money L=2 C=2	C Goal Less airline money L=1 C=3	L Goal Safety L=4 C=2	N Total (neutral weights)	L Total (liberal weights)	C Total (conservative weights)
C Alternative Reduce labor & equipment cost	4	4	2	20	20	24*
L Alternative Pay high labor & equipment cost	2	2	4	16	22*	18
N Alternative In between	3	3	3	18	21	21
SOS Alternative 1. Non-wage benefits 2. Subsidy for high safety & low cost systems	2	5	5	24	29**	29*

ing) emphasizes higher safety. The neutral position compromises between monetary cost and safety. The SOS position might emphasize subsidies to develop technologies that could provide greater safety than we currently have at even lower cost. Such technology might make more use of computerized flight control, including computer-assisted flying (like computer-assisted instruction) from take-off to landing. Such assistance could be provided by flight control towers, as well as within planes. Doing so could save salary costs while providing increased benefits similar to the computer-assisted instruction.

Another example is given in Table 7.3. This example is about applying the general methodology to environmental policy, as contrasted to education or transport policy. All three policy fields (as well as other policy fields) have in common the possibility of increasing benefits and reducing costs through new technologies or new systems for achieving desired goals. In environmental policy, the conservative alternatives tend to emphasize relying on the marketplace. Liberal alternatives tend to emphasize punishing business wrongdoers. Neutrals may also advocate punishment or regulation, especially where toxic pollution is involved, but often with many exceptions and procedural loopholes, thereby considerably lessening the punishment threat.

One SOS alternative in the past has been to have well-placed subsidies to get manufacturing firms to adopt anti-pollution devices. Doing so could reduce pollution even better than the best expectation of liberals. Likewise,

Table 7.3   Dealing with the pollution of Archer Daniels Midland

Alternatives \ Criteria	L Goal Reduce pollution	C Goal Preserve employment & tax base	N Total (neutral weights)	L Total (liberal weights)	C Total (conservative weights)
C Alternative Marketplace	2	4	12	10	14*
L Alternative Punish business wrongdoers	4	2	12	14*	10
N Alternative Exceptions	3	3	12	12	12
SOS Alternative	5	5	20	20**	20**

Notes: The components of the SOS package might include (a) improve the manufacturing process to reduce pollution and simultaneously reduce expenses, which makes the business more profitable; (b) find commercial by-products for the undesirable waste; (c) better communicate the non-toxic nature of the pollutions, but still reduce or eliminate their smell.

doing so could be even more profitable to business than the best expectations of conservatives, especially if the subsidies more than cover the costs. This kind of 'well-placed subsidy' may not be so beneficial to the taxpayer even with the reduced pollution if a better subsidy might exist. Such a subsidy could go to improving the manufacturing process so as to reduce pollution and simultaneously reduce manufacturing expenses, thereby making the business both cleaner and more profitable. This kind of pollution prevention technology is likely to be adopted by business firms without liberal threats, relatively inefficient subsidies or the largely irrelevant marketplace. The new manufacturing process gets adopted because it is more efficient, not because it is cleaner or more legal. That is generally the best kind of incentive to do what is socially desirable.

Still further examples could be given, especially if one broadly defines the concept of reducing costs and increasing benefits. There is an overlap between this approach and some of the others, although it is better to have overlap in a checklist than to have gaps that would miss opportunities to achieve SOS solutions. One can consider the jury size problem to be related if one considers the goals to be increasing the benefits of convicting the guilty and decreasing the costs of convicting the innocent. An alternative way of phrasing the goals would be (1) to increase the benefits of acquitting the innocent and (2) to decrease the costs of acquitting the guilty. The solution of videotaping the trials to aid the jurors' memories involves technology, but the SOS solution of note taking does not. Thus the method of reducing costs and increasing benefits may involve improving the efficiency of procedures without necessitating technological innovation.

The last example is especially relevant to those who argue that SOS solutions are only possible with unrealistic increases in resources or unrealistic new technologies. The reality of many situations is that resources can often be increased and that new technologies can be developed. More important is the fact that many of these examples involve neither increased resources nor new technologies. Instead, they involve thinking more imaginatively along unconventional but potentially productive lines, such as thinking about ways in which costs can be reduced and benefits can be increased simultaneously. Doing this can result in all major viewpoints coming out ahead of their best initial expectations.

8 Early Socialization

Constitutional Law and Free Speech

Judicial Review

Judicial review means allowing the courts in a nation or province, especially the higher courts, to have the power to declare null and void governmental acts that the courts find to be contrary to the constitution. No judicial review means that the legislators and chief executives shall decide for themselves whether they are complying with the constitution. As of the 1990s, in the US context, this issue tends to apply only to civil liberties cases. It formerly applied to economic regulation cases, but has not done so since the 1930s.

The conservative goal in civil liberties matters tends to endorse majority rule regarding free speech, due process for people accused of crimes and equal treatment for groups that have been discriminated against. Conservatives as of the 1990s therefore tend to advocate judicial restraint, rather than vigorous judicial review. The liberal position advocates a more activist judicial review in terms of nullifying governmental acts that conflict with constitutional rights. A neutral position might advocate judicial review subject to having a two-thirds concurrence rule, elected judges on the Supreme Court, or fixed terms to make the courts more responsive to the majority. (See Table 8.1.)

An SOS solution might involve educating the majority better than it has been in the past on how the majority benefits from free speech, due process and equal opportunity. By sensitizing legislators, administrators and the general public to the importance of civil liberties, more might be done to protect these rights than can be done through judicial review alone.

This analysis assumes that both conservatives and liberals endorse constitutional rights, but differ as to the need for and desirability of judicial review to protect such rights. The idea of supplementing restrained judicial review with the appropriate socialization should appeal to both conservatives who emphasize majority rule in civil liberties and liberals who emphasize minority rights.

Table 8.1   Constitutional law: judicial review

Criteria Alternatives	C Goal Popular responsiveness C=3 L=1	L Goal Sensitivity to minority rights C=1 L=3	N Total (neutral weights)	L Total (liberal weights)	C Total (conservatives weights)

C Alternative
  No constitutional
  review
	3	1	8	6	10

L Alternative
  Concurrent
  constitutional
  review
	4	2	12	10	14*

N Alternative
  Judicial
  constitutional
  review
	2	4	12	14*	10

SOS Alternative
  Sensitize legislators,
  administrators
  & public
	5	5	20	20**	20**

Restrained judicial review means that the courts follow such rules as *not* declaring a law unconstitutional (1) if it can be found to be illegal on other grounds, (2) if the law is not presented in the form of a case which involves a litigant who is being hurt by the enforcement of the law, or (3) if the benefit of the doubt does go in favor of the legislature in a close case.

First Amendment

Evaluating ways of handling freedom of speech   The neutral position does well on both the liberal totals and conservative totals, better than a more liberal or conservative position. This may be so because free speech is not an issue that divides liberals and conservatives the way economic issues do. (See Table 8.2.)

A policy that involves government funding and facilitates minority view-points would facilitate creative ideas and constructive criticism of government, but it seems politically unfeasible since the Supreme Court does not require it and a majoritarian Congress is not so likely to appropriate funds. The closest provision is probably requiring radio and television stations to give minority parties free time when the major parties receive free time, and

Table 8.2   Alternative ways of handling freedom of speech

Policies \ Goals	Allow creative ideas	Encourage constructive criticism of government	Protect due process, privacy and equity rights of others	No undue burden on the taxpayer	Political or constitutional feasibility	Totals
1 Provide funding and facilities for minority viewpoints	5	5	4	2	1	17
2 Allow unlimited free speech	4	4	2	3	2	15
3 Limit free speech only when another fundamental right is jeopardized	4	4	5	3	3	19*
4 Limit free speech when no fundamental right of others is jeopardized but when the speech does not do anything constructive concerning societal improvement	2	2	3	3	4	14
5 Limit free speech when it is critical of prevailing government, religious or other establishment ideas	1	1	2	2	1	7

Notes:

1   A policy that involves government funding and facilitates for minority viewpoints would facilitate creative ideas and constructive criticism of government, but it seems politically unfeasible since the Supreme Court does not require it and a majoritarian Congress is not so likely to appropriate funds. The closest provision is probably requiring radio and TV stations to give minority parties free time when the major parties receive free time, and likewise with federal presidential funding, provided that the minority parties are substantial.

2   Unlimited free speech would allow invasions of privacy, prejudicial pre-trial publicity and unlimited campaign expenditures, which neither the courts nor Congress endorse. Those rights of privacy, due process and minimum equality in political campaigning are the fundamental rights which allow free speech limitations under Policy 3.

3   Examples of limitations under Policy 4 include pornography, libel, false pretenses and advocacy that leads to physical harm. All those free speech exceptions have been substantially limited over the last 20 years or so.

4   Policies 2 through 5 are mutually exclusive. Policy 3 outscores the others on the above goals.

likewise with federal presidential funding, provided that the minority parties are substantial.

Unlimited free speech would allow invasions of privacy, prejudicial publicity and unlimited campaign expenditures, which neither the courts nor Congress endorse. These rights of privacy, due process and minimum equality in political campaigning are the fundamental rights which allow free speech limitations under Policy 3.

Examples of limitations under Policy 4 include pornography, libel, false pretenses and advocacy that leads to physical harm. All these free speech exceptions have been substantially limited by the Supreme Court. For example, a libel suit is likely to be discussed if the plaintiff is a public figure unless the defendant deliberately lied or committed gross negligence. Likewise, pornography widely circulates partly owing to increased public tolerance but also to the increased reluctance of the Supreme Court to find that the alleged pornography has no redeeming social value.

The super-optimum solution may be to have virtually unrestricted free speech with the exceptions under the neutral alternative emphasizing conflicts with other rights in the Bill of Rights. To win support from the conservative business community, it is important to allow for free speech in advertising products, prices and services, especially among the professions, union organizations and business competition.

Klu Klux Klan rallies   The terms 'conservative' and 'liberal' are used here to refer to narrowing free speech rights versus broadening them. The terms have nothing to do with endorsing Klan purposes. (See Table 8.3.) The conservative approach is to prohibit or attack the Klan rally in order to prevent it from occurring. The liberal approach is to have a counter-rally or demonstration in order to show that anti-Klan feeling is stronger and more meaningful than pro-Klan feeling. A neutral approach might be to try to ignore the rally. This has the effect of allowing it to go unchallenged, and thereby to make it appear that pro-Klan opinion is stronger than anti-Klan opinion.

The conservative position is seeking to minimize the extent to which the Klan has an audience or outlets to obtain an audience. The liberal position is seeking to allow diverse ideas and is fearful that prohibiting some ideas on the basis of content can set a bad precedent regarding the prohibition of other dissident ideas.

The SOS position may endorse the counter-rally in the short run. As a long-run solution, the SOS position may seek to remove the causes of Klan support from either participants or an audience. This can be done partly through having a prosperous economy that does not generate hatred of minorities as scapegoats for lack of jobs and other opportunities. It can also be done through childhood socialization and education which emphasizes

Table 8.3 Dealing with abhorrent speech

Alternatives	L Goal More creative ideas	C Goal Protect from upset	N Total (neutral weights)	L Total (liberal weights)	C Total (conservative weights)
C Alternative Prohibit abhorrent speech & no funding	1	5	12	8	16
L Alternative Allow abhorrent speech like other speech & no funding	5	1	12	16	8
N Alternative No funding, but tolerate unless riot	4	2	12	14	10
SOS Alternative Remove causes: Nazism, pornography	5	5	20	20	20

Notes: Abhorrent speech refers, for example, to pro-Nazi speeches in Skokie, flag burning or funding of the pornographic or sacrilegious.

the importance of judging people on the basis of individual merit in order to have a productive and cooperative society.

Socialization and Public Policy

Risk takers are generated among little children in the first five years of their lives, depending on whether they are allowed to take chances or are treated in such a way that they never come into contact with anything that might hurt them. There is certainly a need for encouraging more experimentation on the part of children, within reason: more rebelliousness, more trying out to see what will happen if you push your food off the highchair on to the floor without being punished for doing so, to see if the bowl will break or not. This does not necessarily mean that you jump off the third story balcony to see if your head will break.

Socialization could be discussed across every field of public policy. If one is going to have a super-optimum society, the kinds of attitude children have with regard to discrimination, poverty, world peace, crime, education, consumer–merchant relations, labor–management relations, free speech and fair procedure are important. One could even say that the key purpose, or a key purpose, of public policy is to provide for a socialization environment in which children have socially desired attitudes in every field of public policy. If that is done properly, then a good number of the problems as to what policies to adopt will take care of themselves because the need for public policy will be lessened. If children, for instance, are imbued with the idea of judging each other in terms of their individual characteristics rather than in terms of ethnic characteristics, we have less need for public policies dealing with racism because there is likely to be a lot less of it.

Liberals have a lot of trouble with talking about socialization because it sounds like brainwashing people. It can be done in a brainwashing way, or it can be done in a way that encourages children to think things out for themselves to some extent. It is one thing to have a child 'parrot' back some kind of catechism to the effect that 'thou shalt not discriminate against blacks or Hispanics'. It is another thing to use approaches similar to *Sesame Street* or any kind of child teaching that involves the children being involved in working out and deducing what is the right thing to do, instead of being told what it is and to memorize some appropriate words that they do not understand.

If we go down the list of public policy problems, we could talk about appropriate attitudes and then later worry about how instilling those attitudes can be best implemented in a way that constitutes self-development rather than useless brainwashing, which does not even succeed in washing anybody's brain in the sense of making them into equalitarians or work-oriented people, or what have you.

Economic Problems

On the matter of *employment*, this raises the attitude of the work ethic, where people enjoy the work they do and do not look forward to the end of the work day or the end of their careers when they retire. One might say that depends on what kind of job one has, implying that the problem is mainly in the stimulus, not the response. If people are oriented toward doing constructive work as a satisfying way of spending time, indeed as the most satisfying way of spending time, they are likely to find constructive work for them to get themselves into. In other words, the attitude leads to the enjoyable work. The enjoyable work does not seek out people with work-oriented attitudes.

On the matter of *consumer–merchant attitudes*, it is important to get across to little children that in business transactions one seeks to provide quality and reasonable quantity when one is on the selling end, and that it should be expected. We could talk about the opposite attitude on each of the above. The opposite attitude on the work ethic is for people to have as their goal to not have to work at all, to be independently wealthy, win a lottery and just loaf away the rest of their lives. The opposite on the consumer–merchant attitude is that a good seller is one who makes a profit perhaps tricking the buyer into thinking he is getting quality. The person who is oriented toward making a profit by providing low quality or a low quantity in return for a high price acts to the detriment of society, as contrasted to the Japanese philosophy of making big profits by providing high quality and high quantity in return for profitable prices. The Japanese system seeks high profits by (1) raising income through large volume sales as a result of being able to lower prices owing to the modern technology of mass production which also stimulates sales by improving the quality, safety and durability of products; and (2) lowering labor expenses by using more machines and by encouraging worker efficiency through good salaries, working conditions and fringe benefits. The American system traditionally seeks high profits by (1) getting prices up and relying on monopoly and collusion to guarantee captive customers; and (2) getting expenses down by fighting unions, minimum wages, minimum workplace safety and maximum hours.

On *labor relations*, it is the same kind of attitude. The Japanese philosophy is that you do not make money by paying low wages and having relatively cheap working conditions. Instead, you make money by motivating workers, partly with high wages and lots of fringe benefits, including recreation facilities and teamwork. The idea of expecting, as a worker or as a future employee, to work together rather than in conflict is an important attitude with regard to a society doing well.

Technology Problems

On *environmental matters*, little children can easily acquire respect or disregard for the idea of conservation. This comes in under environment, energy and land use. The American attitude has traditionally been one of waste rather than conserving. Conserving at a child's level can simply mean not throwing away litter. However, one does not want to put across the idea of overemphasis on individual responsibility, which may be difficult to deal with at the pre-school level. One cannot so easily communicate to a child that society would do a lot more good if it were to do things to encourage the existence of non-biodegradable litter rather than putting up signs saying that we should put the litter in the wastebasket. Pre-school children do not understand the concept of government and public policy. It is meaningful for them to understand individual responsibility; individual responsibility is not in conflict with collective responsibility. It may even lead to thinking in more collective terms later, when they understand what the collectivity is all about. At the pre-school level, they cannot be expected to have much understanding of how to deal with water pollution or air pollution, although there is no reason why parents cannot indicate their own negative attitudes, if they have them, toward air pollution and water pollution.

Social Problems

On the matter of *poverty*, little children do run into others that are poorer or richer than they are. The traditional American attitude is to look down upon those who are poor and to be jealous of those who are richer. There might be something to be said for the fundamentalist idea of hating the way of doing things and loving the sinner. It is not so meaningful to expect little children to love poor people and love rich people but to hate the idea that society makes for such big disparities. That is too abstract. The key attitude toward poverty is to instill the idea that it is wrong for some people to go without food or shelter or decent clothing and that some day maybe the child who is being socialized will be in a position to do something about it. The idea of doing something about rich children in a negative way is not in conformity with super-optimum solutions, as contrasted to more traditional thinking about class conflict. The SOS thinking says there is nothing wrong with having lots of rich people, so long as there are no deprived people below a minimum level. The more traditional thinking on class conflict objects to rich people as something objectionable in itself.

On the matter of *racism*, parents are the main source of racism in children through their racist examples. Studies show that racist children are that way by about the age of four or five and it has nothing to do with their peer group contacts or elementary school or high school, although those contacts may be reinforcing, especially if those contacts also have racist parents. On this matter of socialization, we are not just talking about parental socialization, we are talking about the socialization that can come through nursery schools, daycare or public television, all with regard to a democratic progressive way for children to learn, and all with regard to values that most people pay lip service to, even if they do not practice them. Very few people are going to object openly to an integrated pre-school program that seeks to encourage respect for other ethnic groups, even if the people themselves do not have respect for other ethnic groups. As of the 1990s, people are embarrassed to admit to racist attitudes, whereas they were highly open as recently as the 1960s. In fact, as recently as the 1960s, people would have been embarrassed in many parts of the country not to be racist. The term 'racist' did not exist, but being thought a 'nigger-lover' or 'Jew-lover' would mean a non-racist being ostracized by the community.

On the matter of *criminal justice*, it is important to instill basic ideas of due process, meaning that when people are accused of wrongdoing they should have an opportunity to defend themselves. They should be told what they have done wrong. They should have an opportunity to call upon others to defend them. The person who is doing the accusing should not be the same person who decides whether they are guilty or not. On the matter of criminal behavior, we need a broader notion of wrongdoing and it needs to be treated with a very negative attitude: this applies to traditional criminal behavior, negligent behavior that causes injuries to others and exploitative behavior that is now grounds for at least civil, if not criminal, action.

Political Problems

Free speech is extremely important. Children need to be encouraged to speak up and object to what they are told to do. There are people with authoritarian minds who would object to this kind of childhood training. Prior to the 1960s, authoritarianism was much more accepted than it is now. A generation ago there were no free speech rights in the United States, although there was a free speech clause in the First Amendment. But not until the 1930s and the 1950s was it made applicable to the states or even made applicable in any significant way in the federal government. And really not until the 1960s did people have any constitutional right to speak out vigorously against government policy.

Regarding attitudes toward *world peace*, the idea of going to war needs to become almost as unthinkable as the idea of robbing banks or murdering people. There is a movement in that direction, to some extent, but little children still play with war toys, although it is more on an individual basis than one country versus another. It is still not as bad as it was formerly. The United States has been moving away from being an oppressive world bully ever since the early 1900s. In the year 1900, President McKinley declared that it was the Manifest Destiny of the United States to bring the American economic system, form of government and religion to developing nations like the Philippines, Cuba, Puerto Rico, Central America, and other places, regardless of what they wanted. We do not have that kind of colonialism any longer. Vietnam was a contrary example, but maybe the final lesson that no such war could ever be fought again by the United States, as was seen when the Reagan administration sought unsuccessfully to repeat Vietnam in Nicaragua. It is important to get across to children the need to resolve disputes through peaceful means rather than through violence. At the same time, there is a need to get across the idea of being capable of defending oneself.

There are a number of policy problems that are basically variations on *poverty* policy. For example, little children can have the attitude that it is highly undesirable for some people to go without food, shelter or adequate clothing, and also adequate health care. Health care for those who cannot afford it is the most important health policy issue. Another health policy issue is developing cures and preventatives for various diseases. This gets back to the work ethic and risk taking as applied to health policy. The work ethic and risk taking cut across all policy fields, in the sense of encouraging children to work to solve problems, including finding cures for diseases.

Reforming government structures is rather abstract, but it can have its concrete aspects. Basically, in the world of the pre-school child, it means decision making through democratic means where children participate in making decisions in their pre-school environments at nursery school. The most important government structure is democracy, with its emphasis on majority rule and universal participation. Democracy also means minority rights, especially free speech to convert the majority. That is a separate point.

Pre-school Education

In addition to elementary, secondary, higher on-the-job training (OJT) and adult education, there is a need for those in schools of education to show more interest in pre-school education. This subject is not being adequately covered by people in child psychology, sociology of the family, social work or other disciplines which have an interest in pre-school children. The emphasis in schools of education has been on elementary and secondary schooling, which only covers pupils from about age five to age 18, although people need to continue to learn from age 18 to the end of their lives. Possibly more important, the first five years may shape one's attitudes for learning in life, so that a little extra educational effort then could have a big subsequent payoff.

Table 8.4 presents an SOS analysis of the subject of pre-school education. The conservative alternative is to provide no government support or government interference. The liberal alternative is to provide a substantial amount of government support and possibly a paternalistic concern for the tender psyches of pre-school children. The neutral compromise is in between on support and concern.

A key conservative goal is to decrease tax expenses. A key liberal goal in this context involves government subsidies especially oriented toward doing something for the poor, as with the Headstart Program in the United States. A key liberal goal in other contexts is to promote civil liberties, and a key conservative goal is to promote productivity, with neutrals especially liking peaceful dispute resolution.

Table 8.4 Evaluating policies toward pre-school education

Criteria ⟍ Alternatives	L Goal Civil liberties	C Goal Productivity	N Goal Peaceful dispute resolution	C Goal Decrease tax expenditures	L Goal Do something for the poor	N Total (neutral weights)	L Total (liberal weights)	C Total (conservative weights)
C Alternative No government support	3	3	3	4	2	30	28	32*
L Alternative A lot of government support	3	3	3	2	4	30	32*	28
N Alternative In between	3	3	3	3	2	28	27	29
SOS Alternative Package	5	5	5	2	4	42	44**	40**

Note: The SOS package involves the following in pre-school education: (a) non-violent dispute resolution, (b) allowing differing ideas, (c) allowing someone accused of wrongdoing to defend himself or herself, (d) reward on the basis of merit, (e) a productive work ethic.

The conservative alternative does well with conservative weights for the goals since it does so well on saving tax money, at least in the short run. The liberal alternative does well with liberal weights since it does well on doing something for the poor, at least in the short run.

The SOS package does involve the expenditure of money, but to help create pre-school facilities for both the poor and the middle class. Pre-school facilities in this context can mean subsidizing learning modules and teachers as part of daycare centers. A requirement for receiving such subsidies would be that the daycare centers do not discriminate on the basis of race or religion and that they provide tuition waivers for those who cannot afford the tuition but who otherwise qualify.

In the United States, the learning modules to be developed with grants from the National Institute for Education might emphasize (1) having a productive work ethic, which should please conservatives, (2) encouraging non-violent dispute resolution, which should please neutrals, and (3) allowing differing ideas, opportunities to defend oneself when accused, and rewards on the basis of merit, so covering free speech, due process and equal treatment under law, which should please liberals and civil libertarians.

9   The Technological Fix

Environmental Technology

The Developmental Policy Studies Consortium was approached in the spring of 1992 to offer conceptual insights relevant to the Earth Summit Conference to be held in Brazil in June 1992. In response to the call for three levels of conceptual insights, we indicated that we would be pleased to contribute our insights regarding the relevance of super-optimizing policy analysis to the problems of economic development versus a clean environment in developing nations.

As for three levels of relevant insights, the first level would be to *communicate what super-optimizing policy analysis is*. It is a new and exciting approach to dealing with public policy dilemmas whereby conservatives, liberals and other major viewpoints can all come out ahead of their best initial expectations simultaneously. Table 9.1 summarizes some of the basic concepts. The basic alternatives are in the rows. The goals to be achieved are in the columns. Relations between alternatives and goals are shown in the cells, tentatively using a 1–5 scale where a 5 means highly conducive to the goal, a 4 means mildly conducive, a 3 means neither conducive nor adverse, a 2 means mildly adverse and a 1 means highly adverse.

This tabular explanation of the nature of super-optimizing analysis has been given elsewhere in this book. This is a new and important form of public policy analysis which is worth repeating. Its newness is indicated by the lack of prior literature. Its importance is indicated by the fact that both sides or all sides in a policy dispute or other dispute would prefer to come out ahead of their best expectations if possible. That is clearly preferable to a lose–lose situation where both sides come out worse than their worst expectations. Such a result often occurs when one side seeks a total victory and thereby provokes a war, strike, expensive litigation or other lose–lose situations. A win–win result is also preferable to a compromise where all sides lose something but come out ahead of their worst expectations.

Overall totals for each alternative are shown in the columns at the right. They include a neutral column where all the goals are given a middling

155

Table 9.1   An SOS analysis of economic development versus a clean environment in developing nations

Criteria / Alternatives	C Goal Rapid economic development C=3 N=2 L=1	L Goal Clean environment C=1 N=2 L=3	N Total (neutral weights)	L Total (liberal weights)	C Total (conservative weights)
C Alternative Unregulated economic development	4	2	12	10	14*
L Alternative anti-pollution regulations	2	4	12	14*	10
N Alternative Compromise regulations	3	3	12	12	12
SOS Alternative Improved manufacturing & agricultural processes	>4	>4	>12	>14**	>14**

weight of 2 on a 1–3 scale of importance. The third total column involves conservative totals where the conservative goals are given a weight or multiplier of 3, and the liberal goals are given a weight or multiplier of 1. The second set of totals are the liberal totals where the conservative goals are given a weight of 1, and the liberal goals a weight of 3. The conservative alternative wins on the conservative totals, and the liberal alternative wins on the liberal totals. The object is to develop an alternative that does even better on the conservative totals than the previous conservative alternative, and simultaneously does better on the liberal totals than the previous liberal alternative.

The second level of insight is to *communicate a recognition that such super-optimum solutions are realistically possible* and not just conceptually possible. A good example relates to the ozone problem and the use of fluorocarbons in hairsprays and other aerosol containers. In about 1985, such devices represented a serious threat, depleting the ozone layer and thereby causing a substantial increase in skin cancer throughout the world. The solution was *not* to rely an unregulated marketplace, which normally provides almost no incentives to manufacturers to reduce their pollution. The solution was *not* regulation or prohibition, which tends to be evaded, expensive to enforce and enforced with little enthusiasm, given disruptions that might occur to the economy. The most exciting aspect of the solution (although the problem is not completely solved) was the development of new forms of spray propellant which are less expensive for manufacturers to use and simultaneously not harmful to the ozone layer.

This kind of solution tends to be self-adopting since manufacturing firms, farmers and others who might otherwise be polluting the environment now have an important economic incentive to adopt the new low-polluting methods because they reduce the expenses of the business firm. This approach does require substantial research and substantial government subsidies for research and development as contrasted to paying the polluters not to pollute, which is even more expensive and often not so effective since they may take the money and pollute anyhow. The business firms generally do not have capital for that kind of research and development, or the foresight or forbearance which public policy and governmental decision making may be more capable of exercising. This includes international governmental decision making, as well as those in developing nations.

The third level of insight is to *communicate that such solutions may be well worth pursuing to resolve the dilemma of economic development versus a clean environment* in developing nations. In the case of Brazil, for example, this may mean research and development to make better use of the rain forests as a source of low-polluting fuel for industries in Brazil and elsewhere, instead of wastefully burning off the rain forests and thereby having an adverse effect, with global warming. The rain forests could conceivably be exploited as if they were a form of coal mine and possibly even analogously to the harvesting of crops. The carbons could be economically converted into relatively clean fuel. This would be an expansion of the ideas of ethanol as a source of fuel for cars. Money invested into this kind of research could simultaneously aid Brazil in its economic development and produce a cleaner environment for both Brazil and other parts of the world.

Other R&D subsidies could go into such ideas as developing ways of processing Brazilian crops to reduce simultaneously the pollution effect of the waste products and the processing costs. This is the kind of research activity that the United States Environment Protection Agency is encouraging in such fields as soybean processing in central Illinois by the ADM Manufacturing Company. It is the kind of research that seeks to find pesticides and herbicides that are even more effective than traditional ones in dealing with undesirable insects and weeds, but are simultaneously less expensive than traditional ones. The University of Illinois Agricultural Engineering Department is at the forefront of this kind of research. The Materials Science and Engineering Department (formerly the Department of Mining and Metallurgy) is also leading the way in developing new polymers and other materials which are less expensive, more effective and less polluting in the manufacturing process than traditional metals. Its work may be relevant to developing more effective, less expensive and less polluting ways of mining gold on the Amazon River than the current methods which add to the mercury content of the river.

Research on the development of these improved manufacturing and agricultural processes is in need of a lot more money than it is receiving from such sources as the Illinois state legislature. There is a need for the Big Seven countries (Canada, France, Germany, Italy, Japan, the United Kingdom and the United States) and other international economic communities to devote more funding to this kind of SOS research. This does mean investing in ideas that may take longer to pay off than investing in a profitable but pollution-producing factory, but the payoffs are likely to be well worth the investment in terms of being able to combine economic development and a clean environment simultaneously. This is in contrast to having to compromise or have tradeoffs which result in both less economic development and a less clean environment.

On environmental policy, this is viewed as a form of business regulation by conservatives and resisted as much as any kind of business regulation. Liberals like environmental regulation, partly because, traditionally, they do not especially like business, and they like to see business regulated. There are thus rather negative motivations on both sides. A more positive motivation would be for both sides to recognize how much better off everybody is with clean air and clean water as the two main kinds of environmental protection. The same is true of concern about toxic waste, acid rain, ozone problems, greenhouse effects, noise pollution, radiation pollution and conservation. The latest problem may be radon pollution, which is not the first natural pollution (as opposed to man-made pollution) that has serious public health consequences. Regardless of the source, and radon pollution seems relatively unimportant compared to other forms of pollution, they are all potentially subject to subsidies, tax breaks and other devices to encourage socially desired behavior.

Technological Innovation

Preserving the patent system (as it is currently operating) tends to stifle some creativity by providing for a 17-year monopoly, renewable once but frequently renewed repeatedly with slight variations. It also stifles creativity by being the basis for lawsuits designed to obtain injunctions against creative competition. Abolishing patents can harm the creativity of people who develop new inventions in order to obtain a monopolistic patent although, as

Table 9.2   The patent system and encouraging inventions

Criteria / Alternatives	L Goal Creativity	C Goal Lower taxes	N Goal Increased GNP	N Total (neutral weights)	L Total (liberal weights)	C Total (conservative weights)

C Alternative
  Preserve
  patents
	2	4	3	18	16	20*

L Alternative Abolish patents	2	4	3	18	16*	20
N Alternative Change systems	2	4	3	18	16	20

SOS Alternative
  Well-placed
  subsidies to
  encourage
  technology
	5	2	5	24	27**	21**

of the 1990s, these new inventions may be relatively small matters rather than new forms of transport, communication, energy or health care. (See Table 9.2.)

Well-placed subsidies could mean calling a conference of leading scientists and engineers to develop a list of 50–100 important needed inventions. The government could then announce the availability of grants and other monetary rewards to encourage the development of these inventions. The rewards could be worth more than a monopolistic patent while encouraging (rather than stifling) competition.

Changing the system by shortening the patent monopoly, requiring licensing or having the government as an insurer against product liability can be helpful, but not as helpful as well-placed subsidies to encourage needed inventions.

10 Contracting Out

Socialism versus Capitalism

The changes that are occurring in eastern Europe and in many other regions and nations of the world provide an excellent opportunity to apply systematic policy analysis to determining such basic matters as how to organize the economy, the government and other social institutions. Super-optimum solutions refer to public policy alternatives that can enable conservatives, liberals and other major viewpoints all to come out ahead of their best initial expectations simultaneously. The problems of privatization and inflation can illustrate what is involved in super-optimum solutions.

Alternatives

Table 10.1 analyzes the fundamental issue of *socialism versus capitalism* in the context of government versus private ownership and operation of the basic means of producing industrial and agricultural products. The essence of socialism in this context is government ownership and operation of factories and farms, or at least those larger than the handicraft or garden size, as in the Soviet Union in 1960. The essence of capitalism is private ownership and operation of both factories and farms, as in the United States in 1960. The neutral position or middle way is to have some government and some private ownership/operation, as in Sweden in 1960. The year 1960 is used because that is about the time that the Soviet Union began to change, with the advent of Nikita Khrushchev. The United States also underwent big changes in the 1960s, with the advent of John F. Kennedy.

Table 10.1 refers to government ownership/operation as the liberal or left-wing alternative, as it is in the United States and in world history, at least since the time of Karl Marx. The table refers to private ownership/operation as the conservative or right-wing alternative, as it is in the United States and elsewhere at least since the time of Adam Smith. In recent years in Russia and in China, those favoring privatization have been referred to as liberals, and those favoring retention of government ownership/operation have been

Table 10.1 Government versus private ownership and operation

Criteria / Alternatives	C Goal High productivity	L Goal Equity	L Goal Workplace quality	L Goal Environmental protection	L Goal Consumer protection	N Total	L Total	C Total
	$C=3$ $L=1$	$C=1$ $L=3$	$C=1$ $L=3$	$C=1$ $L=3$	$C=1$ $L=3$	(neutral weights)	(liberal or socialistic weights)	(conservative or capitalistic weights)
L Alternative Government ownership & operation (socialism)	2	4	2	2	2	24	32*	16
C Alternative Private ownership & operation (capitalism)	4	2	2	2	2	24	28	20*
N Alternative Some govt & some private	3	3	2	2	2	18	24	18
SOS Alternative 100% govt. owned & 100% private operation	>3	>3	>3	>3	>3	>30	>39**	>21**

referred to as conservatives. The labels make no difference in this context: the object of Table 10.1 is to find a super-optimum solution that more than satisfies the goals of both ideologies or groups, regardless of their labels.

Goals and Relations

The key capitalistic *goal* is high productivity, in terms of goods producing income substantially above what it costs to produce them. The key socialistic goal is equity, in terms of the sharing of ownership, operation, wealth and income. Other goals that tend to be more socialistic than capitalistic, but are less fundamental, consist of (1) workplace quality, including wages, hours, safety, hiring by merit and worker input, (2) environmental protection, including reduction of air, water, radiation, noise and other forms of pollution, and (3) consumer protection, including low prices and goods that are durable, safe and of high quality.

The *relations* between each alternative and each goal are shown on a 1–5 scale, where 5 means highly conducive to the goal, 4 means mildly conducive, 3 means neither conducive nor adverse, 2 means mildly adverse and 1 means highly adverse to the goal. We have here a classic tradeoff.

Going down the *productivity* column, the liberal socialistic alternative does not score so high, for lack of profit-making incentive and a surplus of bureaucratic interference, in comparison with the capitalistic alternative, assuming that the level of technology is held constant. The empirical validity of this statement is at least partially confirmed by the fact that the capitalistic countries of Japan and West Germany are more productive than their socialistic counterparts of China and East Germany, although they began at approximately the same level at the end of World War II. Going down the *equity* column, the liberal socialistic alternative does score relatively high. By definition it involves at least a nominal collective sharing in the ownership and operation of industry and agriculture, which generally leads to less inequality in wealth and income than capitalism does.

On the goals that relate to the *workplace, the environment and consumers*, the socialists traditionally argue that government ownership/operation is more sensitive to these matters because it is less profit-oriented. The capitalists traditionally argue that private ownership/operation is more sensitive in competitive marketplaces because of the need to find quality workers and to increase the number of one's consumers. The reality (as contrasted to the theory) is that, without alternative incentives or regulations, both government managers and private managers of factories and farms are motivated toward high production at low cost. That kind of motivation leads to cutting back on the expenses of providing workplace quality, environmental protection and consumer protection. The government factory manager of the Polish steelworks may be just as abusive of labor as the private factory manager of the US steel company. Likewise, the government factory managers in the state factories of China may be just as insensitive to consumer safety and durability as their monopolistic counterparts in the American car industry.

A Super-optimum Solution

As regards the super-optimum solution, it involves government ownership, but all the factories and farms are rented to private entrepreneurs to develop productive and profitable manufacturing and farming. Each lease is renewable every year, or longer if necessary to get productive tenants. A renewal can be refused if the factory or farm is not being productively developed, or if the entrepreneur is not showing adequate sensitivity to workers, the environment and consumers.

To cite some of the *advantages* of such an SOS system, it is easier to not renew a lease than it is to issue injunctions, fines, jail sentences or other negative sanctions. It is also much less expensive than subsidies. The money received for rent can be an important source of tax revenue for the government, to provide productive subsidies elsewhere in the economy. These subsidies can be used in particular for encouraging technological innovation and diffusion, the upgrading of skills and stimulating competition for market share, which can be so much more beneficial to society than either socialistic or capitalistic monopolies. The government can more easily demand sensitivity to workers, the environment and consumers from its renters of factories and farms than it can from itself. There is a conflict of interest in regulating oneself.

This SOS alternative is *only available to socialistic countries* like Russia, China, Cuba, North Korea and others, since they already own the factories and land. It would not be economically or politically feasible for capitalistic countries to move from the conservative capitalistic alternative to the SOS solution by acquiring ownership through payment or confiscation. This is an example where socialistic countries are in a position to decide between socialism and capitalism, perhaps by compromising and winding up with the worst of both possible worlds: the relative unproductivity of socialism and the relative inequity of capitalism. The socialistic countries are also in a position to decide between the two basic alternatives by winding up with the best of both possible worlds. This means retaining the equities and social sensitivities of government ownership, while having the high productivity that is associated with profit-seeking entrepreneurial capitalism. It would be difficult to find a better example of *compromising versus super-optimizing* than the current debate over socialism versus capitalism.

Legal Services for the Poor

The Washington newsletter of the American Bar Association reports that Legal Services Corporation was given a five-year authorization during the Bush administration.

Progressive Contracting Out of Legal Services

The idea of competitive bidding or contracting out of legal services raises some interesting questions. One question is simply whether it is possible for a Democratic Congress to trust a Republican administration with handling competitive bidding. In theory, this could be a highly liberal kind of privatization. The specification of the contract on which bids are taken could be like the following.

Whoever gets the contract must agree to devote half their money to *law reform cases* before the Supreme Court or other courts. Such cases are designed to improve substantially the legal rights of the poor as consumers, tenants, welfare recipients, public housing recipients, voters, arrested persons, employees, health care recipients, students in elementary and high schools, family members, clients of lawyers and other frequent roles.

Perhaps more important than improving rights is just seeking *clarification and enforcement of existing rights*.

A strong *affirmative action program* must be adopted to seek out qualified lawyers who are women, members of minorities, disabled, from poor backgrounds and so on. The affirmative action program should not award any preference or points to those people. The emphasis should be on affirmatively seeking out those who are qualified.

There should be a lot of *public education* in the contract, informing the general public about the legal rights of the poor and the legal rights of consumers, tenants and so on, regardless of whether they are poor.

The contract should include active activities on the part of the firm that is awarded the contract in terms of *seeking legislation* designed to better clarify and enforce the legal rights of the poor, and not just court cases.

There should be activity at *law schools* across the country designed to bring law students into the program according to the theory that this will give them an involvement that will carry on for the rest of their lives and help to shape favorably their attitudes toward legal services for the poor.

In addition to counseling activities, litigation activities, legislative activities, law reform and negotiation, there should be encouragement of activities that involve the *writing of law review articles or books*. This is more a matter of educating the bar and influencing the legal system than it is of public education.

In other words, just because the system is turned over to private enterprise does not mean that poor people are going to be hurt. It all depends on what the contracting out provides for in the contract. If it has provisions like the above, it is much better than government ownership and operation. This is really a good example of cases where liberals have a kneejerk negative reaction to privatization as somehow being inherently reactionary.

Progressive Contracting Out in General

Privatization does not mean an inherent conflict between government ownership and operation, and private ownership and operation. It can mean government ownership and private operation through a progressive system of contracting out, as contrasted to a reactionary system.

A progressive system involves contracting out with contract provisions requiring environmental protection, workplace safety and consumer protection. It also involves contracting out to more than one supplier of the service in order to provide competition. It further involves relatively short-term contracts that come up for renewal and are not renewed if they are not being complied with. Also there should be provisions in the contract for terminating it before the term is up if violations are severe enough.

A reactionary system involves contracting out, leaving the private entrepreneur free to do anything they want with regard to the environment, workplace or consumers. Worse, they are given a monopolistic franchise that leads to even more abuses than would result from simply not having any contract provisions against them. It is also highly undesirable that the contract be for an indefinite time or a definite time that is so long that the idea of non-renewal gets lost in inertia, or that the contract provide for a relatively short time but there is no monitoring of it to see if it is being well complied with, and renewal tends to be automatic.

The concept of contracting out normally refers to the reactionary version and therefore it tends to be opposed by liberals. A progressive version of contracting out, though, can be even better for promoting liberal values than government ownership and operation. The progressive version is also politically and administratively feasible. It is politically feasible because it represents a move away from government ownership and operation, which conservatives should endorse. It is politically feasible for liberals, given the liberal provisions. It is administratively feasible because there will be entrepreneurs who will be pleased to accept these contracting provisions if what they are supplying in the way of services or other activities involves substantially less expense on their part than what they are being paid to do. If the contract is highly profitable, they can easily absorb the environment, workplace and consumer provisions.

Even though the entrepreneurs are making a profit, the government and taxpayer may also be coming out well ahead. This is so because the private entrepreneur may be reducing expenses through the incentive of competition and the private profit motive. These incentives may also be substantially improving the quality of what is being provided, beyond what a monopolistic government agency could provide.

A recent new form of contracting out is the running of the public schools in a city or school district by a private enterprise firm. The contract provides that the firm receives payment equal to 90 per cent of the previous tax costs. The contract also provides for various standards designed to determine how well the students are learning at the beginning of the contract and at the end of each academic year. The contract can be awarded through open bidding, and is up for renewal or rebidding every few years. This arrangement may improve the quality of the schools, but generally does nothing for the integration of students from different economic classes.

11   International Economic Communities

IECs in General

An exciting new development with regard to international interaction to deal with shared policy problems is the international economic community (IEC). It involves a group of countries agreeing to remove tariff barriers to the buying and selling of goods among the countries as a minimum agreement to constitute an IEC. The agreement may also provide for removal of immigration barriers to the free flow of labor and a removal of whatever barriers might exist to the free flow of communication and ideas. The European Economic Union is a good example, but other examples are developing in North America, Africa, Asia and eastern Europe.

Table 11.1 shows how IECs can be viewed as super-optimum solutions where conservatives, liberals and other major viewpoints can all come out ahead of their best initial expectations simultaneously. The conservative alternative emphasizes nationalism and separatism. The liberal alternative emphasizes one world or world government. The neutral alternative emphasizes regional government which involves political institutions more than an economic community.

The conservative goals emphasize national identity and stature. The liberal goals emphasize quality of life in terms of jobs and consumer goods. The conservative alternative does better on the conservative goal, as one would expect, and the liberal alternative does better on the liberal goal. Thus the traditional alternatives result in a tradeoff, where the overall winner depends on whether one has conservative goals or liberal goals.

The alternative of having an economic community does well on the conservative goal of preserving national identity since no sovereignty is lost in an IEC, as contrasted to the sovereignty that is lost in a world government or a regional government. The IEC may also add to the national stature of the component parts by giving them the increased strength which comes

Table 11.1   International economic communities and super-optimum solutions

Criteria / Alternatives	C Goal National identity and stature C=3 L=1		L Goal Quality of life in terms of jobs and consumer goods C=1 L=3		N Total (neutral weights)	L Total (liberal weights)	C Total (conservative weights)
C Alternative Nationalism and separatism	12 (4)	4	2 (2)	6	12	10	14*
L Alternative One world or world government	6 (2)	2	4 (4)	12	12	14*	10
N Alternative Regional government	9 (3)	3	3 (3)	9	12	12	12
S Alternative Economic community	15 (5)	5	5 (5)	15	20	20**	20**

Notes:
1. The relations between each alternative and each goal are shown on a 1–5 scale or circled score. A 5 means highly conducive to the goal, a 4 means mildly conducive, a 3 means neither conducive nor adverse, a 2 means mildly adverse and a 1 means highly adverse to the goal.
2. The conservative goal (C column 1) is given a weight or multiplier of 3 by conservatives (upper left-hand corner) on a 1–3 scale, but a weight of 1 by liberals (lower right-hand corner).
3. The liberal goal (L column 2) is given a weight or multiplier of 1 by conservatives (upper left-hand corner), but a weight of 3 by liberals (lower right-hand corner).
4. A single asterisk shows the alternative that wins on the liberal totals (column 4) and the conservative totals (column 5) before considering the SOS alternative.
5. A double asterisk shows the alternative that wins after the SOS super-optimum solution is considered. The SOS should score higher than both the former conservative winner on the conservative totals (column 5) and simultaneously higher than the former liberal winner on the liberal totals (column 4).

from being part of an important group. Thus France may have more national stature as a leader in the European Union than it has alone.

Likewise, the alternative of having an economic community does well on the liberal goal of promoting quality of life in terms of jobs and consumer goods. Jobs are facilitated by the increased exporting that the IEC countries are able to do. Jobs may also be facilitated by free movement to countries in the IEC that have a need for additional labor. Consumer goods are facilitated by the increased importing that the IEC countries are able to do without expensive tariffs.

Thus the IEC alternative does well on both the conservative goal and the liberal goal. It is therefore able to be a winner on both the liberal totals and the conservative totals. In that sense it has the qualities of a super-optimum solution in the realm of international interaction designed to deal with important economic policy problems.

An additional feature of an IEC might be periodic meetings to plan a division of labor among the member countries. This involves allocating countries to certain kinds of exporting and importing in order to recognize (1) their different abilities and (2) the consumer demands within the IEC and the external world. Some aspects of ways to allocate countries to exporting and importing that have super-optimizing characteristics are discussed in the Appendix at the end of this chapter.

Super-optimizing Applied to Russian Secession

Table 11.2 shows the application of SOS analysis to the problem of the proposed secession of Chechnya from the Russian Soviet Federated Socialist Republic (RSFSR). This application was developed in collaboration with Edward Ojiganoff, the Head of the Policy Analysis Division of the Supreme Soviet of the RSFSR. The Chechnyian problem is partly analogous to the secession of Croatia from Yugoslavia or the secession of any ethnic region from a larger country of which it had been a part.

The alternatives in the RSFSR–Chechnya situation are as follows.

1 Deny independence to Chechnya. This can be considered the relatively conservative position because it seeks to conserve the country, state or political unit as it is.
2 Grant independence to Chechnya. This can be considered the relatively liberal position because it is more tolerant of dissident attitudes.
3 Retain Chechnya as a sub-unit within the RSFSR, but grant Chechnya more autonomy than it currently has. This can be considered the relatively neutral position.

The goals in the Chechnya situation are the following.

1 A key conservative goal is to favor greater Russia and seek a high national income for Russia.
2 A key liberal goal is to help Chechnya, including a high national income for Chechnya.

Table 11.2　Secession of Chechnya from the RSFSR

Criteria / Alternatives	C Goal Greater Russia & high RSFSR GNP	L Goal Chechnya independence & high Chechnya GNP	N Total (neutral weights)	C Total (conservative weights)	L Total (liberal weights)
C Alternative Deny independence	3	1	4	7*	5
L Alternative Grant independence	1	3	4	5	7*
N Alternative More autonomy	2	2	4	6	6
SOS Alternative Economic union	≥2.5	≥2.5		≥7.5**	≥7.5**

Note: On a 1–2 weighting scale, conservative would be likely to give the first goal a weight or multiplier of 2 and the second goal a weight of 1. Liberals would be likely to give the first goal a weight of 1 and the second goal a weight or multiplier of 2.

More goals, and possibly more alternatives, can be added later. For the sake of simplicity, however, we will begin with three basic alternatives and two basic goals.

The relations between these three alternatives and these two goals can be expressed in terms of a 1–3 scale. In that context, a 3 means that the alternative is relatively conducive to the goal; a 2 means neither conducive nor adverse; a 1 means relatively adverse or negative to the goal. Relations can also sometimes be expressed in dollars, miles, 1–10 scales, question marks or other units.

Denying independence to Chechnya is perceived as being at least a mildly positive 3 on the goal of favoring greater Russia. Granting independence to Chechnya is perceived as being at least a mildly negative 2 on favoring greater Russia. More autonomy is in between, with a neutral score of 2. On the other hand, granting independence to Chechnya is scored a 3 on the goal of helping Chechnya. Denying independence is scored a 1 on helping Chechnya. More autonomy is in between on that goal, with a neutral score of 2. These perceptions and scores are likely to be approximately held by both conservatives and liberals in this context.

There are three total scores that can be generated from these data. The total scores are neutral, conservative or liberal, depending on the relative importance of the two goals. If the two goals are considered to be of equal importance, the neutral totals are 4 for each of the alternatives. If the conservative goal is considered more important than the liberal goal, we can count the conservative column twice. That results in totals of 7 for denying independence (3 + 3 + 1), 5 for granting independence (1 + 1 + 3) and 6 for more autonomy (2 + 2 + 2). Thus, with conservative weights for the goals, the conservative alternative wins on the conservative goals.

Likewise, if the liberal goal is considered more important, we can count the liberal column twice. That results in totals of 5 for denying independence (3 + 1 +1), 7 for granting independence (1 + 3 + 3) and 6 for more autonomy (2 + 2 + 2). Thus, with liberal weights for the goals, the liberal alternative wins on the liberal totals. The single asterisk shows the winning alternative on each total column before the SOS alternative or super-optimum solution is taken into consideration.

Appendix: Allocating Countries to SOS Exporting and Importing

To: People Interested in International Economic Communities
From: Stuart Nagel
Date: The 1990s
Subject: Publishing and Related Opportunities

I shall greatly appreciate your informing me that you might like to serve on an advisory committee of the Developmental Policy Studies Consortium dealing with international economic communities.

Enclosed are three items that indicate some of the initial activities of the consortium regarding international economic communities:

1 The closing chapter, 'Global Policy Studies and Economic Communities', from the forthcoming consortium book, *Resolving International Disputes Through Win–Win or Super-Optimum Solutions*. Such solutions can enable all sides to come out ahead of their best initial expectations simultaneously. The IEC idea has the potential for being an SOS solution for many international disputes.
2 An announcement entitled 'A 3-Year, 4-Continent PSO Workshop Program'. This announcement tentatively divides Africa, Asia, Latin America and East Europe into six sub-regions per continent for the purpose of developing workshops in systematic policy analysis, including super-optimizing analysis. These sub-regions can be considered tentatively as the basis for 24 possible international economic communities.
3 A chapter entitled 'Using Management Science to Assign Judges and Lawyers to Types of Cases' from the book, *Microcomputers as Decision Aids in Law Practice* (Greenwood–Quorum, 1987). The methodology described in that chapter involves allocating criminal cases and civil cases to two lawyers in a law firm. The same methodology and related software could be used to allocate the production of approximately 400 basic products to 170 nations of the world and then aggregate their production figures to determine the production of the 24 or so international economic communities.

I am now in the process of obtaining the following information in order to implement the ideas above:

1 The production figures for each of the 170 countries are expressed in GDP dollars. These would be the row totals for a 170 by 400 matrix.
2 The production figures for each of the 400 products, also expressed in dollars. These would be the column totals for the matrix.

3   A 1–5 relation score or quality score for each of the 170 countries on each of the 400 products. This is determined by observing what percentage of the column totals for item 2 above are attributable to each country. The countries in the top quintile get a score of 5, in the second quintile a score of 4, and so on down to the bottom quintile, which gets a score of 1. This scoring operates on the assumption that, if a country is producing and scoring a large portion of the world's production of Product X, it must in general produce Product X reasonably well.

4   The operations research software that I have for assigning people to tasks or countries to products is not very high-powered. I am seeking software that can handle a 170 by 400 matrix possibly for use on the supercomputer.

5   After using this kind of analysis to determine roughly what each IEC should possibly be producing, I would then like to commission an economist, political scientist or other social scientist from a university in that IEC region to draft a chapter dealing with the meaningfulness of the allocation results for that IEC region, and dealing with other related political and economic issues in a regional context.

6   These 24 chapters, grouped by continents, could constitute a meaningful book on international economic communities and global policy studies.

In your role as a formal or informal member of the advisory group, I would welcome learning from you whatever ideas you have on the following:

1   Where can the production figures mentioned in Items 1, 2 and 3 be obtained?

2   Where can operations research (OR) assignment software be obtained that can handle a 170 by 400 matrix? Have you had some relevant experience with such software?

3   What relevant literature are you aware of that deals with problems like these, including literature in international economics and applications of the theory of comparative advantage?

4   What about relevant literature on the politics of trying to overcome economic and political nationalism in the formation of international economic communities?

5   Would you be interested in contributing to a book on international economic communities and global policy studies by authoring a cross-cutting chapter or one with a regional perspective?

6   Do you have some ideas regarding relevant people to whom I should send a copy of this letter?

7   Maybe you have some ideas regarding additional relevant questions that should be asked in order to aid in seeing the big picture of a world

consisting of international economic communities across Africa, Asia, East Europe, Latin America and elsewhere, facilitating a higher quality of life for people in general as a mutually beneficial super-optimum solution to what otherwise has been a history of sins of commission and omission regarding international relations?

I look forward to hearing from you on these important matters. I welcome your responding by way of a short or long note with or without enclosures. I shall be pleased to keep you informed of developments on this potentially exciting and useful project. Thank you for whatever help you can provide. Best wishes for our shared interest in the application of political science, economics and other social sciences to improving the quality of life across developing and industrialized countries.

P.S. It would also be useful if we could get consumption figures (as well as production figures) for each of the 170 countries on each of the 400 products. With that combination of information we could say meaningful things about exports and imports. Thus, if the comparative allocation shows that the United States should be producing 50 units of wheat, and the United States consumes 70 units, then the United States should be importing units. On the other hand, if the United States consumes 35 units of wheat, it should be exporting the remaining 15 units out of the 50-unit production figure. The idea of 400 countries comes from the Leontiev input–output analysis, which tends to work with 400 industries in dealing with the economy of a single country like the United States.

12 SOS Allocation by Increasing the Relation Score

Win–win solutions to budget problems usually consist of one of two kinds. The first is to expand the budget available so that there is more than enough money to satisfy both conservatives and liberals. Consider the example of a $100 budget with the conservatives asking for $150 and the liberals also asking for $150. Each side gets more than its best expectations if $201 can be found to add to the $100 budget. The second solution to budget problems involves working within the present budget but expanding the efficiency of how the budget is allocated.

The General Method

Increasing the relation scores first of all means operationalizing the target that we are striving for, just as we did in talking about increasing the budget in Chapter 3. Table 12.1 summarizes what is involved. The top part of the table refreshes our memory regarding what the relation scores are between (1) dollars spent for the police and crime reduction, (2) dollars spent for the courts and crime reduction, (3) dollars spent for the police and fair procedure, and (4) dollars spent for the courts and fair procedure.

The bottom part of Table 12.1 indicates how the neutral, conservative and liberal allocations in combination with those relation scores produce varying degrees of goal achievement on the goals of crime reduction and fair procedure. In this context, the relation scores might be called effectiveness, efficiency or elasticity coefficients in order to get at the idea that they are like slopes or marginal rates of return which show, for an incremental dollar, how much crime reduction or fair procedure is generated, but in a relative rather than an absolute sense. To be more specific, the 2 which relates $P to crime reduction can be interpreted as meaning that, if there is a 1 per cent in the amount of money spent on the police, there will be a 0.2 per cent

Table 12.1 The SOS allocation based on increasing the relation scores

Goals / Budget categories	C Goal Crime reduction	L Goal Fair procedure
C Item $ police	2	1
L Item $ judges	1	3
N Alloc. Goals achievement	\$P \$J 2 ($92) + 1 ($108) 184 + 108 = 292	\$P \$J 1 ($92) + 3 ($108) 92 + 324 = 416
C Alloc. Goals achievement	2 ($112) + 1($88) 224 + 88 = 312 = X	1 ($112) + 3 ($88) 112 + 264 = 376
L Alloc. Goals achievement	2 ($71) + 1 ($129) 142 + 129 = 271	1 ($71) + 3 ($129) 71 + 387 = 458 = Y
SOS Alloc. Goals achievement	313 = X+1	459 = Y+1

Notes:
1. The left side of each allocation is dollars for the police and the right side is dollars for the judiciary.
2. The relation scores can be considered as proxies for relative slopes, marginal rates of return, elasticity coefficients or other concepts that get at the degree of effect of incremental expenditures on incremental crime reduction or fair procedure. A more complicated alternative would treat the relation scores as exponents and then multiply the sub-parts, rather than add them.
3. The super-optimum solution involves improving at least one of the two relation scores associated with crime reduction, and at least one of the two relation scores associated with fair procedure. Doing so will cause the goal achievement on crime reduction to exceed the conservative allocation, and the goal achievement on fair procedure to exceed the liberal allocation.
4. The next step is to analyze ways of making the police or the courts more efficient on crime reduction, and ways of making the police or the courts more efficient on fair procedure.

increase in crime reduction. This is the same as saying that, if there is a 100 per cent increase in the amount of money spent on the police or a doubling of the police budget, there will be a 20 per cent increase in crime reduction.

The neutral allocation is $92 for the police ($P) and $108 for the courts ($J). The conservative allocation is $112 and $88, whereas the liberal allocation is $71 and $129. A relevant question is how one determines what difference it makes in terms of crime reduction and fair procedure which of those three allocations is used. There is no way of answering this question in terms of the lower number of rapes, murders or burglaries that would be obtained as a result of the different allocations. There is likewise no way of answering it in terms of the number of innocent people who would be saved from conviction or guilty people who would be rightfully convicted when they otherwise might be acquitted. However, it is not necessary to determine those specific facts in order to decide which allocation is best for crime reduction and which allocation is best for fair procedure. The conservative allocation is obviously best for crime reduction, because it gives the most money to the police and the police generate a higher marginal rate of return on crime reduction than the courts do, although with diminishing returns. The liberal allocation is best for fair procedure, because it gives the most money to the courts, and the courts generate a higher marginal rate of return on fair procedure than the police do, although again with diminishing returns.

The question that we want to answer as part of our concern for efficiency improvement is what we have to do to get even more crime reduction than the conservative allocation provides and to get even more fair procedure than the liberal allocation provides. In the first SOS allocation approach (Table 3.1), we concentrated on the alternatives or budget categories, and said we would have a super-optimum solution if we gave $113 to the police and $130 to the courts. We are now concentrating on the goals and saying that it may be possible to exceed both the conservative and liberal best expectations on their respective goals within the $200 budget or even at less than $200. The key place to look in Table 12.1 for what is needed in terms of the arithmetic is the cell marked X on crime reduction and the cell marked Y on fair procedure. These cells indicate the targets that we need to exceed when we emphasize goal achievement, as contrasted to the X and Y targets in Table 12.1 that relate to exceeding the dollar allocations.

The X figure is a relative crime reduction of 312. That is a purely relative number. It cannot be translated into any quantity of crimes. It is like the relative number that says the police are twice as effective on crime reduction as the courts are; that 2 versus 1 is compatible with an infinite set of pairs, all of which involve a 2 to 1 ratio. The 312 is arrived at by recognizing that we can obtain a relative crime reduction figure by adding the conservative $Police allocation of $112 to the conservative $Judges allocation of $88, when both dollar amounts are multiplied by the relation scores.

With an arithmetic calculator, one can calculate the relative goal achievement on crime reduction by simply using the formula $2 (\$P) + 1 (\$J)$, in which $P is the amount allocated to the police, and $J is the amount allocated to the courts. The 2 and the 1 are the relative scoring for $P and $J on crime reduction. Likewise, one can calculate the relative goal achievement on fair procedure by using the formula (1 ($P) + 3 ($J). It is similar to the crime reduction formula, except that it uses the 1 and 3 relation scores from the fair procedure column.

One could use more complicated formulas that would treat the relation scores as exponents, and then multiply the sub-parts, rather than add them. Doing so would not improve the analysis sufficiently to offset making it more complicated. The conservative allocation will still win on crime reduction, and the liberal allocation will win on fair procedure. The relative size of the gap in comparison with the neutral allocation will still be about the same. Most important, the percentage of improvement needed by police efficiency or judicial efficiency on crime reduction of fair procedure will still be about the same under either set of formulas. We are still considering diminishing returns in doing the allocating. The part/whole percentages (which are the essence of this allocation system) are based on the assumption of non-linear diminishing returns. That is why the allocations give something to each budget category, rather than give everything to the most effective budget category, as would be done under a linear allocation system.

With those two formulas of 2 ($P) + 1 ($J) and 1 ($P) + 3 ($J), one can see that a super-optimum solution focusing on conservative and liberal goal achievement needs to do better a 312 on crime reduction and simultaneously better than a 458 on fair procedure. As previously mentioned, the SOS allocation in this context must exceed those best expectations by improving on the relation scores of 2 or 1 for crime reduction, and 1 or 3 for fair procedure. As with the approach that increases the budget, this analysis does not yet give us a substantive answer (as of this point in the chapter). It does, however, give us a methodological orientation that helps in finding the substantive answer or answers.

Substantive Ideas

The next logical question is, what are the substantive answers to the problem of improving those relation scores or elasticity coefficients enough to exceed both the conservative best allocation and the liberal best allocation? As with ways of increasing the budget, there are many answers. The Policy/ Goal Percentaging (P/G%) decision-aiding software can be helpful in deciding among them or what combination is best. The alternatives in this context might include ideas that (1) increase police efficiency on crime reduction, (2) increase court efficiency on crime reduction, (3) increase police efficiency on fair procedure or separating the guilty from the innocent, and (4) increase court efficiency on fair procedure.

First, with regard to increasing the efficiency of the police on crime reduction, that means developing suggestions whereby, at a given dollar or even a reduced dollar, crime reduction can be increased so that the police are even more than twice as effective in reducing crime than the courts are. One proposal that might make sense is to make better use of modern technology which enables one police officer to survey a greater territory than maybe five or ten police officers formerly could.

Again it is often useful to reason by analogy from the private sector to the public sector and vice versa, or from one government agency to another. A good analog in this context is the way in which a large hotel patrols every floor simultaneously with one security guard. That is the equivalent of 20 streets if the hotel has 20 floors. The system which is in common use is to provide an out-in-the-open television camera on each floor that sees down the whole floor with or without the camera turning. A single security guard sits in the basement, for example, observing 20 television screens simultaneously. It is quite difficult to watch 20 television programs simultaneously, but it is easy to see in the middle of the night that on screen 12 somebody is crowbarring open a door or is assaulting someone who has just got out of the lift. Better yet, nobody crowbars any doors or assaults people because the television cameras have a deterrent effect by being out in the open. They are like police cars on the highway with their lights flashing, rather than hiding behind billboards.

The analog is to have a long-distance television camera on a high post or rooftop every mile or so on as many streets as one wants to have covered. The camera is equipped with a lens that makes it almost the equivalent of a U2 high-flying photography plane, although it does not have to be that powerful. What the long-distance camera sees is fed into the police station where anything suspicious becomes the basis for directing a police car to go to the scene when the car would otherwise not have known about the suspicious event. This does not violate civil liberties. These are not x-ray cameras that see into people's bedrooms. They are not able to see anything that a police officer could not see from a police car; the only difference is that they do the work of numerous police cars. They thereby increase crime reduction efficiency while saving substantial cost.

Second, with regard to increasing the efficiency of the courts on crime reduction, one suggestion that might be made is to have the courts pass longer sentences. In some other context, that might be a good suggestion. In the present context, we are talking about ways of making the legal system more efficient without spending more money, and possibly by spending less money. Longer sentences can be very expensive. One could argue that they are not expensive to a budget that only covers the police and the courts. Whatever budget covers the police and the courts probably also covers the prison system. Longer sentences are thus not so appropriate in this context because they would increase the $200 budget or increase the broader anti-crime budget which includes prisons.

We want a way that will enable the courts to reduce crime at no substantial extra cost beyond the $200 budget, and maybe even save money. One such suggestion relates to a frequent type of crime, the crime that is committed by a person who is released on bond pending trial. That kind of crime is especially undesirable because it breeds disrespect for the legal system on the part of both criminals and the citizens whose support the legal system needs. It breeds disrespect by criminals because they often suffer no additional negative sanctions as a result of committing a crime while released since their original crime may be more serious and that may be the only one for which they will be prosecuted and imprisoned. It also breeds disrespect because of the feeling on the part of criminals that they have go away with something extra when they have succeeded in committing a crime even while they are theoretically under court supervision. Crime-committing while released on bond causes ordinary citizens to feel the courts are being too soft on arrested people. The general public may not adequately understand the presumption of innocence, or they may have an awareness of it but feel that it is being abused by anyone who commits a crime while released on bond and by any judge who releases such a person. As a result, the general public becomes less supportive of other important safeguards for the innocent besides pre-trial release, such as right to counsel, right to trial by jury and right to appeal.

Crime-committing by people released on bond can be reduced by the judicial system adopting various inexpensive procedures such as the following.

1   Make use of the point systems that other courts have developed for screening arrested people to determine whether they are good risks to release. These point systems take into consideration whether a person is married and has a family, whether they have lived in the community for a while, and whether they have a job, as contrasted to more subjective and possibly discriminatory criteria that rely on the defendant's appearance. The experienced-based point systems are also better than rules of thumb that relate the size of the bond and thus the likelihood of being released almost entirely to the severity of the charges, rather than to indicators of the probability of crime-committing and escaping.

2   Have the released person report to the courthouse once a week or once every two weeks to sign in. This costs virtually nothing, but it is quite

meaningful in letting the defendant know that his whereabouts are of concern to the court.

3 When the time comes for the hearing or trial, remind the defendant by mail or phone to be in court. Doing this substantially reduces the crime of escaping. It also indicates to the defendant that the court is keeping track of him or her and thereby reduces other forms of crime-committing. It costs very little to send a postcard or to make a quick phone call, especially relative to the benefits received.

4 Occasionally go after and prosecute some of the people who escape instead of waiting for them to commit a crime while released. By waiting in this way the criminal justice system encourages such crimes. It also encourages escape because the chances of being prosecuted for escaping are so low if one has already been charged with a serious crime for which one was originally arrested and then another serious crime that is part of the second arrest.

5 Maybe most importantly, shorten the length of time between arrest and trial. If the time is short, there is not much opportunity to escape or commit a crime. For a few weeks after being arrested and released, a person may be on particularly good behavior for fear that the judge will be especially harsh if he or she is rearrested so soon after being released. There are many ways in which such delay can be reduced without the expensive hiring of more judges and without denying one a hearing or a day in court. A system of efficient sequencing of cases with priorities for criminal cases over other cases can be helpful.

Third, with regard to increasing the efficiency of the police on fair procedure or separating the innocent from the guilty, in most jurisdictions the police only have two choices when faced with someone who is misbehaving. They can either arrest the person or reprimand, warn and scare the person before letting them go. This may result in a lot of innocent people being arrested, as partly indicated by the fact that such a small percentage of arrested people are ever convicted of anything. What may be needed is a middle alternative between arresting and releasing, so that the police officer does not feel he or she has to arrest such a high percentage of those who are misbehaving. Some jurisdictions are now making frequent use of the summons to appear, which is like a traffic ticket. It can be used for misdemeanor cases where the police officer feels the individual is likely to show up in court and the crime is not very severe.

Some liberals may object to such a system on the grounds that the police officer cannot be trusted with that kind of discretion: the system will be abused. That might be quite true if we were talking about giving police the discretion to shoot people on the spot where they feel that the person would or should probably eventually get executed anyhow. In other words, we are not talking about increasing the police discretion to be more punitive toward the people they deal with, but rather increasing police discretion to be less punitive. At present, they do not have, in most jurisdictions, the choice of issuing a summons to appear. They must in effect arrest a lot of people to whom they might otherwise give summonses. They do have an incentive to give a summons because it saves them the time and trouble of having to bring someone to the police station to be officially booked. Such a system is wasteful of money and in terms of crime reduction, as it means police officers spending so much time bringing people to the police station for booking.

Whether a public policy is liberal or conservative sometimes cannot be determined very easily by just examining the policy out of context. One has to be aware of what the previous prevailing policy was. Thus passing a law providing capital punishment for all murderers is liberal if the previous law provided capital punishment for pickpockets and shoplifters, as English law did before the reforms around 1800. Capital punishment for all murderers would be rather conservative now in England, since that country has virtually abolished capital punishment, except for unusual situations such as murdering a guard while one is serving life in prison. Likewise, giving the police discretion to issue summonses would be conservative if they previously only had the authority to give warnings. It is liberal, though, if for all practical purposes they previously mainly had the authority to make arrests. More importantly, the summons to appear enables the police to separate the innocent from the guilty more efficiently by providing for a gray area, and it simultaneously saves the criminal justice system money in terms of police time and jail time.

Fourth, with regard to increasing the efficiency of the courts in separating the innocent from the guilty, perhaps the most inefficient aspect of the criminal court system relates to the way jury trials are conducted. By inefficiency, in this context, we are not talking about spending money on jurors, since they get very little, or delay due to jury trials, since they tend to occur only in trials that would take a long time anyhow. Instead, we are talking about inefficiency in separating the innocent from the guilty. More specifically, in recent years, a number of suggestions have been made for ways in which jurors could perform that separation function more accurately. One way is allowing them to take notes, since jurors may often make mistakes because they cannot remember all the testimony, instructions and other relevant inputs. In most states, they are prohibited from taking notes as a carry-over from medieval times, when few jurors could read or write, and it was felt that those few who could take notes would then dominate the juries. In the 1990s, most people can write and can therefore take notes. Changing the rules to allow for note taking would increase the efficiency of the courts in separating the innocent from the guilty.

One could go further and require videotaping of all jury trials or even bench trials. One purpose would be to save a lot of money that is otherwise spent on court reporters and transcribing. The more important purpose in this context is that the videotapes would be available to the jurors or to the judge in order to better review what was presented at the trial. The videotape preserves what one can hear and see even better than note taking. It enables controversies to be resolved accurately where one juror thinks a witness said the defendant was present at a certain time, and another juror thinks it was a different time. The idea of videotaping jury trials and bench trials is a good example of how to increase the efficiency of the courts on separating the innocent from the guilty without additional costs. It is also one of many examples that could be given of how to obtain greater benefits at lower costs (or at least not substantially higher costs) in the criminal justice system or in other public policy fields. What is needed is more of a mental orientation toward looking for procedures that increase benefits and decrease costs simultaneously. Likewise, we need a frame of mind that seeks solutions to choosing and allocating problems which can exceed the best expectations of both liberals and conservatives simultaneously.

PART III
MORE COMBINATIONS OF ALTERNATIVES

13 Big Benefits on One Side, Small Costs on the Other

SOS in the Migrant Labor Case

The illustrative example which follows involves a leading grower in the Peoria, Illinois, area (who employs approximately 70 farmworkers a year) being sued by the Migrant Legal Counsel which is a legal services agency that specializes in the legal problems of migratory farm workers in the United States. The workers, as a large class action, were suing to recover approximately $3 000 000 in wages that had been deducted to pay for loans, rents and other expenses without proper legal authorization. The money had actually been loaned or advanced to the workers, but the procedures designed to prevent illegal exploitation had not been followed. The growers insisted they should pay nothing, since the money they deducted was for loans actually made. The best expectations of the workers in terms of net gain would be rather low, since whatever they collected they would have to repay, with the possible exception of about $50 000 in compensation to some of the named plaintiffs who were fired or quit their jobs, unless unlikely punitive damages could be obtained. The best expectations of the growers would be to spend $50 000 or more going to trial and win with no liability. Thus the object for an SOS court mediator would be to come up with a settlement that would be worth more than $50 000 to the farm workers and would simultaneously save more than $50 000 in litigation costs for the growers.

What follows is a description of the super-optimum solution in this specific case. The essence of the solution is that the growers agree to deposit $100 000 to begin an employee credit union. Depositing $100 000 costs nothing to the growers since it is insured by the federal government and can be withdrawn after an agreed upon time period, possibly even with interest. The $100 000, however, serves as the basis for the beginning of an economic development fund which enables the workers, through real estate leveraging, to obtain a mortgage for building over $500 000 worth of housing for the workers as a big improvement on their current housing. The existence of the credit union also enables them to avoid having to get advances from the growers, which generates a lot of friction as a result of alleged favoritism in giving and collecting the advances. There are other elements involved, such as new grievance procedures and reports regarding compliance with other rules governing the working conditions of migratory labor. The essence of the solution, though, is that both sides come out ahead of their original best expectations.

Preliminary Elements

1   The establishment of a kind of bill of rights for the workers and an institutionalized grievance procedure with a grievance committee and provision for mediation and arbitration of grievances.
2   The submitting of a nine-part report by the lawyers for the growers as to exactly how the growers are now in compliance with the nine sets of violations listed on pages 7 and 8 of the complaint.
3   Compensation for the named plaintiffs for the special out-of-pocket expenses that they incurred. It is definitely desirable right from the start to have the clients and not just the lawyers present. Otherwise, for this kind of solution, the lawyers would logically say that they have to go back and consult with their clients.

The Main Element: The Economic Development Credit Union

1   It will be partly funded as a result of deposits made by the grower. The deposits need to be determined as to the amount, the length of time and the interest. The amount is about $100 000 for the first year, with subsequent amounts to be determined. The length of time that the money will be kept on deposit needs to be fairly substantial, maybe as long as five years, in order for the money to be available for loans. The interest rate would be the normal rate given under credit union provisions.
2   A board of directors will be established. It will include mainly representatives of the workers and a least one representative of the growers. There will also be expertise supplied by professors of business administration or economics.
3   The money should be used for loans especially for economic development projects, not consumer goods. These projects will include housing for workers, education programs and business investments that will benefit the community.
4   Help in establishing the credit union is available from the Illinois Finance Agency. Help is also available for training workers.

5   The Illinois Credit Union League puts out a useful set of materials.

Features that are Attractive to the Plaintiff

1   Being able to borrow money without begging for it or being discriminated against.
2   Being able to pay back the money under reasonable repayment arrangements, rather than in large amounts.
3   The economic development projects will benefit the workers in areas such as housing, education and business.
4   The solution can apply to former workers who are eligible to borrow.
5   It involves money from the defendant, possibly other farmers, and possibly grant money from the federal government, especially the Departments of Agriculture and Commerce.
6   A benefit to the workers is that, by the farm not going bankrupt, their jobs continue to be available.
7   The plaintiff's side also gets psychological rewards from having originated the idea rather than having it imposed from the outside.

Features that are Attractive to the Defendant

1   A release from being sued, which entails the risk of substantial judgment concerning deductions and possible penalties.
2   A release from expensive litigation costs.
3   Better relations with the workers.
4   Being relieved of being in the lending business, of giving advances to future workers and present workers.
5   The possibility of the prestige that goes with inviting other farmers to participate in this credit union in order to have a lending institution that would relieve them of lending burdens.
6   Avoidance of what could be a revenge-oriented lawsuit or one designed to make an example of the grower.
7   Avoidance of possible bankruptcy.
8   Some psychological rewards from having improved upon the idea, especially with the funds on deposits, the other farms and the federal grants.
9   Both sides may take considerable pleasure in the idea's being adopted elsewhere in the country, or even in other countries which have problems between farm workers and growers.

It is important to get people in a super-optimum solution frame of mind by emphasizing that we are looking for mutually beneficial solutions and not compromises and not determinations that one side is in the right and another is in the wrong.

SOS in the Product Liability Case

Computer-aided mediation can be considered to have officially begun in November 1987, because that is when the first court case was known to have been settled as a result of computer-aided mediation. The case involved an American insurance company suing a foreign electronics company in the Federal Court of the Northern District of Illinois. The purpose of this section is to describe briefly what the case involved, as a good example of computer-aided mediation in general.

Figure 13.1   Settle versus trial from the plaintiff's perspective

Notes:
1. The expected value of settling from the plaintiff's perspective is $1 099 000, as described in the text (first column).
2. The middle column shows that the plaintiff's first demand or best expectation was $700 000.
3. The expected value of going to trial from the plaintiff's perspective is only $290 000, as described in the text (third column).

A Case

The subject matter of the case was products liability. The names of the litigants are confidential. Some of the facts have been simplified or made more general for methodological purposes. The case can be used in particular to indicate how computer-aided mediation can facilitate super-optimum settlements, or at least ordinary settlements.

Figures 13.1 and 13.2 illustrate what is involved in a super-optimum settlement. The plaintiff demands $700 000 as a minimum in order to settle. The defendant offers $350 000 as a maximum in order to settle. The object of a super-optimum settlement is to provide the plaintiff with more than $700 000 while simultaneously not having the defendant pay more than $350 000. In other words, the problem is to find a number that is simultaneously bigger than $700 000 and smaller than $350 000, which are roughly the best expectations of the plaintiff and defendant, respectively.

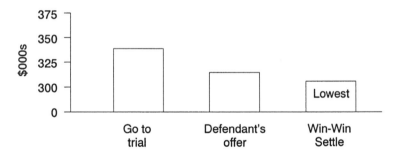

Figure 13.2   Settle versus trial from the defendant's perspective

Notes:
1. The defendant's first offer or best expectation is $350 000 (first column).
2. The expected value of going to trial from the defendant's perspective is $330 000 (second column).
3. The value of settling from the defendant's perspective is only $326 000 (third column).
4. Note that the settlement is lower and thus better than the defendant's best expectation from the defendant's perspective.
5. The $326 000 settlement figure could be substantially lower and still bring the plaintiff to a settlement in view of the big gap in Figure 13.1 between the settlement value and the trial value from the plaintiff's perspective.

A Settlement

Such a settlement can be arrived at by considering additional settlement criteria beyond the exchange of money. In almost every damages case, the defendant is an insurance company, a manufacturer, a transport company or some other kind of company that can offer something of a considerable value to the plaintiff, but having relatively low cost to the defendant. In this case, it was possible for the defendant to consider offering electronic equipment, insurance claims and insurance annuities to the plaintiffs and their insurance companies. This combination of equipment, claims and annuities had an estimated cost value of only $326 000 to the defendants, as indicated by Figure 13.2. However, it had an estimated purchase value of $1 099 000 to the plaintiffs.

Notes

On big benefits for one side and low costs for the other as a method of arriving at super-optimum solutions, see the alternative dispute resolution literature that discusses each side giving on issues that are not so important to it and receiving on other issues that are important to it. See, for example, Ury *et al.* (1988), Susskind and Cruikshank (1987), Nagel and Mills (1990) and Nagel and Mills (1991).

On mediation as a special form of dispute resolution in contrast to win–lose procedures, see Kressel and Pruitt (1989), Folbert and Taylor (1984) and Moore (1986). Win–win solutions can be arrived at without third-party mediation if one or more of the negotiators successfully pursues a win–win or super-optimum solution, as described in Fisher and Ury (1981) and Jandt (1985).

14   Combining Alternatives

Higher Education

Almost every university in the United States is an example of public and private mixed – at least, every so-called 'private university' is. About half of their funds come from alumni and student tuition and half from government grants. It is about the same with so-called 'state universities' that are now more dependent than they have been in the past on alumni and student tuition. The difference between public colleges and private colleges is lessening in the United States. They are all a mixture of private funds (from students and alumni) and public funds (from either direct state tax dollars or lots of indirect federal aid to education). This includes, in particular, grant money from government agencies for research, although the more research-oriented universities get more research grant money. Smaller colleges get fewer big grants, but the percentages of their total annual budget may consist of a sizable percentage of grant money, even though it does not amount to a lot of money compared to that of the large state universities.

This is an example of the kind of SOS that involves combining liberal and conservative alternatives where they are not mutually exclusive. The liberals want public schools and public universities supported by tax money and open to the general public. The conservatives want private elitist schools that are more exclusive. There are state universities that will only admit the top 10 per cent of their classes, being more snobbish than most second-rate Ivy League schools, and certainly more so than Lake Forest College, which is considered a snobbish school in Illinois but will admit people of lower qualifications than the University of Illinois. American state universities, like Berkeley, Michigan and Wisconsin, are now the snobbiest places in the country, as compared to the small totally private liberal arts colleges that have relatively little intellectual prestige. On the other hand, those small liberal arts colleges that have lost their private character are highly dependent on federal funds. Thus American higher education is achieving the goals of conservatives by providing for aristocratic schools that are the envy of the world, while at the same time achieving the liberal goal of making them open to the public, as opposed to being open only to the children of aristocrats or people with the 'right' ethnic backgrounds. They also follow the liberal goal of making them oriented toward the public interest, partly because they receive so much government money for which they are supposed to do worthwhile things.

One can also say that American higher education is an SOS, not just because it simultaneously satisfies liberal and conservative goals, but because it is viewed as superior to the higher education systems of any other country. One indication of this is that a high percentage of the top Chinese communist government leadership is now sending their children to American schools, even though the United States ideologically is at one end of a continuum and communist China is at the other. What this shows is that they think or recognize that American schools (notwithstanding that they may turn their children against their Communist Party parents) are worth sending their children to so they can become better engineers, scientists, business people and so on. It is indeed a compliment to the system when its enemies want to go there, or especially when its enemies want their children to go there, even though they know doing so may turn their children against them.

The higher education area is an example where public money and private money coexist very comfortably. One could say that defense contracting is another example (but not one to be especially proud of) where the government pours in a lot of money and private stockholders take it home with them. The defense contracting industry is not an example of efficient economic organization. It is an example of a highly subsidized industry that might collapse totally if it had to sell only to the private market.

Under the higher education example (Table 14.1), the alternatives are as follows.

1   Private-sector or, better put, private schools. This is the conservative solution. It was previously the system in England and much of western Europe.
2   State-owned colleges and universities. This is the liberal solution. All are state-owned at the university level in China, Russia and other communist countries, with minor exceptions. All the major universities in the United States between California and the east coast are also state-owned. There is no prominent major university, with the exception of Northwestern and the University of Chicago, between the Ivy League and Stanford. Once one gets west of Harvard, Yale, Princeton or the University of Pennsylvania, which is still in theory private, there are few major private universities. On the west coast, Stanford is the only exception. There is no world-class university on the west coast other than Stanford that is private.

Table 14.1 Combining public and private higher education

Criteria / Alternatives	L Goal Highly educated	L Goal Produce new knowledge	C Goal Lower tax cost	L Goal Equity	N Total (neutral weights)	L Total (liberal weights)	C Total (conservative weights)
C Alternative Private schools	2	2	4	1	18	19	17*
L Alternative State-owned schools	4	4	1	4	26	37*	15
N Alternative Some private & some state	3	3	2.5	3	23	29.5	16.5
SOS Alternative Public money to private/private money to public	5	5	2	5	34	47**	21**

197

3   The compromise position would be simply to have some private schools and some state-owned schools. That was the case in the late 1800s and early 1900s, when the United States did not have much of a university system.
4   The SOS (although still subject to improvement) is the kind of mix we have now, which involves every major private school receiving lots of tax money. Harvard University is considered to be the leading private university in the United States. It probably gets more federal money than any other public school in the United States, with the possible exception of Michigan, Illinois, Berkeley and a couple of others. The federal money goes where the quality professors are. It has nothing to do with whether the school is public or private.

Likewise, the University of Illinois would collapse if it were not for private alumni contributions and student tuition, including high student tuition that Abraham Lincoln would not have condoned when he set up the land grant college system. It is not oppressive, though, because students who cannot afford it can get financial aid. The SOS is thus public money to private schools and private money to public schools, providing a great mix of resources that makes the American higher education the envy of all countries. Also there is a mix in the sense of democratic admissions that are not based on race, class or nepotism, with at the same time lots of meritocracy elitism that would appeal to the most elitist British educator. The top students at Berkeley, for instance, probably score higher on entrance exams and other exams than the top students at Oxford and Cambridge do. The professors at Berkeley also score higher in contributing to the world's knowledge than the professors at Oxford and Cambridge do.

The goals are (1) to have a highly educated population, (2) to have universities that produce new knowledge, (3) to be relatively inexpensive in terms of burden on the students and burden on the taxpayer, and (4) the equity criterion of being available to everybody regardless of demographic background. These goals thus comprise two measures of effectiveness, one of efficiency and one of equity.

Legal Services for the Poor

The purpose of this section is to describe how a new microcomputer program, called Policy/Goal Percentaging (abbreviated P/G%), can be used to aid in dispute resolution. In that regard, the essence of the program is to be able to show disputants quickly the effects of alternative proposals on their respective criteria. Doing so can facilitate arriving at dispute-resolving compromises, including optimizing compromises where all the disputants come out ahead of their original maximum positions.

The program is called Policy/Goal Percentaging because it relates policies (or alternatives) to goals (or criteria), and it often uses part/whole percentaging to deal with the occurrence where the goals may be measured on different dimensions. The program is designed to process a set of (1) goals to be achieved, (2) alternatives for achieving them, and (3) relations between goals and alternatives in order to choose the best alternative or combination for maximizing benefits minus costs of the disputants or other users. P/G% is a form of expert systems software, since it seeks to capture the essence of what good decision makers do implicitly in making decisions. That includes what good mediators do in mediating decisions. P/G% is also a form of multi-criteria decision making (MCDM), since it tends to work with multiple goals. Doing so facilitates finding satisfying compromises because concessions can be made to each side on different goals. An MCDM perspective also facilitates bringing in new goals and new alternatives on which both sides might be able to reach agreement.

The kind of dispute resolution with which this chapter is especially concerned is with regard to disputes over public policies that ought to be adopted in dealing with various social problems. In such circumstances, the disputants are likely to be liberal and conservative policy makers, generally serving in a legislative body. They could also be associated with administrative agencies, courts, interest groups or political parties. Examples could be taken from the public policy fields that relate to environmental protection, poverty, criminal justice and other social problems.

A good example of the microcomputer program in action is applying it to the highly emotional controversy of how to provide legal services for the poor. This example can be helpful in understanding (1) how to determine initial alternatives, criteria and relations, (2) how to attempt to resolve deadlocks by weighting the criteria and averaging the alternatives, (3) how to determine what it would take to convince the other side, (4) how to resolve deadlocks by adding an alternative, (5) the concept of optimizing compromise as a goal to seek in dispute resolution, and (6) various other means for achieving optimizing compromises. All the examples should be viewed in terms of the general ideas which they illustrate and which are applicable to a wide variety of dispute resolutions in public policy evaluation.

At the outset one should clarify that the concept of dispute requires persons, groups, ideologies or other entities to be in conflict over how a matter should be resolved. A problem is not necessarily a dispute, since it may only involve one person or entity trying to decide what to do. The major processes whereby disputes are resolved are through forms of negotiation, mediation, arbitration or adjudication. In negotiation, the two or more sides interact to try to come to an agreement, which may be considered mutually desirable or may be forced by one party on the other through threats of negative sanctions. In mediation, a non-disputant tries to bring or force the disputants to reach an agreement. If the non-disputants have the power to impose a solution on the parties, then they are generally referred to as arbitrators, where chosen by the parties, or as judges, where the non-disputants are imposed on the parties. Mediators generally seek solutions that will be considered mutually satisfying by the parties. Arbitrators and judges seek solutions that are considered correct in accordance with a body of past practice, common sense or rules, and the solutions may not be mutually satisfying. Arbitrators, as compared to judges, tend to place more emphasis on past custom and less on past recorded cases. They also place more emphasis on uncodified common sense and less emphasis on codified rules.

The P/G% program can facilitate either individual problem solving or dispute resolution. It can facilitate dispute resolution through negotiation, mediation, arbitration or adjudication. The emphasis in this chapter is on dispute resolution through microcomputer-facilitated negotiation and mediation. Other materials deal with microcomputer-facilitated arbitration and adjudication.

This section is organized in terms of the following ideas:

1   In resolving disputes through the multi-criteria decision making of the P/G% program, one needs
    (a)   to indicate the alternatives to choose among,
    (b)   to indicate the criteria for judging the alternatives,
    (c)   to indicate how the alternative relate to the criteria,
    (d)   to bear in mind that all three elements may be subject to change.
2   If clarifying the alternatives, criteria and relations results in a deadlock or continued dispute, then MCDM and P/G% may be able to resolve the dispute through the following means:
    (a)   averaging the alternatives with or without weighting the criteria,
    (b)   determining what it would take to convince the other side,
    (c)   adding a new alternative.
3   The idea of an optimizing compromise or a win-plus solution, where each side comes out ahead of its original best expectations can be illustrated by:
    (a)   the dispute over how to provide legal service to the poor,
    (b)   criminal and civil litigation,
    (c)   other legal policy controversies such as sentencing, pre-trial release and housing for the poor,
    (d)   legislative redistricting.

4 Microcomputer-based procedures for resolving disputes can be generalized to cover:
   (a) changing the alternatives,
   (b) changing the criteria,
   (c) changing the relations,
   (d) using P/G% to decide among the methods for resolving disputes.

The Alternatives

The basic alternatives in the public policy dispute over how to provide legal
services to the poor are a volunteer system versus salaried government
lawyers. The government administration has repeatedly proposed that legal
services for the poor should be provided by volunteer lawyers with no
federal appropriation. Congress has repeatedly voted in favor of salaried
government lawyers working for the Legal Services Corporation. An interesting aspect of this dispute is that the disputants generally agree on (1) the
conflicting alternatives, (2) the basic criteria for determining the best alternative, and (3) how the alternatives score on each criterion. Yet they disagree on which alternative is best, largely because they disagree on the
relative importance of the various criteria. Until recently, they have not
adequately explored dispute-resolving alternatives.

    There are other ways of providing legal services to the poor besides
salaried government lawyers or volunteer attorneys. Those two general ways
are, however, the leading contenders in the dispute between the White
House and Congress over how to provide legal services to the poor. Another
approach that at one time was considered an important third alternative is a
Judicare system, which involves poor people going to whatever lawyers will
take their cases, and the government then paying the expenses incurred,
possibly in accordance with a fee schedule. This is analogous to the Medicare system for providing medical services to the poor. It has been largely
rejected by conservatives as too expensive, and by liberals as only covering
routine case handling, with no organized law reform elements.

    Each of the basic alternatives has a number of variations. The volunteer
system, for example, could involve (1) mandatory volunteering in order to
have one's license renewed, although mandatory volunteering sounds contradictory; (2) volunteering with substantial federal funds to coordinate and
train the volunteers; and (3) volunteering to handle cases for a fee, the way
federal criminal cases are handled for indigent defendants, although paid
volunteers also sounds contradictory. The salaried government program has
such variations as (1) a program that is restricted to routine cases with no
suing of government officials, no law reform and no research back-up
agencies; (2) a program that is subject to being vetoed by local politicians

and bar officials, which may thereby limit its independence, (3) a circuit-riding program designed to cover a wide territory, with lawyers being present in different places on different days, (4) a program that combines civil and criminal cases, and (5) a program that emphasizes law reform, with routine cases being handled through a Judicare system. The Judicare system has such variations as (1) not allowing the clients to go to any lawyer, but just to certain firms that have a contract with the federal government to represent poor people, (2) a reimbursement system without fee control or with it, and (3) private sector lawyers only for certain types of cases, only in desolate geographical areas, or with other restrictions.

In this section, partly as a form of shorthand, the position which favors a system of volunteer attorneys is often referred to as the conservative position. The position which favors a system of salaried government attorneys is often referred to as the liberal position. The conservative position has internal diversity, since volunteer systems can range from (1) traditional legal aid with no government funding or incentives to participate to (2) heavily funded volunteer systems with attractive compensation for volunteering or sanctions for not volunteering. The conservative position, however, mainly refers to traditional legal aid. Likewise, the liberal position has internal diversity, since salaried government attorneys can range from (1) attorneys who are restricted to doing only routine civil cases with no research back-up, appellate capacity, legislative drafting or testifying, group representation, or government defendants to (2) attorneys who are authorized to engage in all these activities. The liberal position, however, mainly includes as many of these activities as can be authorized.

The Criteria

The basic criteria are four in number.

1   Inexpensiveness: both liberals and conservatives favor inexpensiveness or efficiency in the sense that, if quality legal services can be provided for 100 million, then 150 million should not be spent. Liberals and conservatives may disagree as to what should be done with the extra 50 million. Liberals might favor urban programs, and conservatives might favor defense programs. Neither side, however, would favor spending 150 million for what could be obtained for only 100 million.

2   Accessibility: the program should be accessible and visible to poor people. If one is sincerely interested in having a legal services program for the poor, it should be a program that will be used and not one that is relatively unknown and/or especially difficult to make use of.

3   Political feasibility: the program should be capable of (a) getting through

Congress and (b) not being vetoed by the president or capable of surviving a veto through a two-thirds congressional vote.

4 Competency: the attorneys in the program should be reasonably competent. They should be willing and able to go to court if necessary to provide adequate representation to their clients.

Other criteria could be added, but they are not likely to resolve the dispute by enabling either alternative to become a clear winner. For example, liberals might include accountability to poor clients and to representatives of the poor on the governing boards of the legal services agencies. On the other hand, conservatives might include the importance of accountability to the bar and local government officials. These two criteria tend to offset each other since accountability to the poor tends to favor salaried government lawyers, whereas accountability to the bar and city hall tends to favor a volunteer system, especially one run by local bar associations.

One might raise the question of how a problem is dealt with if some of the disputants do not accept the basic criteria as being relevant criteria. There are, for example, some people who are so opposed to providing legal services to the poor as an inherently trouble-making activity that the less accessible the program is and the more incompetent the attorneys are, the more they might like the program. Such people are probably too small a segment of the opposition to salaried government lawyers to be given substantial consideration. Republican presidents, like Nixon, Reagan and Bush have indicated that they are not opposed to the idea of legal services for the poor, including accessible competent legal services, but only to legal services that are provided through salaried government lawyers.

If one has a dispute in which two or more sides differ, not just in the weight they give to the criteria, but also on what criteria they use, this creates no special problems for multi-criteria decision making. It just means that, in analyzing how each offer and counter-offer does in light of the conservative, liberal or other criteria, one uses different criteria. Table 14.2, for example, would thus show different criteria in B for conservatives than the criteria shown in C for liberals. The object is still the same, namely to find an alternative that both sides will consider to have a high overall score in light of their respective criteria, regardless of what those criteria are.

The Relations

Table 14.2(A) shows how the two alternatives score on the four criteria. Each criterion involves a simple 1–2 scale, where 1 means relatively low, and 2 means relatively high. The scoring of the relations between the alternative and the criteria are as follows.

Table 14.2   Volunteer versus salaried legal services

	Inexpensive	Accessible	Polit. Feas.	Competency
A With unweighted criteria				
Volunteer	2.00	1.00	2.00	1.00
Salaried	1.00	2.00	1.00	2.00
B With conservative-weighted criteria				
Volunteer	4.00	1.00	4.00	1.00
Salaried	2.00	2.00	2.00	2.00
C With liberal weighted criteria				
Volunteer	2.00	2.00	2.00	2.00
Salaried	1.00	4.00	1.00	4.00

1   Inexpensiveness: the volunteer system is clearly less expensive than a system of salaried government lawyers.

2   Accessibility: the salaried government lawyer in the context of the Legal Services Corporation is especially accessible by way of storefront neighborhood law offices. Volunteer legal aid has traditionally been relatively inaccessible because of the difficult procedures for contacting the volunteer attorneys. For example, in Champaign County, before the Legal Services Corporation (LSC), poor people would (a) phone the United Fund and (b) be referred to the office of the Bar Association, where they would (c) be referred to the chairperson of the Legal Aid Committee who would (d) refer them to a member of the Committee who might then be unavailable or who would (e) refer them to law students in their office. The system processed about 50 cases a year before LSC, which was almost immediately processing about 100 cases a week as a result largely of increased visibility and accessibility.

3   Political feasibility: the volunteer system is more politically feasible in the sense that no one in Congress is likely to object to attorneys being willing to volunteer to help poor people. On the other hand, there are objections to paying government salaries to such attorneys, especially if they spend a substantial amount of time developing test cases and new legal policies concerning the legal rights of the poor against landlords, merchants, employers and government officials, as contrasted to more routine family-oriented legal aid matters.

4   Competency: the salaried system tends to generate more competent

attorneys who work full-time in the field of poverty law. The volunteer system tends to bring out new attorneys who are looking for experience, or older attorneys who are trying to be helpful, but who are not so knowledgeable about poverty law matters.

One might object to using a scale of relatively low and relatively high for measuring how the alternatives score on the criteria. Such a scale has the advantage of simplicity for better understanding the dispute resolution methodology. There is no need to use more complex measurement if simple measurement will achieve the same bottom-line results. The analysis of the data will make clear that there would still be a virtual deadlock between conservatives and liberals on the volunteer system versus the salaried government system. This is so even if (1) expensiveness were measured in exact dollars; (2) accessibility were measured in average miles from the homes of the poor population to participating law offices, or were measured in terms of awareness scores on the part of the potential clients; (3) political feasibility were measured in terms of the percentage of House or Senate members who would be likely to vote for allowing the alternative to exist; and (4) competency were measured by average Law School Admission Test (LSAT) scores, grade point averages, bar exam scores, years of relevant experience, aggressiveness or other measures of attorney competence in this context. The results would still be that those with conservative values or weights would support the volunteer system, because it would score more highly on inexpensiveness and political feasibility. Likewise, those with liberal values or weights would still support the salaried government system because it would score more highly on accessibility and competency. These results go back to the definition and empirical nature of volunteer attorneys and government salaried attorneys.

Weighting the Criteria and Averaging the Alternatives

Table 14.2(A) shows that, with those four reasonable criteria and with the reasonable scoring of the alternatives on them, there is a deadlock tie of 6 points apiece for each alternative. At first glance, one might think the tie could be broken and the dispute resolved by recognizing that the criteria should not all receive equal weight. Table 14.2(B) uses conservative weights. Such weights put relatively more emphasis on inexpensiveness and political feasibility. Doing so means doubling the scores on those two criteria to show that they have more importance than accessibility and competency. Doing so in Table 14.2(B) shows that the volunteer system receives 10 points and the salaried system receives only 8 points from a conservative perspective.

Table 14.2(C) uses liberal weights. Such weights put relatively more emphasis on accessibility and competency. Doing so means doubling the score on those two criteria to show that they are more important than inexpensiveness and political feasibility. Table 14.2(C) shows that the volunteer system receives only 8 points and the salaried system receives 10 points from a liberal perspective. If we average the conservative 10 and the liberal 8 for the volunteer system, we obtain 9. Likewise, if we average the conservative 8 and the liberal 10 for the salaried system, we also obtain 9.

Thus weighting the criteria does not resolve the deadlock here. It might have do so if liberals were to like the salaried system more than conservatives like the volunteer system, or vice versa, assuming liberals and conservatives have an equal say in this controversy. In this situation, however, their value weights are diametrically opposed in both direction and magnitude.

The results of the weighting here merely tell us that, if one has conservative values, one is likely to prefer the volunteer over the salaried system, and that, if one has liberal values, one is likely to prefer salaried over volunteer lawyers for providing legal services to the poor. One might, therefore, conclude that systematic policy analysis is a sham, especially with microcomputers, because it merely tells us that the results depend on one's values. This legal services dispute, however, turns out to be one of the real success stories of systematic policy analysis, as we will shortly see.

Determining What it Would Take to Convince the Other Side

Another way of sometimes resolving such disputes, besides the system of weighting and averaging, is to have one side convince the other side to adopt the other position. The P/G% software is especially helpful in showing what changes are needed in the scoring of the relations or the weighting of the goals in order to move the liberals to adopt the volunteer system or the conservatives to adopt the salaried system.

Table 14.3(A) shows what it would take to bring the salaried system up to the level of the volunteer system, given the conservative values. Table 14.2(B) previously showed the salaried system receives a score of 8. Thus there is a two-point gap that the liberals need to make up in order to convince the conservatives that the salaried system is as good as the volunteer system. Table 14.3A shows 12 ways that the gap could theoretically be made up. Reading down the columns, those ways are as follows. First, on *inexpensiveness*, (a) the volunteer system receives a 'no', (b) the salaried system receives a 'yes', (c) inexpensiveness receives a weight of zero. Any one of these three changes would generate a tie by bringing the volunteer system from a score of 10 down to an 8 (possibility a), by

Table 14.3 What it would take to convince the other side

A Bringing the salaried system up to the level of the volunteer system, given conservative values

	Inexpensive	Accessible	Polit. Feas.	Competency
Volunteer	1.00	-1.00	1.00	-1.00
Salaried	3.00	4.00	2.00	4.00
Weight	-0.000	3.000	-0.000	3.000

B Bringing the volunteer system up to the level of the salaried system, given liberal values

	Inexpensive	Accessible	Polit. Feas.	Competency
Volunteer	4.00	2.00	4.00	2.00
Salaried	-1.00	1.00	-1.00	1.00
Weight	3.000	0.000	3.000	0.000

bringing the salaried system from a score of 8 up to a 10 (possibility b), or by bringing both down to a score of 6 (possibility c). All three possibilities, however, are quite unrealistic. Conservatives are not going to perceive that the volunteer system is really an expensive system or that the salaried system is an inexpensive one, or that inexpensiveness is of no importance.

Second, on *accessibility*, (a) the volunteer system receives a -1, but that is impossible since the scale only goes as low as 1 and as high as 2, (b) the salaried system receives a 4 on accessibility, which is also impossible; (c) accessibility receives a weight of 3. That is not impossible. It is, however, unlikely that accessibility would receive more weight than inexpensiveness and political feasibility in the values of conservatives.

Third, on *political feasibility*, there are three possibilities: the same unrealistic possibilities that were previously discussed under inexpensiveness.

Finally, on *competency*, there are the same impossible and unlikely possibilities discussed under accessibility.

Table 14.3(B) shows what it would take to bring the volunteer system up to the level of the salaried system, given liberal values. Table 14.2(C) previously showed that, with the liberal weights, the salaried system receives a score of 10 and the volunteer system receives a score of 8. Thus there is a two-point gap that the conservatives need to make up in order to convince the liberals that the volunteer system is as good as the salaried system. Table 14.3(A) shows 12 ways that the gap could theoretically be made up. Reading down the columns, these ways are as follows.

1   Inexpensiveness
   (a)   The volunteer system receives a 4; that, however, is beyond the 1–2 scale.
   (b)   The salaried system receives a–1; that, however, is also beyond the 1–2 scale.
   (c)   Inexpensiveness receives a weight of 3. However, it is unlikely that inexpensiveness will receive more weight than accessibility or competency in the values of liberals.
2   Accessibility
   (a)   The volunteer system receives a 2; liberals, however, are not going to perceive that the volunteer system scores as high as possible on accessibility.
   (b)   The salaried system receives a 1; liberals, however, are not going to perceive that the salaried system scores as low as possible on accessibility.
   (c)   Accessibility receives a weight of zero, but liberals are not going to agree that accessibility is of no importance.
3   Political feasibility. There are three possibilities here: the same impossible and unlikely possibilities discussed under inexpensiveness.
4   Competency. There are also three possibilities here: the same unrealistic possibilities discussed under accessibility.

Thus the probability seems low that liberals could convince conservatives to accept salaried legal services, or that conservatives could convince liberals to accept a volunteer system. The kind of sensitivity analysis shown in Table 14.3, however, is often helpful in indicating to disputants what they should emphasize in order to convince the other side. This is a sensitivity analysis in the sense that it shows how sensitive the conclusion is to various changes in the weights of the criteria and the relations between alternatives and goals. It just so happens that, in this situation, all of the threshold or break-even values shown in Table 14.3 are either conceptually impossible to obtain or empirically unrealistic. Thus the deadlock is not likely to be resolved by one side convincing the other.

Resolving Deadlocks by Adding an Alternative

A third alternative that has been discussed in the past is a Judicare system analogous to Medicare or Medicaid whereby poor people would go to existing private sector lawyers who would then be compensated by the federal government. That alternative, however, is not a compromise in the sense of being a fallback second choice to the volunteer system for conservatives, or to the salaried system for liberals. Instead, it is probably a third choice for both sides. Conservatives now reject the Judicare system because it is substantially more expensive than salaried legal services. The LSC program tends to pay lawyers an annual salary of about $25 000 for which they process numerous cases, including maybe as many as 300 divorce cases a year. If each case were handled by a private sector lawyer at approximately $300 apiece, that would be $90 000, just for divorce cases. Liberals reject the Judicare system because it tends to handle only routine cases, such as family law cases. Salaried legal services attorneys tend to look for precedent-setting test cases that will have high leverage in developing the legal rights of the poor.

Looking back at Table 14.2(A) stimulates ideas as to what a deadlock-resolving alternative might involve. It would probably have to build on the existing salaried LSC, since it is already in place, as contrasted to starting from scratch. Whatever is built on the existing LSC program should seek to reduce the expensiveness of salaried government lawyers, and improve upon their political feasibility, since those are the two criteria on which salaried attorneys admittedly do not do so well. Likewise, whatever is built on the existing LSC program should seek to improve upon the lack of accessibility of volunteer attorneys and their relative lack of competency, since those are the two criteria on which volunteer attorneys admittedly do not do so well.

In 1982, Professor Gerald Caplan of George Washington University was appointed Acting Director of the Legal Services Corporation. He was an excellent compromise, for a number of reasons. He could appeal to liberals, being one of the founders of the original Legal Services Program of the Office of Economic Opportunity under Lyndon Johnson, and being a professor with credentials in both law and social science. He could appeal to conservatives, having been a leader in developing anti-crime policy in the Law Enforcement Assistance Administration under Richard Nixon and Gerald Ford. He is an arch-conservative, but in a libertarian sense, who believes the government should get off the backs of poor people as well as business people. He also made clear that he would only be a temporary acting director just long enough to try to salvage what was becoming a shambles at LSC owing to the inability of the White House and Congress to resolve their dispute.

Partly following the reasoning suggested by the above analysis of Table 14.2, Gerald Caplan proposed to require that all legal services agencies spend 10 per cent of their budgets for the development of a meaningful volunteer system. The money would be used mainly for two purposes. The first purpose would be to make volunteers more accessible. A survey should be made in each community of all the attorneys to determine (1) which ones are willing to do some volunteer work, (2) what their specialties are, and (3) what days and times they are available. The second step involves maintaining a well-organized cardfile of relevant information on volunteers. Appointments can then be scheduled for them with legal services clients who have problems that relate to their specialties at the regular legal services agency office. The volunteers are therefore just as accessible to the clients as the regular attorneys. The clients are unable to tell the difference. Also the volunteer attorneys do not suffer the frustration of having no clients, irrelevant clients or long waiting periods with nothing to do.

The second purpose of the 10 per cent funding would be to provide training to improve the competency of the volunteers. These well coordinated volunteers, however, would not need so much training since they would be handling cases in fields with which they are already familiar, rather than across-the-board poverty law. Nevertheless, they could benefit from materials and workshops that relate their fields to the problems of poor people. Thus a real estate lawyer may not be completely aware of special statutes and precedents that relate to poverty tenants, and a lawyer who is an expert on the Commercial Code may not be completely aware of procedures that relate to poverty consumers. The volunteers could also benefit from training that relates their fields to the broader context of poverty law.

Even if this works, one might argue that it still shows how arbitrary public policy is, since the 10 per cent figure seems to have been pulled out of the air, but, to the contrary, the 10 per cent represents approximately the maximum amount that could possibly be spent on coordinating the accessibility and improving the competency of the volunteer attorneys. The Legal Services Program is funded at approximately $300 million a year, so 10 per cent represents $30 million. For $30 million, one can buy all the coordinating surveys, cardfiles, training manuals and workshops that it is possible to buy. A stubborn skeptic might argue that the $30 million taken away from other LSC activities may mean laying off some regular LSC lawyers or other personnel. That is true, but if spending $30 million brings in $60 million worth of accessible and competent volunteer attorneys, the investment will have been well worth it.

Optimizing Compromises or the SOS Solution

Table 14.2 shows how the 10 per cent compromise compares with the other two alternatives. Table 14.3 is the same as Table 14.2 since the scoring of the volunteer and salaried systems has not changed. On all four criteria, the compromise system does well. On *inexpensiveness*, the compromise system is not so inexpensive as a volunteer system. It is, however, less expensive than a salaried system in two ways. First, it reduces the appropriation for the purely salaried system by 10 per cent. Second, and more important, the 10 per cent compromise produces a better benefit/cost ratio. The cost can be considered the same, at $300 million. If, however, the amount of valuable attorney labor goes up as a result of adding the volunteer component, the total system is more economic and is less expensive for the value received. Therefore we score the 10 per cent compromise at 1.5 on inexpensiveness, between the 2 for the volunteer system and the 1 for the salaried system.

As regards *accessibility*, there is no reduction in accessibility as a result of adding volunteers who meet poor clients during regular hours at the regular offices of the legal services agency. They are thus just as accessible to the clients as the regular attorneys, as previously mentioned.

Political feasibility tends to be a matter of either having it or not having it, and not so much a matter of degrees. The salaried government attorney system lacks political feasibility in the sense that (1) it is strongly opposed by the White House, (2) it has substantial difficulty getting through both houses of Congress without considerable anguish and friction, and (3) it runs into administrative problems due to the White House hostility. The 10 per cent compromise system has, however, manifested its political feasibility by not being so strongly opposed by the White House, by getting through Congress more easily and by having less administrative sabotage and turmoil.

On *competency*, adding the volunteer component does not substantially lower the competency if the volunteers work primarily in their specialties and receive appropriate training. They may sometimes even add useful specialized knowledge to the regular attorneys who are more generalists in poverty law.

Given the scores on the compromise row of Table 14.2, the 10 per cent compromise receives a total score of 7.5 as compared to the 6 of the volunteer system and the 6 of the salaried system. One might, however, question the value of such a compromise by referring to it as everybody's second choice when the conservative and liberal values are taken into consideration, as is so often the case with compromises.

Table 14.3 shows how the 10 per cent compromise scores on the four criteria, given the conservative weights which emphasize inexpensiveness and political feasibility. Table 14.3 differs from Table 14.2 in that the raw scores are doubled on the inexpensiveness column and on the political feasibility column. The result is that the volunteer system receives a score of 10 and the salaried system receives a score of 8, as mentioned in discussing Table 14.2. Note, however, that the compromise alternative receives a total score of 11, which is even higher than the previous first choice using conservative values.

Table 14.4 shows how the 10 per cent compromise scores on the four criteria, given the liberal weights which emphasize accessibility and competence. Table 14.4 differs from Table 14.2 in that the raw scores are doubled

Table 14.4   An example of computer-aided mediation

		Inexpensiveness	Accessibility	Political feasibility	Competence
A	With unweighted criteria				
	Volunteer	2.00	1.00	2.00	1.00
	Salaried	1.00	2.00	1.00	2.00
	Compromise	1.50	2.00	2.00	2.00
B	With conservative values				
	Volunteer	4.00	1.00	4.00	1.00
	Salaried	2.00	2.00	2.00	2.00
	Compromise	3.00	2.00	4.00	2.00
C	With liberal values				
	Volunteer	2.00	2.00	2.00	2.00
	Salaried	1.00	4.00	1.00	4.00
	Compromise	1.50	4.00	2.00	2.00

Notes:
1. The alternative ways of providing legal counsel to the poor include:
   (1)   Volunteer attorneys, favored by the White House
   (2)   Salaried government attorneys, favored by the Congress
   (3)   A compromise that involves continuing the salaried system, but requiring that 10 per cent of its funding go to making volunteers more accessible and competent.
2. The criteria are inexpensiveness, accessibility, political feasibility, and competence. Each alternative is scored on each criterion on a 1–2 scale.
3. Conservatives values involve giving a weight of 2 to inexpensiveness and political feasibility when the other criteria receive a weight of 1. Liberal values involve giving a weight of 2 to accessibility and competence when the other criteria receive a weight of 1.
4. With conservative values, the volunteer system wins over the salaried system 10 points to 8. The compromise is an overall winner with 11½ points.
5. With liberal values, the salaried system wins over the volunteers system 10 points to 8. The compromise is an overall winner with 11½ points.
6. The '10 per cent compromise' is thus a super winner in being better than the original best solution of both the conservative and the liberals.

on the accessibility and competency columns. The result is that the volunteers receive a score of 8, salaried attorneys receive a score of 10 and the compromise system receives a still higher score of 11.5 using liberal values.

This is a good illustration of the concept of an optimizing compromise which is an additional alternative that is better than the previous first choice of either set of disputants using their own values to weight the criteria and their own perceptions to score the alternatives on the criteria. Acceptable compromises that are everybody's second choice are often difficult to achieve, although the P/G% microcomputer program does facilitate such compromises by clarifying the criteria, the alternatives, the relations and, especially, the effects of changing any of those components on the bottom line conclusion as to which alternative is best. The incremental difficulty of achieving optimizing compromises should be more than offset by the incremental gain in terms of satisfying conservative and liberal disputants and in terms of benefiting the recipients of the public policies that are adopted.

Notes

On combining liberal and conservative alternatives, there is a literature dealing with the process of compromising and collaborating which is partly relevant. See Dobel (1990) and Gray (1989). More relevant literature, however, deals with ways to combine non-mutually exclusive alternatives so that nothing is lost from either side and possibly a new higher synthesis is gained. That literature includes 'Hegel: Dialectic and Nationalism' and 'Marx and Dialectical Materialism', which are Chapters 30 and 33, respectively, in Sabine (1950). The idea of thesis, antithesis and synthesis in Hagel and Marx leads to what one could consider to be a super-optimum solution, rather than a compromise. For further details on American higher education as providing a kind of super-optimum synthesis of the public and private sectors, see Gove and Stauffer (1986).

On the alternative ways of providing legal services for the poor in general, see Legal Services Corporation (1980), Berney *et al.* (1975), Jarmel (1972), Garth (1983), Brickman and Lempert (1976) and Chilton Research Services (1971).

On non-American alternative for providing legal services for the poor, see Blankenburg and Meier (1980), Cappelletti and Garth (1978), *Windsor Yearbook of Access to Justice* (1980–), Zemans (1979) and Jarmel (1972).

15   Developing a Multifaceted Package

Pre-trial Release

One of the first stages in criminal proceedings which seems to call for judicial reform is the stage at which a decision is made about an arrested suspect prior to his or her trial. The basic alternatives involve releasing or not releasing him prior to trial depending on (1) whether he can offer a sufficient money deposit to serve as a guarantee or incentive that he will return for trial, or (2) whether his characteristics are such that he is likely to return for his trial rather than risk being prosecuted as a trial jumper. The first alternative is referred to as the traditional bail bond system, and the second alternative as release on one's own recognizance or the ROR system. In past years, the bail system was by far the dominant method. This was so partly because of the belief that individuals were economically motivated and partly because the system favored middle-class people whose interests tended to dominate legal rule making. The reform trend is increasingly toward a more objective and scientific ROR system, for a number of reasons.

Studies by the Vera Institute in New York City have shown that, by carefully screening arrested suspects into good risks and bad risks (largely on the basis of their roots in the community and the seriousness of their crimes), one can obtain at least as low a percentage of trial jumpers as one does with the traditional money deposit system. Trial-day mail or phone reminders also help reduce trial jumping. These studies have further shown that, with the screening and notification system, a far higher percentage of arrested suspects can be released from jail pending their trial than under the money deposit system. Such release means these good risks can (1) continue their jobs, (2) better prepare their cases to establish their innocence, (3) save the taxpayer money by not occupying jail space, and (4) be less bitter than if they spent time in jail and were then acquitted. The money deposit system so inherently discriminates against the poor that the United States Supreme Court may someday declare it to be in violation of the equal protection clause of the constitution.

One objection to the ROR system is that it might result in releasing a number of arrested suspects who will commit crimes while awaiting trial. One response to this objection is that truly dangerous persons should be kept in jail pending a speedy trial, regardless of how able they are to offer a large money deposit. Another response is to point out that pre-trial crimes are more often due to long delays prior to trial than to poor screening or the lack of a bail bond requirement. The delay problem, however, is a separate area of judicial reform.

Pre-trial Release of Arrested Defendants: Spreadsheets

Table 15.1 analyzes how the criminal justice system might handle the problem of pre-trial release of arrested defendants. The prevailing compromise policy is to hold people in jail prior to trial unless they can provide a money deposit to allow their release. The proposed conservative policy of the Reagan administration was to hold more people in jail by explicitly adding the probability of crime-committing as a criterion regarding pre-trial release. The SOS policy which has been increasingly adopted is to hold fewer people in jail, while holding constant or improving the court appearance rate by better screening, supervision, notification, prosecution and delay reduction.

The goals in the pre-trial release context include avoiding or minimizing undesirable occurrences such as (1) the embittering experience of being held in jail prior to trial without ever being convicted, (2) the arbitrary subjectivity which tends to be associated with who gets released and who is held, (3) jail riots due to the bitterness and overcrowding often associated with pre-trial detention, (4) convictions of innocent defendants who agree to plead guilty in order to be released from pre-trial detention with a sentence equal to the time already served, (5) the expense of having to expand overcrowded pre-trial jails, (6) lost gross national product, (7) increases in welfare cases owing to pre-trial detention of family income producers, (8) non-appearance in court of released defendants, and (9) crime-committing by released defendants.

Table 15.1 shows the relations between the policies and the goals using the same 1–5 scoring system as was used in other tables. The Reagan proposal scores low on the liberal and neutral goals, but high on the conservative goals. The liberal policy scores high on the liberal and neutral goals, but low on the conservative goals. The prevailing compromise policy scores in the middle on all the goals. The SOS package scores high on all the goals.

Table 15.1 Evaluating policies toward pre-trial release

Criteria / Alternatives	C Goal High show-up rate	C Goal No crime-committing	N Goal Fewer tax costs	L Goal Less lost productivity	L Goal Less bitterness	N Total (neutral weights)	L Total (liberal weights)	C Total (conservative weights)
C Alternative High holding rate	4	4	2	2	2	24	24	32*
L Alternative Low holding rate	2	2	4	4	4	32	36*	28
N Alternative Middling holding rate	3	3	3	3	3	30	30	30
SOS Alternative Low holding, high appearance, without crimes	5	5	5	5	5	50	50**	50**

Note: The SOS package includes (1) screening of arrested persons to determine risk of release, (2) having them check in at the courthouse while released, (3) notifying released persons when the court date arrives, (4) prosecuting those who fail to show up and, especially, (5) reducing delay, which thereby reduces both the releasing costs and the holding costs.

217

Under the differential weighting system, liberals give liberal goals a weight of 3 and conservative goals a weight of 1, as contrasted to conservatives giving liberal goals a weight of 1 and conservative goals a weight of 3. The SOS reform policy receives the highest overall score under all three weighting systems. Like the winning proposals in all these problems, it represents a way of achieving both the conservative and liberal goals simultaneously. The average defendant will appear even more in court without being arrested while released, which should please conservatives. The proposals also result in holding fewer people in jail prior to trial, which should please liberals.

The dollar cost of these reforms was not included as a goal, although this could easily be added. The dollar costs, however, are quite low with regard to doing a minimum amount of (1) screening to separate good and bad risks, (2) supervision by way of having released defendants report periodically to the courthouse prior to trial, (3) notification by postcard or other means immediately before the trial date, (4) selective prosecution of those who do not show up, to make examples of them, and (5) reduction of the delay from arrest to trial so as to reduce the expense of holding defendants in jail and to reduce the probability of released defendants disappearing or committing crimes. With the costs being relatively low and the benefits being relatively high in terms of goals achieved, it is understandable that these SOS reform measures have become widely adopted, although perhaps not widely enough.

Out-of-court Settlements in Criminal Cases

Evaluating Policies toward Plea Bargaining

Lenient plea bargains tend to occur when the defendant is capable of paying for a defense that will greatly tie up the prosecutor's scarce resources in motions, trial time and appeals. Severe plea bargains tend to occur when the defendant is held in jail pending trial and is willing to plead guilty to time already served in order to be able to go home, even though waiting for a trial might result in an acquittal or a lighter sentence if the defendant were not being held in jail.

Plea bargaining with results similar to sentences that might occur from a bench trial or a jury trial can be obtained through a five-part package that comprises (1) special funding for the prosecutor to deal with difficult defendants, (2) special services such as appellate services for the public defender to be able to defend and bargain effectively, (3) a higher rate of pre-trial release, with provision for decreasing the number of those who do not show up and crime-committing, (4) flat sentencing, so that both sides know what sentences are likely to be given, and (5) access to data showing probabilities of convic-

Table 15.2 Evaluating policies toward plea bargaining

Criteria / Alternatives	C Goal Deserving sentences	N Goal Fewer taxes	N Goal Respect for legal system	N Goal Reduce delay	L Goal Separate innocent	N Total (neutral weights)	L Total (liberal weights)	C Total (conservative weights)
C Alternative Abolish lenient plea bargains	4	1	4	1	4	28	28	28
L Alternative Abolish severe plea bargains	4	1	4	1	4	28	28	28
N Alternative Maintain as is	2	4	2	4	2	28	28	28
SOS Alternative Settlements with jury results	5	2	5	4	5	42	42**	42**

219

tion and average sentences, so that both sides are less likely to be fooled into thinking the probable sentence will be substantially higher or lower.

A Simplified SOS Analysis of Plea Bargaining

Both conservatives and liberals endorse sentencing that is deserved by the convicted defendant. Conservatives tend to believe more severe sentences are deserved, and liberals tend to believe less severe sentences are deserved. Both would like to see money saved as a result of reducing the number of trials when out-of-court settlements can produce results that are similar to what trials would produce. (See Table 15.2.)

If overly lenient bargains can be lessened, conservatives would be pleased. These are the bargains that are arrived at by defendants who may have enough financing to afford expensive legal counsel and threaten to tie up the prosecutor if a bargain is not struck. If overly severe bargains can be lessened, liberals would be pleased. These are the bargains that are arrived at by defendants who have no funds for private counsel and possibly no funds for bail. They are thus highly vulnerable to pleading guilty and accepting a sentence when they might not be found guilty if they were better represented.

The SOS alternative should please conservatives by providing county prosecutors with special funding from the state to deal with defendants who are well financed. The SOS alternative should please liberals by providing the public defender with special funding to represent defendants at least on appeal where the public defender feels an innocent person might otherwise be convicted. The liberal position should also welcome a higher rate of pre-trial release, since being held in jail prior to trail makes defendants especially vulnerable to offers from the prosecutor. Both conservatives and liberals should welcome guidelines on sentencing and access to prior data. (The 'prior data' refers to information on the average prior sentences for various crimes and also the percentage of cases of various types that result in convictions.) These procedures enable both sides to predict better how the cases will be decided, and thus they can arrive at plea bargains which better reflect those likely decisions.

Note

For general literature dealing with the approach of trying to develop a package of alternatives, one could look at the literature that attempts philosophically to defend eclecticism (see Titus, 1947). For further details on the example of developing a package of alternatives for dealing with pre-trial release, see Hall (1984), Thomas (1976) and Flemming (1982).

16 Sequential SOS

Business Development

The business development problem is very time-oriented in that it talks about small businesses as a stepping-stone over time to big businesses. The shortsighted say that we have unemployment, especially unemployed women. We must give them something to do and so give them dead-end jobs making clothes and selling clothes or, even worse, growing fruit and vegetables and selling those.

The people with more of a time horizon say that the big problem is not eating a fish for today but learning how to fish or doing some kind of activity that has some payoff beyond today of this week. In that context it may involve sending the women to school to learn how to be computer operators. The business development context, as contrasted to the education and skills upgrading context, is 'Let's start them out in a small machine shop where they make spark plugs'.

However, you cannot make spark plugs as fast as you can make dish-cloths or as fast as you can go into the countryside and pick wild rhubarb to sell: to make spark plugs, first of all, you have to get the machines to make them with and you have to learn to operate the machines. Maybe no income will come in for a couple of months, whereas income can be immediate in selling sweaters or casaba plants. After a few months, spark plugs are being made and sold, maybe with more income, although with more expense than selling fruits and vegetables, so that at first making spark plugs is even less profitable.

The key thing, though, is that making spark plugs can lead to having a factory. It can lead to the manufacturing of spark plugs on a larger scale or can lead to manufacturing of other car parts. That in turns leads to the employment of more people, both men and women. It may even lead to producing more spark plugs than the local economy can buy because the local economy does not have many cars or trucks. That could mean exporting the surplus spark plugs to places that supply foreign money – hard currency for buying bigger machines for making, say, hubcaps, headlights,

221

windshield wipers and maybe even cars eventually, although not necessarily.

Making cars in developing nations is frequently not productive: it is just a status symbol activity. Cars can be made better in Japan or even in the United States. Making cars is getting into something very complex that involves lots of components coming from different places. A spark plug may be nothing but some porcelain and some metal, and one machine makes the whole spark plug. There is no such thing as a machine that makes a whole car.

The super-optimum solution is deliberately choosing small businesses that have a high or, relatively speaking, higher capability of becoming big businesses even though it takes a while for even the small business form to pay off (see Table 16.1). That is part of long-term thinking. It is the idea of delayed gratification and also of taking one step back in order to take two steps forward later. It is a way of thinking that has not been very common in equatorial countries, where there is a tradition that, if you want to eat, you do not have to do a lot of planting in the springtime and wait until autumn to harvest and eat it. Instead, you just go out and shake a pineapple plant or coconut tree and you have food. That works fine with pineapples and coconuts. It does not work so well with pharmaceuticals. There is no pharmaceutical tree, although developing nations do sometimes make good use of herbs. There is certainly no car tree.

Nobody worried about cars a hundred years ago because they did not exist. Africa was blessed with being on the equator and having no need for heavy clothes, heavy houses or heavy agriculture. The climate was warm all year round and wild food was plentiful. That has partly become something of a curse in the sense of creating limited time horizons with regard to delaying gratification. The concern of the Africa Development Bank for long-term development is well-placed. Africa is less concerned with long-term development than any other of the four regions, partly because it has more land mass and more people along the equator than does Asia or Latin America, and certainly a lot more than eastern Europe, which is a long way from the equator. Eastern Europe may be faced by almost the opposite problem, as it is sometimes so cold that people are prevented from doing much of anything. At the equator people are disinclined to do anything because in the past there has been so little need to do things.

One point that must be strongly emphasized is that this is not climatic determinism, because human beings are quite capable of overcoming whatever climate they happen to live in. Climate may have shaped things in prehistoric times, but modern people can live luxuriously on the equator in central Africa, or in the Antarctic if they want to do so. We have refrigerators for central Africa and we have effective heating devices for the Antarc-

Table 16.1   Business development and Africa

Criteria / Alternatives	C Goal Easy feasibility	L Goal Value to economy	N Total (neutral weights)	L Total (liberal weights)	C Total (conservative weights)
C Alternative Large business	2	4	12	10	14*
L Alternative Small business	4	2	12	14*	10
N Alternative Medium business	3	3	12	12	12
SOS Alternative Small to large (especially manufacturers)	>3.5	>3.5	>14	>14**	>14**

tic. To a considerable extent, it is a matter of public policy stimulating the use of appropriate technology.

The term 'appropriate technology' is sometimes used by backpackers to mean virtually no technology at all. It should be used to mean that what is good technology for the Antarctic may not be good technology for central Africa, but that humans have developed technologies that can deal with any climate or any kind of geographical factors. People could live luxuriously at the top of the Himalayas or well below sea level, as long as they are not under water. In fact, if necessary, we could even live under water and pump oxygen in.

Energy Sources

Nuclear power plants and nuclear waste deposits should be as far from centers of populations as possible, with more concern than has been shown for the safety factors. Such power plants do seem worth developing in view of (a) relatively low air pollution compared to coal or even oil burning, (b) unlimited sources of supply, (c) potential inexpensiveness, especially from breeder reactors if they can be safely developed and especially when oil and coal become scarce and thus even more expensive. (See Table 16.2.)

Coal pollution can be reduced through gasification and such a simple device as coal watering. The pollution of the land from strip mining can be reduced by government-enforced replacement which still leaves coal stripping profitable, given the increased demand for coal as oil becomes more

Table 16.2 Evaluating energy policy alternatives

Criteria / Alternatives	C Goal More energy business	C Goal Business use of energy	N Goal Lower tax cost	N Goal Technological feasibility, short run	N Goal Technological feasibility, long run	L Goal Environmt, safety & IR	L Goal Consumer interest & equity	N Total (neutral weights)	L Total (liberal weights)	C Total (conservative weights)
C Alternative Nuclear & oil	4	2	2.5	3.5	3	2	2	38	36	40
L Alternative Solar & synthetic fuels	2	3	2.5	2.5	3.5	4	3	41	43*	39
N Alternative Coal & mixture	3	3	3	2.5	3	3	3	41	41	41*
SOS Alternative Sequential combination, well-placed subsidies	5	5	2	3.5	5	5	5	61	61**	61**

224

Notes:

1. 'IR' stands for international relations. It means that reliance on oil disputes affects our foreign policy activities. For example, we may have to be nice to feudalistic Saudi Arabia when we otherwise would not be. Reliance on coal does not disrupt our foreign policy.

2. 'Environment' refers to the fact that coal, especially soft sulfur coal, is highly polluting to breathers generally and to coal miners in particular, where as nuclear fuel is not. Nuclear power, however, raises more serious safety problems than any of the other fuels, although there are safety problems in coal mining too.

3. One should note that each policy has sub-policies which are not shown here:

   (a) nuclear can be divided into uranium (the most common form), plutonium and hydrogen;
   (b) oil can be divided into known deposits and unknown deposits;
   (c) coal can be divided into high polluting (the most common form) and low polluting;
   (d) synthetic fuels can be divided into natural (like oil shale) and artificial (like garbage);
   (e) solar can be divided into small-scale and large-scale.

4. One should note the big drawback for each energy source:

   (a) nuclear, especially nuclear waste, lacks sufficient safety;
   (b) oil lacks long-term value;
   (c) coal is bad on pollution;
   (d) synthetic fuels have high continuing costs;
   (e) solar has high start-up costs for large-scale operations.

5. The choices can be best viewed in terms of three tracks:

   (a) oil is best on the short-term track;
   (b) coal and synthetic fuels make the most sense on the intermediate track, with a need for developing more economic synthetic fuels;
   (c) solar and nuclear make the most sense on the long-term track, but there is a need for developing safer nuclear energy and for research on implementing large-scale solar energy.

225

expensive and as the stripping technology becomes more economically feasible. This is analogous to taconite mining of iron ore.

Price regulations may require government ownership or at least yardstick ownership. Such ownership of an electric company is partly for the purpose of better informing government regulators on what private electric companies should be charging for various kinds of electricity. Government price regulation of privately owned and operated oil development, and probably coal development, results in stultifying management which may actually bring higher prices through more expensive operations. Such government ownership may bring prices down without expensive and stultifying regulations, but obtaining ownership may be politically unfeasible. The only way it could become politically feasible would be for the oil business to become a depressed business, as passenger rail services have become. So long as the business is increasingly profitable, or at least profitable, a government takeover is unlikely, although the enforcement problems of government price regulation may be preferable to monopolistic pricing that would otherwise occur in this essential industry if it were unregulated.

Taxes on petrol do decrease some consumption. A tax policy to discourage excessive consumption, however, needs to distinguish between wasteful use of petrol in cars that get low mileage versus those that get high mileage. That would require differential energy conservation taxes on cars by size, which the Carter administration was unable to put through. That kind of tax policy could be applied to other energy users besides car owners. For example, there could be a tax on oil use of so much per gallon, depending on what it is to be used for. In effect, that would be like a rationing system where different kinds of uses would be given different priorities and the lower priority uses would be subjected to a higher tax in order to give them a lower allocation. This kind of plan is also politically unfeasible because it would antagonize both individual and company consumers, as well as producers of energy.

The Carter administration was actively trying to reduce the proliferation of nuclear energy, or at least limiting or attempting to limit the proliferation to peaceful uses. The main thing, though, that will keep countries from converting their nuclear energy technology to a nuclear bomb technology is a feeling that they do not need to develop nuclear bombs, not an attempt to hide the technology from them. On the shifting of the balance of power, due to increased importance of oil locations, the Carter administration's foreign policy does seem to have been at least partly designed to curry favour among countries that have extensive oil reserves, such as the Arabian countries (today possibly with the addition of China). The best way to decrease the pivotal importance of such countries, though, is to develop alternative energy sources.

Oil productivity does not need any governmental stimulation, but a profit motive provides plenty of stimulation. The government needs to stimulate development of alternatives to oil. Tighter government regulations could decrease oil spills and pipeline accidents. The oil business is so profitable that it is ridiculous for the oil companies to argue that they cannot afford the safety technology that has been developed through oil transportation at least within a reasonably low risk level.

The corrupting influence of oil and other energy lobbyists has been reduced as a result of the decreased need for government subsidies such as the depletion allowance, import quotas and pro-rationing supply restrictions by the states. The only way to eliminate completely this influence is to put the oil industry under government ownership, which is not a politically feasible suggestion. Ironically, the more industry is regulated the more corrupting it becomes, because it then has more incentive to try to buy off legislators to decrease the regulatory influence.

The long-run solution does seem to require the government to stimulate the development of safer nuclear energy and new energy forms, particularly solar energy, and new substitutes for the internal combustion engine that do not require so much petrol, with the side benefit of substantially reduced pollution. This requires substantial government subsidies, which probably have not been large enough hitherto because the pressures have not been great enough.

Obtaining domestic self-sufficiency in energy in the United States would require (1) more use of low sulfur or gasified coal, (2) more development of safe nuclear energy, (3) more development of new energy sources such as solar energy, (4) more conservation of energy, not in the sense of doing without and thereby lowering standards of living, but in the sense of de-creasing wasteful uses such as excessive petrol-burning cars and lack of use of good public transport, and (5) more reliance on nearby oil sources in Alaska and Mexico.

On energy policy, a 'microwave in the sky' can provide cheap energy for residences, which should please liberals, given their consumer orientation. Like a lot of the super-optimum solutions, though, this requires spending big money to make money. It requires taking risks and making big invest-ments in order to improve thing substantially. The money can come from reductions in other forms of government spending and, in some instances, from cross-national cooperation. It is a matter of having the will to act collectively, even though few business firms would be willing to invest in something that would take many years to pay off, although the number of years is not that great. Anything that takes more than about 10 years to pay off may as well take infinity in terms of the willingness of most American businesses to put big money into it. Only the government, by and large, is willing to do that sort of thing. While it is losing on an investment that does not pay off for 10 years, it is gaining from other sources, including general tax revenues. The government does not have to pay dividends to stockholders and it does not need to show a profit on current investments in order to pay government executives.

Sequential Analysis

Conflicting SOS Solutions Handled Sequentially

One could also make a case for saying that sometimes one SOS can conflict with another.

Commuter congestion   One example in the transport field is the idea of dispersing job opportunities to the suburbs as being a good idea for relieving commuter congestion. It does run contrary to the inner city poverty SOS which includes enterprise zones that involve attracting business opportunities away from the suburbs to the inner city. The businesses can be attracted away from other places besides suburbs. That is not so good if they are attracted from inner cities, like moving job opportunities from the inner city of Detroit to the inner city of Chicago. One can also argue that inner city jobs tend to be factory-oriented, whereas suburban jobs tend to be office-oriented. A counter to that is that inner city people should also have access to office jobs. The counter to that is that, for now, they can better qualify generally for factory jobs than for office jobs.

Land redistribution   The land reform problem involves an SOS of giving land to the peasants along with systems for producer cooperatives so that smaller landholdings are not so inefficient. Giving land to the peasants runs contrary to the SOS of facilitating movement from rural areas where farmers are less needed than in the past, to go elsewhere. The elsewhere does not have to be the central cities. It can be to regional cities. What the peasants may need more than land is an upgrading of their skills so they can make more money and possibly be happier doing something that relates to office work, although not necessarily factory work.

Both problems   What the above illustrates is that doing something for one problem may complicate another problem. Doing something for commuter congestion may hurt the poor in the inner cities; doing something for landless peasants may hurt the need for a transition from so much farming into non-farm occupations. The sequential idea and its relation to incrementalism may be important. One can turn landless peasants into land owners but then make provision for educating their children so that they can hold down non-agricultural jobs. Likewise the inner city problem may be partly a temporary situation to provide some immediate jobs. The long-run solution sequentially is to facilitate moving out of the inner city to a more middle-class environment, partly through housing vouchers. The two problems are closely related. One gives farmers land and agricultural jobs, but anticipates that at least their children will be in more productive non-agricultural work. Likewise, the government gives inner city people factory jobs, in the inner city, but anticipates that their children will move out. Their movement will be facilitated by housing vouchers, or government house buying, loans or subsidies.

Sequential Business Development in Africa

The first situation involves encouraging small businesses in Africa that have a fair chance of becoming large businesses. It is not meaningful to do large first and then small, although especially big businesses can be broken up. Breaking up big businesses does nothing for efficiency and consumers, unless they compete with each other, as contrasted to being given regional monopolies. There is something inherent in the small to large sequence. One can say it is a matter of economic feasibility. Developing nations cannot afford to go right into large manufacturing. It requires too much capital and more training than their current skills provide for.

Sequencing Energy Sources

The second situation involves sequencing energy sources, with an emphasis on oil, an intermediate emphasis on coal and a distant future emphasis on safe nuclear and mass-solar. Doing safe nuclear and mass-solar white oil is plentiful is not so realistic, since the incentives are not strong.

Sequencing the Inner City Problem

The idea of setting up virtually all inner city people in suburban office jobs is not economically feasible in terms of the monetary costs. Doing so with their children might work without any special monetary incentives. Housing vouchers can also provide good facilitators. They would not be needed if the children were given good enough education, so that on their own they can get good jobs and good housing without a subsidy of housing vouchers or a subsidy to buy a house. One could argue, in the other direction, that the subsidies are needed now to move the inner city people out. Otherwise their children are not going to acquire a sufficient education to break out. The children may be trapped generation after generation unless the cycle is broken. That seems to go contrary to the purpose of the enterprise zone, designated by the government as eligible for special loans to build or relocate factories and other sources of employment. People living in the inner city, however, can be facilitated with regard to moving out, while better jobs are provided for those who stay, temporarily or permanently.

The enterprise zones might thus have to be accepted as a temporary way of dealing with unemployment in the inner city owing to lack of funding for a massive housing voucher program. This is not a problem with regard to opposition to people moving from the inner city to the suburbs on racial grounds or class grounds. They would be moving to apartments or houses on a rental basis, with a rent that they can afford, meaning relatively low-income housing. Also they move into lower-middle class neighborhoods in a dispersed way, not concentrated in time or place. This is not like a building, a high-rise public housing project in Deerfield, Illinois, which did arouse vigorous opposition.

PART IV
INTEGRATION

17 Combining and Summarizing Approaches

Combining Approaches

Examples of Undesirable Policy Analysis

One of the most interesting aspects of the Philippine land reform experience has been the many mistakes (or one might call them learning experiences) that have been made by well-intentioned agricultural experts who may have been overly focused in their expertise. This can be contrasted with policy analysts, who have a more generalist perspective. One should try to see how different policy problems and proposed solutions can interface with each other. Some alternatives have a 'domino effect', where the *unintended consequences* of what otherwise looks like a meaningful approach to increased agricultural productivity become devastating.

Four examples were given by the people associated with agrarian reform in the Philippines. The first example involved telling farmers how they can double their crops through the use of better seeds, pesticides, herbicides, fertilizer and machinery, but not providing for any increased *storage facilities* to put the doubled crop. The result was that much of the increased productivity rotted in the fields.

The second example involved telling farmers how they could arrange for as many as four crops a year, instead of one crop a year, by using special seeds that have a three-month season from sowing to harvesting. However, the farmers were not told how the owner of a one-person farm could *plow, weed and harvest* four times a year and still be able to attend fiestas.

The third example involved supplying the farmers with new pesticides that kill all the crop-damaging insects and weeds, but also kill the frogs and fish that live on the farms that the farmers like to eat. After the frogs and fish were killed, the pesticides and herbicides were withdrawn, following the realization that the farmers did not want to kill the frogs and fish. The result

233

is that the farmers now have no frogs, no fish, and the pests are back. The thing to do might have been to continue with the pesticides, but to give the farmers *food stamps* to buy frogs and fish from the local markets. The economy would then be better off because the increased farm productivity would more than offset the cost of the frog and fish stamps.

The fourth example involved showing the farmers how they can grow more efficiently with a tractor than with an ox. Such a demonstration may, however, fail to recognize that tractors do not make good fertilizer. The demonstration may also fail to recognize that, if you give a tractor to one farmer and not to other farmers in the area, the other farmers, especially his relatives, come to borrow that farmer's tractor. That farmer then has no tractor, no ox and no fertilizer. The correct solution might have been to give the tractor to the whole community *collectively to share*, the way American farmers share grain elevators or Russian farmers share tractors at machine tractor stations.

The idea of one tractor per Philippine farmer is American individualistic capitalism gone berserk, contrary to the realities of farming in the Philippines and other developing countries, or even developed countries. Not all farmers in Champaign County, Illinois, have a combine, and they do not feel deprived. They find it more efficient to hire a combine company, just as every American does not own a U-Haul trailer or a Greyhound, although they use them. Farmers want to own their own land, at least in most developing countries. There are many American farmers, however, who own no land, but who farm for land owners. They often make a lot of money getting paid to do the work with their equipment. Wanting to own one's own land does not mean one wants to own a combine. The land is used almost all year long if you are a farmer. The combine gets used for one week, and it is recognized as wasteful to have to store it, watch it depreciate and make payments on it on a year-round basis. There is a need for *combining individualistic land ownership with collectivistic sharing and renting*.

In a socialistic society like China, the combination of individualism and collectivism might take the form of *retaining government ownership of the land and renting it* to farmers who will personally and productively work the land. The rent they pay serves as a substitute for property taxes. The rent can be lowered to provide a strings-attached subsidy to encourage the adoption of new herbicides, pesticides, farm machinery, hybrid seeds and other biotechnology. There is also the possibility of non-renewal of the one-year lease (or other terms) if the farmer–renter violates reasonable rules relating to the environment, workplace safety, labor relations, consumer relations, employment discrimination or other socially-desired standards of behavior. Non-renewal of the lease is much easier to implement than traditional regulatory measures which emphasize fines, injunctions, litigation, threats and other negative sanctions. This would also deter the buying of land for windfall gains or tax-avoidance purposes, as contrasted to land for food production.

Alternatives, Goals and Relations as Inputs

If we are talking about 100 units of land, the typical conservative *alternative* tends to advocate retaining most of the ownership of the land in the hands of the traditional landed aristocracy. The typical liberal approach tends to advocate turning most of the ownership of the land to landless peasants to farm. The typical neutral or compromise approach is something in between, although not necessarily exactly a 50–50 split of the 100 units, as shown in Table 17.1.

Table 17.1   Land reform in developing countries

Criteria / Alternatives	C Goal Productivity	L Goal Equity	N Total (neutral weights)	L Total (liberal weights)	C Total (conservative weights)
C Alternative Retain land (0 units)	4	1	10	7	13*
L Alternative Divide land (100 units)	1	4	10	13*	7
N Alternative Compromise (50 units)	2.5	2.5	10	10	10
SOS Alternative 1. Buy the land 2. Lots of land 3. Coop action	4.5	4.5	18	18**	18**

Notes:
1.   The SOS package combines an individualistic desire to own land with collectivistic action to make more efficient use of shared technology and ideas.
2.   It is not an SOS package to give farmers technology or ideas out of the context in which the farmers operate, such as the following: (a) ideas on fertilizer for increasing acreage yields without providing increased storage capability; (b) ideas on seeds for multiple crops within a given time period, without providing increased labor or technology to handle the increased work; (c) ideas on pesticides and herbicides for destroying insects and weeds which may also destroy frogs, fish and other edible animals, without providing for food stamps or other replacements; (d) ideas on farm machinery without providing for a fertilizer replacement and a system of sharing the machines if there are not enough machines for every farmer in the area to own one.

The two key *goals* in the controversy tend to be agricultural productivity and a more equalitarian or equitable distribution of land ownership. The conservative alternative (by allowing for economies of scale that are associated with large land holdings) is more productive, but less equitable. The liberal alternative of widespread land distribution is less productive, but more equitable. The neutral compromise is somewhere between these relation scores, just as it is somewhere between the conservative and liberal distribution alternatives.

With those relation scores, we logically have the *result* mentioned above, where the conservative alternative wins with the conservative weights, and the liberal alternative wins with the liberal weights. We are also likely to get the classic compromise, which is everybody's second-best alternative, or worse. The 'or worse' means that sometimes liberals accept the compromise when the conservative alternative actually does better on the liberal weights, or the conservatives accept the compromise when the liberal alternative actually does better on the conservative weights. Each side may accept the compromise even though it is the third-best alternative to them, because they do not want to give in to the other side. That is not the case with Table 17.1, but it does sometimes occur in the psychology of public policy making.

Finding a Super-optimum Package of Policies

The super-optimum alternative seems to involve three key elements. The first is that the *land needs to be bought* from the present land owners, rather than confiscated. If the owners are threatened with confiscation, one possible reaction is to establish death squads, to bring in American military power, or to do other especially nasty things that may easily cost more than the cost of buying the land. The United States probably could have saved a fortune in military and other expenditures on Nicaragua, El Salvador and Guatemala from the 1950s to the 1990s by simply using a fraction of the money spent to buy land from the owners to give to the peasants. The land owners would have probably also saved themselves money and anxiety by paying a substantial portion of the taxes needed to buy the land. Money needlessly or excessively spent by landlords went to the hiring of private armies, bodyguards, thugs, and fortification.

The second element is that *lots of land* needs to be involved. It cannot be a token program. The landless peasants in developing countries are no longer as passive as they one were. They cannot be easily bought off with trinkets, pie-in-the-sky religion, patronizing aristocrats and other relatively worthless bribes of distractions. They have demonstrated a willingness to fight and die for land in pre-communist China, in Central America and in other developing countries, such as the Philippines.

The third element is the need to use *modern technologies in a cooperative way* to overcome the divisive effect of distributing the land in relatively small parcels to the landless peasants. This is where the policy makers can learn from both capitalistic American farmers and communistic Russian farmers. American farmers are highly individualistic, but they recognize that it makes no sense for each of them to own their own grain elevators, combines and other big equipment which they can own collectively through producer cooperatives. In the Soviet Union, agricultural efficiency has been promoted through machine tractor stations, where farmers can share tractors which they cannot afford to own separately. This is true regardless of whether the individual farmers are associated with collective farms or private plots. Cooperative activities also involve the equivalent of county agents who help bring farmers together to learn about the latest seeds, herbicides, pesticides, fertilizers and other useful knowledge. Cooperative action can also include credit unions and drawing upon collective taxes for well-placed subsidies to encourage the diffusion of useful innovations.

With this combination of SOS elements, one can have agricultural *productivity and equity simultaneously*, enabling that combination to be a strong winner on both the liberal totals and the conservative totals. Appropriate timing may also be required in the sense of moving fast to implement these kinds of ideas. The longer the delay, the more difficult such an SOS solution becomes. The reason is that the liberal left may acquire such a negative attitude toward the conservative right that the liberal left would consider buying the land to be a surrender to evil people. Likewise, the conservative right may acquire such a negative attitude toward the peasant guerrillas that they can see no respectable solution other than extermination of what they consider to be terrorists.

Summarizing Approaches

Classifications of SOS

This chapter has reviewed various SOS approaches. Solutions to public controversies can be classified in various ways.

1   There are super-optimum solutions in which all sides come out ahead of their best initial expectations, as mentioned above. At the opposite extreme is a super-malimum solution in which all sides come out worse than their initial worst expectations. That can be the case in a mutually destructive war, labor strike or highly expensive litigation.
2   In Pareto optimum solutions, nobody comes out worse off and at least

one side comes out better off. That is not a very favorable solution compared to a super-optimized solution. A Pareto malimum solution would be one in which nobody is better off and at least one side is worse off.

3   A win–lose solution is one where what one side wins the other side loses. The net effect is zero when the losses are subtracted from the gains. This is typical of the litigation dispute when one ignores the litigation costs.

4   In a lose–lose solution, both sides are worse off than they were before the dispute began. This may often be the outcome of the typical litigation dispute, or close to it, when one includes the litigation costs. These costs are often so high that the so-called 'winner' is also a loser. This is also often the case in labor–management disputes that result in a strike, and even more so in international disputes that result in going to war.

5   At first glance, the so-called 'win–win' solution looks like a solution where everybody comes out ahead. What it typically refers to, however, is an illusion, since the parties are only coming out ahead relative to their worst expectations. In this sense, the plaintiff is a winner no matter what the settlement is because the plaintiff could have won nothing if liability had been rejected at trial. Likewise, the defendant is a winner no matter what the settlement is because the defendant could have lost everything the plaintiff was asking for if liability had been established at trial. The parties are only fooling themselves in the same sense that someone who is obviously a loser tells himself he won because he could have done worse.

One of the most important aspects of SOS for public administration is its capacity to challenge the assumed limitations of customary practice. When we think of improving national productivity, we can consider some of the following alternatives:

1   better child care to allow mothers of pre-school children to work;
2   subsidies to move unemployed people to places where increased job opportunities are available;
3   subsidies for business firms to move where there are pockets of unemployment;
4   subsidies for unemployed people to get more education in order to improve their employability;
5   subsidies for employers to provide on-the-job training to improve the skills of their workers;
6   subsidies for universities and other institutions that develop new technologies;

7   subsidies for business firms to adopt new technologies;
8   subsidies for workers to enable them to adapt to new technologies.

The above list may be too general because it covers all kinds of productivity problem. We can talk about increasing the potential productivity of the elderly, the disabled or people who are not working up to their capabilities. We might prefer a problem such as how to increase the productivity of the American car industry. The national productivity problem could be handled on an industry-by-industry basis, or with regard to different parts of the labor force, or with regard to specific firms. In these situations we could have a list of alternatives and goals, and then come up with a package solution that may be better than anything the liberals or the conservatives were previously pushing. We then call it an SOS and make it row 4 in a standard SOS table, with row 1 the conservative position, row 2 the liberal, and row 3 the compromise. That SOS table then becomes a visual aid for advocacy purposes as well as decision-making purposes and shows the SOS in its best possible light.

Analysis and Advocacy

The SOS approach bridges the usual gap between analysis and advocacy. Analysts are traditionally supposed to be neutral among alternatives. They just present how the alternatives relate to the goals and maybe which alternative is best in light of given goals. They leave it to the decision maker to decide which is best depending on the relative weights of different goals and the decision maker's perceptions of the relations.

In an SOS situation, the analyst plays a different role. The analyst may be the person who comes up with the SOS, which is an act of creativity, not just that of a technician. More importantly, the SOS by definition is not sensitive to whether we use liberal weights or conservative weights. By definition, it is better than the liberal alternative or the conservative alternative using either liberal or conservative goals and weights. In that kind of situation, the obligation of the analyst may be to try to get the SOS adopted – that is, to become more of an advocate. The analyst still has an obligation not to engage in anything that might be interpreted as lawyer-type advocacy or business advertising-type advocacy. That means the analyst has an obligation to show the defects the SOS might have and how they can be overcome. The lawyer and the business advertiser consider themselves as having no obligation to point out good characteristics in their competitor's products or in the other side of the law case. If the analyst knows of a defect in the SOS (even just a possible defect and not a confirmed defect), he or she should have an obligation to indicate it.

Streams of Relevant Ideas and Literature

There are a number of relevant ideas and publications that have played important parts in the development of the concept of achieving super-optimum solutions. One stream of ideas relates to the use of computers to facilitate systematic, evaluative and explanatory reasoning. The key literature includes Humphreys and Wisudha (1987), Gass *et al.* (1986) and Nagel (1989).

The second stream of inspiration has come from people in the field of mediation and alternative dispute resolution. The key literature here includes Susskind and Cruikshank (1987) and Nagel and Mills (1987).

The third stream of inspiration has come from people who are expansionist thinkers. This include the conservative economist, Arthur Laffer, and the liberal economist, Robert Reich, who have in common a belief that policy problems can be resolved by expanding the total pie of resources or other things of value available to be distributed to the disputants. The expansion can come from well-placed subsidies and tax breaks, with strings attached to increase national productivity. This kind of thinking can apply to disputes involving blacks–whites, rich–poor, males–females, North–South, urban–rural and other categories of societal disputants. The key literature includes Magaziner and Reich (1982) and Roberts (1984).

This chapter has identified seven approaches to super-optimum solutions. It can serve as one set of models for further development and analysis. Public administration and public policy and public productivity can only benefit from more expansionistic and multi-criteria decision making.

Bibliography

Agnew, John (ed.) (1980), *Innovation Research and Public Policy*, Syracuse, NY: Syracuse University.

Alberts, D. (1970), *A Plan for Measuring the Performance of Social Programs*, New York: Praeger.

Alperovitz, Gar and Jeff Faux (1984), *Rebuilding America: A Blueprint for the New Economy*, New York: Pantheon.

Bailey, S. (1950), *Congress Makes a Law: The Story Behind the Employment Act of 1946*, New York: Columbia University Press.

Ball, Michael, Michael Harloe and Maartje Martens (1988), *Housing and Social Change in Europe and the USA*, London: Routledge.

Banister, J. (1987), *China's Changing Population*, Stanford, CA: Stanford University Press.

Baumer, D. and C.V. Horn (1985), 'The Politics of Unemployment', *Congressional Quarterly*, Washington.

Bawden, Lee and Felicity Skidmore (eds) (1989), *Rethinking Employment Policy*, Washington, DC: Urban Institute.

Berney, Arthur *et al.* (eds) (1975), *Legal Problems of the Poor: Cases and Material*, Boston: Little, Brown.

Blankenburg, Erhard and Helmut Meier (eds) (1980), *Innovations in the Legal Services*, Cambridge, MA: Oelgeschlager, Gunn and Hain.

Blumstein, A. (ed.) (1978), *Deterrence and Incapacitation: Estimating the Effects of Criminal Sanctions on Crime Rates*, National Academy of Sciences.

Brickman, Lester and Richard Lempert (eds) (1976), *Delivery of Legal Services*, special issues of the *Law and Society Review*.

Butler, Stuart (1981), *Enterprise Zones: Greenlining the Inner Cities*, New York: Universe Books.

Canto, V., D. Joines and A. Laffer (1983), *Foundations of Supply-Side Economics*, New York: Academic Press.

Cappelletti, M. and B. Garth (eds) (1978), *Access to Justice: World Survey*, Authoff and Noordhoff.

Carley, M. (1981), *Social Measurement and Social Indicators: Issues of Policy and Theory*, Boston: Allen & Unwin.

Chilton Research Services (1971), *Legal Services Evaluation Study: Literature Search Report*, Radnor, PA: CRS.

Clark, Mary (1989), *Ariadne's Thread: The Search for New Modes of Thinking*, New York: St Martin's Press.

Cook, T. (ed.) (1986), 'Performance Measurement in Public Agencies', *Policy Studies Review*, symposium issue.

Davis, James Robert Bray and Robert Holt (1977), 'The Empirical Study of Decision Processes in Juries: A Critical Review', in June Tapp and Felice Levine (eds), *Law, Justice and the Individual in Society: Psychological and Legal Issues*, New York: Holt, Rinehart & Winston.

Dermer, Jerry (ed.) (1986), *Competitiveness through Technology: What Business Needs from Government*, Lexington, MA: Lexington-Heath.

Dobel, Patrick (1990), *Compromise and Political Action: Political Morality in Liberal and Democratic Life*, Savage, Md: Rowman and Littlefield.

Dorfman, R. (1964), *Measuring Benefits in Government Investments*, Washington, DC: Brookings.

Duggan, P. (1985), *The New American Unemployment*, Washington, DC: Center for Regional Policy.

Eckstein, O. (1983), *Inflation: Prospects and Remedies*, Washington, DC: Center for National Policy.

Etzioni, Amitai (1983), *An Immodest Agenda: Rebuilding America Before the 21st Century*, New York: McGraw-Hill.

Etzioni, Amitai (1988), *The Moral Dimension: Toward a New Economics*, New York: The Free Press.

Fisher, Roger and William Ury (1981), *Getting to Yes: Negotiating Agreement Without Giving In*, New York: Houghton-Mifflin.

Flemming, Roy (1982), *Punishment Before Trial: An Organizational Perspective of Felony Bail Processes*, New York: Longman.

Folbert, Jay and Alison Taylor (1984), *Mediation: A Comprehensive Guide to Resolving Conflicts Without Litigation*, San Francisco: Jossey-Bass.

Freeman, H., P. Rossi and S. Wright (1980), *Evaluating Social Projects in Developing Countries*, Organization for Economic Cooperation and Development.

Garth, Bryant (ed.) (1983), *Research on Legal Services for the Poor and Disadvantaged: Lessons from the Past and Issues for the Future* (Disputes Processing Research Program) Madison: Wisconsin Law School.

Gass, Saul *et al.* (eds) (1986), *Impacts of Operations Research*, Amsterdam: New Holland.

Gilmartin, K. *et al.* (1979), *Social Indicators: An Annotated Bibliography of Current Literature*, New York: Garland.

Ginzberg, E. (1963), *The Unemployed*, New York: Harper.

Gove, Samuel and Thomas Stauffer (eds) (1986), *Policy Controversies in Higher Education*, Westport, CT: Greenwood.

Gray, Barbara (1989), *Collaborating: Finding Common Ground for Multi-party Problems*, San Francisco: Jossey-Bass.

Hall, Andy (1984), *Pretrial Release Program Options*, Washington, DC: National Institute of Justice.

Hamilton, W., L. Ledebur and D. Matz (1984), *Industrial Incentives: Public Promotion of Private Enterprise*, Aslan Press.

Holzer, Marc and Arie Halachmi (1988), *Public Sector Productivity: A Resource Guide*, New York: Garland.

Holzer, Marc and S. Nagel (eds) (1984), *Productivity and Public Policy*, Beverly Hills, CA: Sage.

Humphreys, Patrick and Aylean Wisudha (1987), *Methods and Tools for Structuring and Analyzing Decision Problems*, London: London School of Economics and Political Science.

Jandt, Fred (1985), *Win–Win Negotiations: Turning Conflict into Agreement*, New York: Wiley.

Jarmel, Eli (1972), *Legal Representation of the Poor*, Albany, NY: Matthew Bender.

Kash, Don (1989), *Perpetual Innovation: The New World of Competition*, New York: Basic Books.

Kassin, S. and L. Wrightsman (1988), *The American Jury on Trial: Psychological Perspectives*, Hemisphere Publishing Corporation.

Kelly, Rita Mae (ed.) (1988), *Promoting Productivity in the Public Sector: Problems, Strategies and Prospects*, New York: St Martin's Press.

Kressel, Kenneth and Dean Pruitt (eds) (1989), *Mediation Research: The Process and Effectiveness of Third-Party Intervention*, San Francisco: Jossey-Bass.

LeBoeuf, Michael (1982), *The Productivity Challenge: How to Make it Work for America and You*, New York: McGraw-Hill.

Legal Services Corporation (1980), *The Delivery System Study: A Policy Report to the Congress and the President of the United States*, Washington, DC.: LSC.

Levine, James, Michael Musheno and Dennis Palumbo (1980), *Criminal Justice: A Public Policy Approach*, New York: Harcourt Brace Jovanovich.

Lindsey, Lawrence (1990), *The Growth Experiment: How the New Tax Policy is Transforming the U.S. Economy*, New York: Basic Books.

Little, I. and J. Mirreesin (1974), *Project Appraisal and Planning for Developing Countries*, New York: Basic Books.

MacRae, D. (1986), *Policy Indicators: Links Between Social Science and Public Debate*, Chapel Hill, NC: Duke University.

Magaziner, Ira and Robert Reich (1982), *Minding America's Business: The Decline and Rise of the American Economy*, New York: Harcourt Brace Jovanovich.

Mills, Lawrence (1973), 'Six-Member and Twelve-Member Juries: An Empirical Study of Trial Results', *University of Michigan Journal of Law Reform*, **6**, 671.

Mitnick, B. (1980), *The Political Economy of Regulation*, New York: Columbia University Press.

Mole, Veronica and Dave Elliott (1987), *Enterprising Innovation: An Alternative Approach*, London: Frances Pinter.

Moore, Christopher (1986), *The Mediation Process: Practical Strategies for Resolving Conflict*, San Francisco: Jossey-Bass.

Nagel, S. (1984), 'Using Positive and Negative Incentives', *Public Policy: Goals, Means and Methods*, New York: St Martin's Press.

Nagel, S. (1989), *Higher Goals for America: Doing Better than the Best*, Lanham, Md: University Press of America.

Nagel, S. (1991), *Developing Nations and Super-Optimum Policy Analysis*, Chicago: Nelson-Hall.

Nagel, S. (1994), *Policy Analysis Methods and Super-Optimum Solutions*, Nova Science Publishers.

Nagel, S. (1997), *Super-Optimum Solutions and Win–Win Policy*, Westport, CT: Quorum.

Nagel, S. (1998), *Public Policy Evaluation: Making Super-Optimum Decisions*, Aldershot: Ashgate.

Nagel, S. and M. Mills (1987), 'Microcomputers, P/G% and Dispute Resolution', *Ohio State Journal on Dispute Resolution*, **2**, 187–223.

Nagel, S. and M. Mills (eds) (1990), *Systematic Analysis in Dispute Resolution*, Westport, CT: Greenwood-Quorum.

Nagel, S. and M. Mills (1991), *Multi-Criteria Methods for Alternative Dispute Resolution: With Microcomputer Software Applications*, Westport, CT: Greenwood-Quorum.

Nagel, S. and M. Mills (1993), *Developing Nations and Super-Optimum Policy Analysis*, Nelson-Hall.

Nagel, S. and M. Neef (1975), 'Deductive Modeling to Determine an Optimum Jury Size and Fraction Required to Convict', *Washington University Law Quarterly*, **933**.

Osborn, Alex (1963), *Applied Imagination: Principles and Procedures of Creative Problem-Solving*, New York: Scribner's.

Palda, Kristian (1984), *Industrial Innovation: Its Place in the Public Policy Agenda*, Toronto: The Fraser Institute.

Penrod, S. (1985), 'Evaluating Techniques to Improve Juror Performance' (unpublished paper presented at the American Judicature Society Conference on The American Jury and the Law).

Raskin, Marcus (1986), *The Common Good: Its Politics, Policies and Philosophy*, New York: Routledge & Kegan Paul.

Roberts, Paul (1984), *The Supply Side Revolution*, Cambridge, MA: Harvard University Press.

Robinson, J. (1991), 'Of Family Policies in China', in Richard Hula and Elaine Anderson (eds), *The Family and Public Policy*, Westport, CT: Greenwood Press.

Ruby, Lionel (1950), *Logic: An Introduction*, Chicago: Ill.: Lippincott.

Sabine, George (1950), *A History of Political Theory*, New York: Holt.

Salamon, Lester (ed.) (1989), *Beyond Privatization: The Tools for Government Action*, Washington, DC: Urban Institute.

Sato, Ryuzo and Gilbert Suzawa (1983), *Research and Productivity: Endogenous Technical Change*, Boston: Auburn House.

Sawhill, Isabel (ed.) (1988), *Challenge to Leadership: Economic and Social Issues for the Next Decade*, Washington, DC: Urban Institute.

Schwartz, H. and R. Berney (eds) (1977), *Social and Economic Dimensions of Project Evaluation*, Inter-American Development Bank.

Sternlieb, George and David Listokin (1981), *New Tools for Economic Development: The Enterprise Zone, Development Bank and RFC*, Brunswick, NJ: Rutgers University.

Susskind, Lawrence and Jeffrey Cruikshank (1987), *Breaking the Impasse: Consensual Approaches to Resolving Public Disputes*, New York: Basic Books.

Thomas, Wayne (1976), *Bail Reform in America*, Berkeley, CA: University of California Press.

Titus, Harold (1947), *Ethics for Today*, New York: American Book Company.

Tornatzky, L. (1980), *Innovation and Social Process: National Experiment in Implementing Social Technology*, New York: Pergamon.

Ury, William, Jeanne Brett and Stephen Goldberg (1988), *Getting Disputes Resolved: Designing Systems to Cut the Costs of Conflict*, San Francisco: Jossey-Bass.

Walker, Samuel (1989), *Sense and Nonsense about Crime: A Policy Guide*, Pacific Grove, CA: Brooks/Cole.

Windsor Yearbook of Access to Justice (1980–), Windsor, Ontario: University of Windsor, Faculty of Law.

Winslow, Robert (1977), *Crime in a Free Society*, Encino, CA: Dickenson.

Zeisel, Hans (1971), 'And Then There Were None: The Diminution of the Federal Jury', *University of Chicago Law Review*, **38**, 710.

Zemans, Frederick (ed.) (1979), *Perspectives on Legal Aid: An International Study*, Westport, CT: Greenwood Press.

Index